A READING OF STEPHEN CRANE

A Reading of
Stephen
Crane

MARSTON LaFRANCE

CLARENDON PRESS · OXFORD

1971

Oxford University Press, Ely House, London W.1

GLASGOW NEW YORK TORONTO MELBOURNE WELLINGTON
CAPE TOWN SALISBURY IBADAN NAIROBI DAR ES SALAAM LUSAKA
ADDIS ABABA BOMBAY CALCUTTA MADRAS KARACHI LAHORE
DACCA KUALA LUMPUR SINGAPORE HONG KONG TOKYO

PRINTED IN GREAT BRITAIN
BY W & J MACKAY & CO LTD, CHATHAM

FOR

MARIE ANN

AND

MARC, LISA and ANDRE

ACKNOWLEDGEMENTS

THIS book owes much to more people than can be named here. Some fifteen years ago, when I first became interested in Crane, one had (with luck) the twelve-volume edition assembled by Wilson S. Follett, a better text of the major prose works in R. W. Stallman's *Omnibus*, the biographies by Thomas Beer and John Berryman, three valuable unpublished theses—by Jean V. E. Whitehead Lang, James B. Colvert, and Thomas A. Gullason—and a handful of worthwhile critical essays. Since then, all texts—novels, short stories, poems, sketches, and letters—have been made readily available, and a reader can now draw upon rich critical resources, for Crane has become firmly established as an important figure in American literature. I have used all these resources to the best of my ability, and my documentation will have to be my thanks to a small body of excellent scholars and editors. Here I would at least point out, with pleasure, that some half-dozen names recur rather often in my references.

Harry Hayden Clark, Professor of English at the University of Wisconsin, directed a first version of this study in the form of a thesis and thus gave me the benefit of his own knowledge of the American 1890s, his unfailing patience, and criticism that I was always happy to accept. Working with him was consistently a pleasure.

Joseph Katz and E. R. Hagemann, among others, have answered promptly and in detail the queries with which I have troubled them, and I have received expert assistance in many libraries. I would thank particularly the members of the library staff who have helped me at Carleton University, the University of Wisconsin, the Butler Library Special Collections at Columbia University, the Bodleian Library, the Free Library of Philadelphia, Syracuse University, the Library of Congress, and the British Museum; to the cost of their time they have saved a great amount of my own.

Parts of this study have appeared, in slightly different form, in

Studies in Short Fiction, and in *Patterns of Commitment in American Literature* (Toronto, 1967); I am grateful to the University of Toronto Press and *Studies in Short Fiction* for their permission to include this material in my book. Also, I sincerely thank the following for permission to quote from unpublished theses: James B. Colvert for his 'Stephen Crane: The Development of His Art', Cornell University for 'The Art of Stephen Crane' by Jean V. E. Whitehead Lang, Will C. Jumper for his 'Tragic Irony as Form: Structural Problems in the Prose of Stephen Crane', Michigan State University for 'Stephen Crane's Social Outlook as Revealed in His Writings' by Andrew W. Hart, Marion L. Shane for his 'The Theme of Spiritual Poverty in Selected Works of Four American Novelists: Twain, Crane, Fitzgerald, and Dreiser', the University of Illinois for 'The Fiction of Stephen Crane and Its Critics' by John C. Bushman, and Max R. Westbrook for his 'Stephen Crane and the Revolt-Search Motif'. I am grateful for being allowed to quote from Søren Kierkegaard's *Concluding Unscientific Postscript*, translated by David F. Swenson and Walter Lowrie, copyright 1941 © 1969 by Princeton University Press; Princeton Paperback, 1968: quotations are reprinted by permission of Princeton University Press and the American Scandinavian Foundation. Crane's own writings, I am told by Alfred A. Knopf, Inc., are now in the public domain.

My dedication thanks some likeable people who have had the ghost of Stephen Crane about their house these eight years past and have made it welcome.

Carleton University,   M.L.
Ottawa, Canada

CONTENTS

Stephen Crane to Willa Cather, January 1895:

> He gave me to understand that he led a double literary life; writing in the first place the matter that pleased himself, and doing it very slowly; in the second place, any sort of stuff that would sell. And he remarked that his poor was just as bad as it could possibly be. He realized [,] he said, that his limitations were absolutely impassable. 'What I can't do, I can't do at all, and I can't acquire it. I only hold one trump.'

'When I Knew Stephen Crane', *Prairie Schooner*, XXIII (Fall 1949), 234–5.

Stephen Crane to John Northern Hilliard, January 1896:

> The one thing that deeply pleases me in my literary life—brief and inglorious as it is—is the fact that men of sense believe me to be sincere. . . . I understand that a man is born into the world with his own pair of eyes, and he is not at all responsible for his vision—he is merely responsible for his quality of personal honesty. To keep close to this personal honesty is my supreme ambition. There is a sublime egotism in talking of honesty. I, however, do not say that I am honest. I merely say that I am as nearly honest as a weak mental machinery will allow. This aim in life struck me as being the only thing worth while. A man is sure to fail at it, but there is something in the failure.

Stephen Crane: Letters, ed. R. W. Stallman and Lillian Gilkes (New York, 1960), pp. 109–10.

I

AWARENESS AND APPRENTICESHIP

STEPHEN Crane's brief literary life lasted only some seven years, from the first publication of *Maggie* in 1893 to his death, at twenty-eight, on 5 June 1900. However, he was writing anonymously for publication as early as the summer of 1887 or 1888 when he began helping his brother, Townley, report seasonal gossip from the Jersey shore at Asbury Park, Ocean Grove, and occasionally Avon-By-The-Sea, for the New York *Tribune*. Whatever literary apprenticeship Crane served thus has to begin with this banal newspaper correspondence and end with the appearance of his Sullivan County tales in 1892, that is, begin when the apprentice was about sixteen and end shortly before he was twenty-one. The apprenticeship terminated abruptly when the *Tribune* published his report of a parade by the Junior Order of United American Mechanics (21 August 1892, p. 22). Although this effort was well below the mark set by some of the pieces Crane had published earlier that summer, an uproar ensued, both Townley and his apprentice—unfortunately no longer anonymous in the offices of the *Tribune*—were fired, and Crane entered upon his precarious journeyman's existence in New York from which he finally emerged with *The Red Badge of Courage*.

Yet if one wishes to begin a study of Crane at the beginning, this apprentice period has to be more narrowly limited. Crane apparently held himself in check during the first two or three summers; it is virtually impossible to identify any of his *Tribune* pieces before 1891, and one is thus left with the scanty work of only two summers. Much more important, however, the 1891 writings are decidedly after the fact, if one is interested in tracing the development of Crane's distinctive ironic view of the world. Certain attitudes or capacities of Crane's mind had already formed, and his ironic vision had been functioning properly long before the summer of 1891. Some of his neglected apprentice work merits a closer look than it has received, but it has to be approached by way of some understanding of Crane's uncanny awareness because, by 1891, his eyes trained upon the Jersey shore establishment suggest a concealed cannon trained upon a complacent and un-suspecting foe. The cannon had been quietly armed and aimed some years earlier, probably with considerable help from his sister Agnes, within the mist of Crane's sparsely documented boyhood.

Apparently the fourteenth and final child of the Reverend Dr. Jonathan Townley Crane and Mary Helen Peck was a born ironist.[1] He has, of course, been called almost everything else, as one scholar wryly observed in 1961—'realist, romantic, naturalist, imagist, existentialist, symbolist, impressionist, expressionist, and *pointilliste* (I may have overlooked some).'[2] Nevertheless, no one would deny that he is an ironist, and this term differs from the other critical labels because a real ironist has little choice in the matter. All manifestations of irony, of course, depend in part upon experience, upon what the exterior world offers for the ironist to work with, and the prevalence of irony in American literature of the period suggests that the offerings of the 1890s were particularly rich. Still, the expression of irony depends ultimately upon the perception or awareness of the ironist. If Crane and Hamlin Garland, for example, were to stroll together through a ten-block stretch of the Bowery the externality they would encounter should be the same for both, yet Crane the ironist could be counted upon to 'see' a great deal more during this walk than would Garland, who was not an ironist. Irony in this decidedly unliterary sense of the term is an organic peculiarity, a distinctive cast of mind. According to Kierkegaard, it

arises from the constant placing of the particularities of the finite [or external] together with the infinite [or internal] ethical requirement,

---

[1] All the Crane children are named and their dates, when known, are given by Robert Wooster Stallman, who finds that only eight were living when Crane was born: *Stephen Crane: A Biography* (New York, 1968), p. 563.

[2] Edwin H. Cady, 'Stephen Crane and the Strenuous Life', *English Literary History*, XXVIII (Dec. 1961), 378.

thus permitting the contradiction to come into being. Whoever can do this with facility . . . must have executed the movement of infinitude in his soul, and in so far it is possible that he is an ethicist . . . solely and exclusively through maintaining an inner relationship to the absolute requirement. Such an ethicist uses irony as his incognito. . . . Irony is a synthesis of ethical passion which infinitely accentuates inwardly the person of the individual in relation to the ethical require- ment—and of culture, which infinitely abstracts externally from the personal ego, as one finitude among all the other finitudes and parti- cularities. This abstraction causes the emphasis in the first attitude to pass unnoticed, and herein lies the art of the ironist, which also insures that the first movement shall be truly infinite. The masses of men live in the converse manner; . . . when the absolute requirement looks in upon them, there they have no taste for accentuating their own persons.

Irony is an existential determination, and nothing is more ridiculous than to suppose that it consists in the use of certain phraseology, or when an author congratulates himself upon succeeding in expressing himself ironically. Whoever has essential irony has it all day long, not bound to any specific form, because it is the infinite within him.[3]

Crane implies much the same definition in less abstract language. He recognizes his uncommon perception when he states that because everyone is born with his own pair of eyes no one can be held responsible for the quality of his own vision. His poems which discuss the god of a man's inner thoughts, the eye of the soul, present his awareness of the infinite ethical requirement as a moral force within himself. Irony serves him as the disguise which pre- serves his own moral life in full view of all the particularities of the American 1890s. His ironic cast of mind is apparently an existential determination: its existence certainly precedes any characteristic expression, and Crane himself did not choose the quality of his own awareness.

Thus endowed with this sort of essential irony the ironist cannot discard it. He can suppress the expression of what it reveals to him, a feat which Crane taught himself to perform successfully; he can simply close his eyes to a painful revelation or look else- where, which Crane never did; and he can in his own mind transcend

[3] Søren Kierkegaard, *Concluding Unscientific Postscript*, trans. David F. Swenson and Walter Lowrie (Princeton, 1941), pp. 448–50.

the contradictions he perceives and thus hold to what Crane calls 'personal honesty' rather than allow his own values to blur towards ambiguity (Swift, for example, probably had little trouble distinguishing Stella or Vanessa from the shadowy image of a woman flayed); but he is unable to perceive in a manner which is not ironic, and Crane may have recognized this helplessness in himself when he said that 'every artist must be in some things powerless as a dead snake'.[4] This ironic vision itself can be described, until it is encountered again and again in Crane's work, as simply the perception or awareness of a double realm of values where a different sort of mind perceives only a single realm. 'The ironist is characterized by his recognition of the antitheses in human experience: his is an interested objectivity; he is detached but not indifferent, withdrawn but not removed. . . . In fact the ironist is deeply concerned with both aspects of the contradictions he perceives.'[5] Crane's late boyhood and early adolescence, according to the available information, seem to have been almost ideally arranged to raise a potential ironist's innate capacity to active function.

Both Crane's parents devoted their lives to the Methodist Church, and every summer Asbury Park became a self-consciously respectable resort, while nearby Ocean Grove became a Methodist camp ground. The Methodism in which the area, and particularly Crane's parents, fairly marinated had seen its finest hour in a frontier environment during the first half of the century; and it was far too narrow, too anachronistic, to provide acceptable nourishment for a precocious boy growing up during the 1880s in urban Asbury Park. In Crane's day its principal fruits, as might be expected from any moribund institution forced to live beyond its time, were innocent acceptance—exemplified by Crane's father—and equally innocent but more or less militant dogmatism —better exemplified by Crane's mother. Crane recorded his own response in a reminiscence dictated the year before his death: 'I

---

[4] Quoted by John Berryman, *Stephen Crane* (New York, 1950), pp. 6, 256.
[5] A. H. Wright, 'Irony and Fiction', *Journal of Aesthetics and Art Criticism*, XII (Sept. 1953), 115, 113.

used to like church and prayer meetings when I was a kid but that cooled off and when I was thirteen or about that, my brother Will told me not to believe in Hell after my uncle had been boring me about the lake of fire and the rest of the sideshows.'[6] The time of Crane's conversion is probably quite accurately dated in this memoir, for Crane was thirteen on 1 November 1884, the year of the death of his favourite sister Agnes.

One seldom hears anything about his other sisters; of the brothers only Will, Edmund, and Townley are usually mentioned, and there is no strong indication that any of them could understand Crane. But Agnes, fifteen when Crane was born, apparently had to assume the parental responsibility not only for the new baby, but for the rest of the household as well, while both parents laboured in the depleted vineyard; and Agnes, out of the entire family, seems to have been the only one psychologically equipped to cope with the needs of her youngest brother. Melvin Schoberlin describes her as brilliant, exacting, severe, painfully sensitive, moody, a rebel—all terms which have been used appropriately to describe Crane himself—and she wanted most of all to write. Moreover, she insisted upon her own definition of 'Christian lady' in a household where, one infers, such an insistence must have been mildly tinged with rebellion.

Upon Stephen, until her death at twenty-eight in 1884, she lavished her boundless affection and understanding. And more than anyone else, it was she who gave direction to his early years. She taught him much of literature and science, and of living; she directed, to a great extent, his reading. . . . Like his sister, Stephen was sensitive and moody and often rebellious. In the midst of 'such an oyster-like family,' as she summed up the household, a strong bond developed between the two rebels. And like her, his outlook on life was inordinately serious.[7]

Crane's father died on 16 February 1880, and if the bond between his two rebellious children had been established before his death it must have grown considerably more intense shortly after: the

---

[6] *Stephen Crane: Letters*, ed. R. W. Stallman and Lillian Gilkes (New York, 1960), p. 242.

[7] Melvin Schoberlin, *The Sullivan County Sketches of Stephen Crane* (Syracuse, 1949), Introduction, pp. 3–4.

eight-year-old boy, instinctively seeking to compensate for the loss of his father, must have turned to Agnes, not to his mother. Crane's father died too soon to have been personally subjected to his son's ironic vision, but Crane's mother was not so fortunate.

According to Thomas Beer, Mary Helen Crane was an 'effective' worker for the Methodist cause, and 'the women of other sects admired her. She has been somewhat wildly described as a religious maniac, but what is known of her shows a fine mind trained in a formula.'[8] The formula, however, must have posed a few problems for young Crane. A copy of *What Must I Do to Be Saved?*, for example, is available in the Columbia University Crane collection; this 'grim unrelenting didacticism', written by Mrs. Crane's uncle, Bishop Jesse T. Peck, and inscribed by the author to Crane's father, was presented to Crane in 1881, the year of his tenth birthday.[9] Beer's implicit distinction between the woman—the fine mind—and the formula becomes explicit in the mature ironist's recollection:

My mother was a very religious woman but I don't think that she was as narrow as most of her friends or her family. . . . My brothers tell me that she got herself into trouble before I was old enough to follow proceedings by taking care of a girl who had an accidental baby. Inopportune babies are not part of Methodist ritual but mother was always more of a Christian than a Methodist and she kept this girl at our house in Asbury until she found a home somewhere. (*Letters*, pp. 241–2)

The double vision thus sharply separates the two elements of his mother's life: 'religious' is used ambiguously to imply both the values Crane accepts and those he rejects, but Beer's woman, the mother who is here caught in a stoic act of simple humanism, has become 'Christian', and the formula, the futile orthodoxy of *What Must I Do to Be Saved?*, has become 'Methodist'. Also, the stigma of 'Methodist' has been deftly removed from the 'Christian' mother and transferred to her more 'narrow' friends and family. It seems quite safe, for at least two reasons, to accept this 1899

[8] Thomas Beer, *Stephen Crane: A Study in American Letters*, introduction by Joseph Conrad (London, 1924), p. 54.

[9] See Daniel G. Hoffman, *The Poetry of Stephen Crane* (New York, 1957), pp. 54–5.

reminiscence as a sincere expression of how Crane felt during the earlier period itself: his choice of 'Christian' to imply unqualified approval—an extremely rare usage in Crane—probably harks back to Agnes's insisting upon her own definition of 'Christian lady'; and his complete rejection of 'Methodist' and all it implies is balanced by the warm humour, the implicit acceptance, in Crane's recollection of his mother—an ironist is deeply concerned with both aspects of the contradictions he perceives.[10]

One need not claim that an eleven- or twelve-year-old did any more than accept some values and reject others. However, the opposing forces in young Crane's life between 1880 and 1884 align themselves clearly within the oyster-like household: on the one side an existing identification between two rebels heightened by the death of their father, and on the other a part-time mother who doubled as a narrow old woman who 'lived in and for religion. . . . You could argue just as well with a wave' (*Letters*, p. 242); on the one side the understanding and discriminating guidance of Agnes, and on the other the love of his mother tempered by the dogmatism of the 'Methodist' who, sooner or later, must have pressed the boy towards an orthodox commitment. As Crane grew into adolescence under such conditions his critical awareness could hardly have remained quiescent. His awareness, however, would also have revealed to him that those values which he rejected were as omnipresent, as perceptibly insistent in human experience, as those he accepted; and thus of necessity he would have had to develop some kind of ethical line of demarcation between the double realm of values he perceived. If the boy could have stated in words the solution to this problem, with some help from Agnes, something such as the following should have resulted: 'certain values exist in so far as people apparently believe in them and uphold them, but I do not, cannot, and will not accept them; to me,

[10] The same contradiction, with the same emphasis on either aspect, is repeated in his niece's memoir of Crane as he appeared shortly after his mother's death: 'His mother's memory was dear to him, he had nothing dearer . . . [but] he did marvel always that such an intellectual woman . . . could have wrapped herself so completely in the "vacuous, futile, psalm-singing that passed for worship" in those days' (Helen R. Crane, 'My Uncle, Stephen Crane', *American Mercury*, XXXI [Jan. 1934], 25).

these values are illusory, and because they are illusory the people and the institutions upholding them are, more or less innocently, ridiculous.' And thus the young ironist would psychologically have become a man.

It is impossible to say just when this psychological coming-of-age occurred. It apparently had occurred by 1884 'or about that', and this would place the first stirrings of self-realization well back into the years when Agnes was alive. If Agnes eventually assumed for the boy the moral and ethical role normally fulfilled by both parents, then Crane could have felt psychologically secure in his developing awareness so long as she was present as the authority, the acceptable sanction, behind the values he perceived. There would have been no real need for him to assert himself, the boy could in fact have remained a boy, as long as Agnes was alive. But if so, her death must have been an appalling loss, a shock even greater than the death of his father, because this time he was left a psychological orphan. Since Crane began asserting himself about 1884, it is safe to assume that he responded to this crisis as, henceforth, he would respond to every crisis in his life—except for some terrible wavering about his return to England after the Spanish-American War. He accepted the inevitable, and psychologically and emotionally turned to no one. The ironist apparently was his own man by about his thirteenth year. And fittingly enough, it was his mother who affixed the seal to his psychological declaration of independence. Her cry of despair, shortly after Agnes's death, innocently pronounces the benediction upon all the love and understanding the dead sister had lavished upon her little brother: 'Stevie is like the wind in Scripture. He bloweth where he listeth' (Berryman, p. 15).

Unless one accepts the fact that Crane was his own master by 1888 when he enrolled at Claverack, the strange tale of his flirtation with higher education will not make much sense. Crane's schooling away from home began when he was thirteen, in the fall of 1885, at Pennington Seminary, where his father had been principal, well-liked and extremely effective, from 1849 to 1858. Although Pennington was a good school, one of its most important purposes was to prepare young men for the ministry; and thus Crane was again surrounded by Methodism properly buttressed by all the banal prohibitions which, later, amused him at Ocean Grove. He lasted two full years and a fall term before he transferred to Claverack, a preparatory school in the Hudson valley near Poughkeepsie, on 4 January 1888; he returned to Claverack the following September and again in September 1889; in September 1890, he moved on to Lafayette College; in January 1891, he transferred to Syracuse University, and in June he left for good—probably with part or all of *Maggie* down in first draft—still four months away from being twenty.[11] Apart from an 'A' in English literature as the only mark he bothered to earn at Syracuse, and a zero in theme-writing at Lafayette, his formal education was undistinguished. He worked at playing baseball, was an important man in Claverack's military drill unit, carefully examined the joys of fraternity life, spent long hours poking about the streets of Syracuse, and attended classes or completed assignments whenever the spirit of conformity to orthodox academic respectability nudged him—which was not often, especially at Syracuse which then was, again, a Methodist stronghold. Thus, the considerable gleanings Crane acquired from his college years were, for the most part, picked up outside the classroom: his total academic experience, but not his formal education, may safely be called extensive. As a result, Crane entered the world of letters 'comme un jeune reporter dont le précoce talent n'a rien à voir avec la culture académique et qui se fie uniquement à ses sens et à son imagination. Et aussi comme un jeune Américain pleinement affranchi des influences britanniques traditionnelles.'[12] And thus he remained, formally ill-educated and comparatively

[11] See Lyndon Upson Pratt, 'The Formal Education of Stephen Crane', *American Literature*, X (Jan. 1939), 460–71; Claude Jones, 'Stephen Crane at Syracuse', *American Literature*, VII (Mar. 1935), 82–4; Harvey Wickham, 'Stephen Crane at College', *American Mercury*, VII (Mar. 1926), 291–7; Jean Cazemajou, 'Stephen Crane: Pennington Seminary: Étape d'une éducation méthodiste', *Études Anglaises*, XX (avril–juin 1967), 140–8; Thomas A. Gullason, 'The Cranes at Pennington Seminary', *American Literature*, XXXIX (Jan. 1968), 530–41.

[12] Georges Remords, 'Un Précurseur des romanciers américains contemporains: Stephen Crane (1871–1900)', *Bulletin de la Faculté des Lettres de Strasbourg*, XXIX (1950–1), 182.

ill-read, until his death. As Willa Cather correctly inferred, 'he seemed to feel that this fuller culture was not for him' (*Prairie Schooner*, 232–3).

Given Crane's ironic vision, that precocious talent which indeed had nothing to do with academic culture, and the fact that he had already decided upon a life of writing—an excellent juvenile piece entitled 'Uncle Jake and the Bell-Handle' survives, dated 1885[13]—college must have appealed to him primarily as just one more aspect of life upon which his vision could work. That it was working effectively is implied by the puzzled remembrances of a classmate at Claverack: Harvey Wickham recalls that Crane was 'peculiar, an oyster beneath whose lips there was already an irritating grain of some foreign substance . . . not tender of other people's vanities . . . given to holding aloof, especially if the human animal was manifesting its capacity for collective action . . . something extravagant in Stephen Crane which only the fabulous can express.' One wonders how Crane could have summoned any motivation for the sort of commitments demanded by scholarship. He must very early have been aware that his vision was not going to be affected appreciably by dean's-list honours in algebra, chemistry, physics, drafting, or even first-year French or German. His zero in theme-writing appropriately foreshadows his later failure to report the essentials of a news event to the satisfaction of editors. Crane, of course, was entirely capable of either of these elementary jobs—he published sketches at both Claverack and Syracuse, and upon the rare occasion when editorial requirements happened to coincide with his own interests he was the best of reporters[14]—but he nowhere reveals the affection for grammar which might have endeared him to graders of freshman themes, and compared with what goes on within the mind of his characters the external facts of a situation, in either his fiction, poetry, or the better news articles,

[13] Daniel G. Hoffman, 'Stephen Crane's First Story', *Bulletin of the New York Public Library*, LXIV (May 1960), 273–8.

[14] See Lyndon Upson Pratt, 'An Addition to the Canon of Stephen Crane', *Research Studies, State College of Washington*, VII (Mar. 1939), 55–8; Olov W. Fryckstedt, ed., *Stephen Crane: Uncollected Writings* (Upsala, 1963), pp. 3–6; for Crane's skill as reporter, see 'Howells Fears Realists Must Wait', New York *Times*, 28 Oct. 1894, p. 20.

are never of any great importance. In fact, the academic aspect of college probably held only one real interest for Crane: even if he had his unique talent and his decision to write, he still had to acquire form and style; and the subject most suitable for his pursuit of this interest would have been English literature. In brief, the evidence suggests that Crane's reaction to college is a repetition of his reaction to his mother: his ironic perception simply split academic life into those values he could accept and those he could not. He accepted sports, military training, fraternity life, other extracurricular activities, and English literature; he rejected, in varying degrees, everything else.

Implicit in the rejection of both his mother's religious orthodoxy and the academic respectability which would have made him a conventional student is the force of what Berryman calls Crane's 'huge' will: the necessary determination to accept, at whatever cost, and act in accordance with whatever values the piercing ironic awareness reveals to him. The cost is isolation in some form, psychological, social, or moral, from the conventionally and institutionally accepted values which the ironist perceives as unacceptable illusions. Hoffman states that 'Isolation and non-conformity, its logical outcome in action, may be achieved either through the activity of the will in conscious opposition to convention, or through the unwilled expression of one's inner nature, a nature that is not in consonance with the assumptions of society' (*Poetry*, p. 8). But it is of some importance to realize that for Crane this matter apparently did not present itself as an either-or proposition. Crane's letter to Hilliard holds a man absolutely responsible for his own personal honesty, that is, for accepting and acting honestly upon the values he perceives with the vision given him, and thus Crane implies that thc will has to be deliberately invoked to carry into action the implications of a man's unwilled perceptions. Such a doctrine seems to offer no concealed difficulties until one realizes that it at least suggests an almost instantaneous relationship between perception and the willed commitment for which man is responsible; what is missing is the whole intellectual process of logical argument which leads most persons through a series of increasingly refined perceptions to a final, reasoned, commitment. In other words, there is some reason to believe that, for Crane, qualitative judgement is implicit in the act of perception itself; and because the ironist cannot help but perceive differently from the majority of his contemporaries, cannot be otherwise than more or less out of consonance with the assumptions of society, the huge will is instantly required merely to *accept* his perception as a valid basis for action which, if he is to be personally honest, will place him in conscious opposition to convention.

Such a conclusion implies that Crane, from the beginning, relied ultimately upon his perception for his essential means of orienting his life, not upon his intellect, education, tradition, or even experience—if one can distinguish between detached perception and actual participative action. A direct acceptance and dependence upon perception, at any rate, best accounts for the odd air of authority that scholars have noted in both the man and his work, an enigmatic aura of psychological security not particularly open to argument in the man and not unduly vulnerable to analysis in his work.

A serious author who will knowingly shock his readers [as Crane did in *Maggie*] is an author confident of the correctness of his vision of life, despite its being out of joint with conventional morality. And an author who will—as Crane did in *The Red Badge*—trust his imaginative conception of the nature of war and its effects on men is just as confident of the validity of his personal vision.[15]

Crane perceived that man's mental machinery is 'weak' in comparison with the forces, both external and internal, with which it has to cope; and his several explorations of this particular perception constitute the essential subject of both his prose and poetry, as will be seen. At this point, however, it is merely necessary to suggest that Crane began his literary life with all the intellectual equipment he needed: the unique awareness of the ironist, the huge will necessary for a direct acceptance of his own perception, and—one has to assume—the stoic fortitude to accept

---

[15] Donald Pizer, 'Romantic Individualism in Garland, Norris and Crane', *American Quarterly*, X (Winter 1958), 473.

whatever kind or degree of isolation resulted from his remaining personally honest during America's mauve decade. By the summer of 1891 his primary need was competence in the craft skills of writing: he still had to acquire an acceptable style, and most of all he had to find some form which would allow him to turn his ironic perception to direct advantage in fiction.

The particular assumptions of the summer society which became the first literary grist for Crane's ironic mill were orthodox, respectable, and unbelievably banal. He began the 1891 season with a feather in his cap when a hoax, a story of an insect plague on the outskirts of Syracuse, written while he was still at university, made the front page of the *Tribune*.[16] Also, his decision to leave college must have contributed to a general sense of release, a relaxed, buoyant mood in which a free intelligence amused itself by studying its antagonist and merely toying with it in print. Such a mood lies behind a few articles which originated at the Jersey shore that summer. The overall impression they convey is ironic amusement, the writer enjoys penning wry comments about the Methodist concern with temperance legislation, and the prose implies an amateur craftsman's stylistic experiments—with imagery, with the comic effect of judicious omissions, the revealing quotation, the flat presentation of sharp details deliberately disconnected. This amused onlooker, for example, reported a sermon by the Reverend Dr. Thomas Hanlon, who happened to be the principal of Pennington Seminary while Crane was a student there:

His theme was 'Individual Responsibility.' 'The tendency to demolish the family,' he said, 'was the great danger that threatened the Nation. Easy divorce was a menace. The purity of the ballot was threatened by the money power, the rum power and the shot-gun power. The money power was worse than the shot-gun power. A foreigner ought to wait twenty-one years before he could vote. I had to wait twenty-one years,' he said. Loud applause was given this sentiment. Dr. Stokes said: 'Say amen as much as you please, but don't let us turn this place into a theatre.' The women ought to have the ballot. He reviewed the

---

[16] 'Great Bugs in Onondaga', New York *Tribune*, 1 June 1891, p. 1.

legislation of New-Jersey for the last three years on the liquor question and denounced it in unmeasured terms.[17]

For the reader able to leap from topic to topic without benefit of transitions, the intelligence of both the preacher and his audience is implied by the 'loud applause' at the absurd analogy attacking a foreigner's right to vote. And this unseemly racket evokes the superbly orthodox admonition from Dr. Stokes. By the time the reader encounters the 'liquor question' he should be able to infer that it will not be finally resolved by such innocent people as these. The same technique is again applied to poor Dr. Hanlon in another snippet. The correspondent begins his report quite properly: 'There were nearly 1,600 present at Dr. Hanlon's Bible class. The lesson was on "The Marriage at Cana of Galilee".' But then everything stops abruptly with the following comment: 'The drift of the discussion was that the wine made by Christ was non-alcoholic.'[18]

However, this correspondent's seasonal masterpiece reports the anniversary celebration of the 'Daughters and Sons of the King'.[19] The organization itself—which forcefully recalls that the 1890s were immensely hospitable to *Trilby* and *Little Lord Fauntleroy*, to Thomas Beer's 'Titaness', Richard Harding Davis, Josiah Holland, Frances Willard, Elbert Hubbard, Richard Watson Gilder, Orison Swett Marden, and dozens more of such intellectually anaemic kinsmen—the wonderful names, the fatuous asides by Stokes and Hanlon, all contributed to what must have been a hilarious day for a young ironist.

This was the third Ocean Grove anniversary of the King's Daughters and Sons, and was a regular field day, beginning at 8 o'clock with a devotional meeting in Thornley Chapel, conducted by Mrs. Margaret Bottome, the founder of the order. An unusual number of members

---

[17] 'Meetings for Worship at Asbury Park', New York *Tribune*, 6 July 1891, p. 2. The Revd. Ellwood H. Stokes was a member of Pennington's Board of Trustees when Crane was a student, and 'the first president (1869–1897) of the Ocean Grove Camp Meeting Association' (Gullason, 'Cranes at Pennington', p. 540).

[18] 'Services By The Seaside', New York *Tribune*, 20 July 1891, p. 3.

[19] New York *Tribune*, 7 Aug. 1891, p. 7.

participated at the young people's meeting. The Rev. George W. Barker discoursed on the necessity of leading souls to Christ, after which the usual promise service took place. D. Fife gave interesting incidents of Southern mission work. Mrs. Bottome conducted a conference of workers in the young people's temple. . . . The Rev. Dr. Stokes welcomed these Royal ladies, saying, 'Were I not a King's son I would be abashed in the presence of so much royalty.' . . . The Rev. Dr. Ganlon [*sic*], principal of Pennington Seminary, said that the organization was the working out of old ideas of personal Christian service. . . . He classed Clara Barton and Dorothea Dix as King's Daughters. Men can be influenced by women and women can be influenced by men, and that is the reason that there are more women in the Church than men. If they had more women preachers there would be more men converts.

These harmless pieces imply a writer sharpening his eye for the sort of detail which will reveal a state of mind; and the details selected are presented disjointedly in either a flat statement or with mildly eccentric colouring, as when the anniversary service of the King's Daughters is called 'a regular field day'. The reader is forced to infer his own transitions and, quite often, considerable context as well—it is safe to assume the Principal of Pennington found more to say of 'The Marriage at Cana of Galilee' than merely that the wine was non-alcoholic. By means of such a presentation, the subject of the article is set in an ironic light so as to reveal the weak mental machinery in action. If one allows for youth, inexperience, and the factual limitations of even such journalistic pap as this, the techniques employed in these pieces are not unlike those found in the Sullivan County tales. Moreover, the details themselves occasionally wear the peculiarly original garb of Crane's images:

Parties from the hotels go on long pedestrian tours along the banks of Shark River, and create havoc among the blithesome crabs and the festive oysters. Sketching parties . . . also love the banks of the river, and they can be seen on fine afternoons painting industriously, while their white umbrellas . . . give the party the appearance of a bunch of extraordinary mushrooms.[20]

[20] 'On the Banks of Shark River', New York *Tribune*, 11 July 1891, p. 5.

Thus the summer of 1891 was largely devoted to stylistic experiment. Crane must have been aware that this summer job was trivial, not in itself worth the effort of restraining oneself, but his mother was still living, and he may have curbed his expression partly out of consideration for her. However, his mother died on 7 December; and the following summer Crane, probably with the rejection of *Maggie* as a spur, was free to draw his ironic arrows to the head.

He began his 1892 campaign with an excellent volley aimed at the vitals of the Methodist citadel in Ocean Grove:

The sombre-hued gentlemen who congregate at this place in summer are arriving in solemn procession, with black valises in their hands and rebukes to frivolity in their eyes. They greet each other with quiet enthusiasm and immediately set about holding meetings. The cool, shaded Auditorium will soon begin to palpitate with the efforts of famous preachers delivering doctrines to thousands of worshippers. The tents, of which there are hundreds, are beginning to rear their white heads under the trees.[21]

This loaded passage effectively sets forth the illusory nature of an obsolete orthodoxy professionally maintained for its own sake. The rebukes to frivolity are presented as an external, and expected, accoutrement which the correct sombre-hued professional will acquire just as he acquires his black valise. The oxymoronic coupling of 'quiet enthusiasm' implies that the quietness, if not also the enthusiasm is, again, professionally orthodox. Together the two sentences convey the innocent unreality of these ominous figures who march in like restrained black riders and then, anticlimactically, merely hold meetings. The auditorium, about to lose its cool and shaded comfort, will soon palpitate with the heat of these quietly enthusiastic preachers handing down—'delivering' —orthodox doctrines (implicitly rebukes to frivolity or, again, a moral version of the professional's ready-made black valise) to innocent 'worshippers'. The reader has to decide for himself whether the object of worship is God, a famous preacher, or some

21 'Meetings Begun At Ocean Grove', New York *Tribune*, 2 July 1892, p. 4.

professionally certified doctrine. Thus **Crane** at once distinguishes the respectable orthodoxy—which he finds absurdly unrealistic—from the men—whom he finds innocently unrealistic—and implies the gullibility of worshippers who hearken to such leaders. And reality, morally a common-sense norm apart from all of this respectably orthodox darkness and yet under the very noses of both preachers and audience, is suggested by the contrasting white of the tents beneath the trees.[22] Whatever else may have contributed to the concentrated efficiency of this attack, which was not present in the 1891 writing, it stems in part from a new sense of focus. By 1892 Crane had recognized that his antagonist's commitment to illusory values was an Achilles' heel, and thus he knew exactly where to direct his fire.

When he carried his attack to the orthodox respectability of the Asbury Park holiday-maker, a money-spending creature at whom hotel proprietors 'smile copiously', he first noted the continuous search for means of providing innocuous amusement:

Asbury Park is rapidly acquiring a collection of machines. Of course there is a toboggan slide. Now, in process of construction, there is an arrangement called a 'razzle-dazzle.' Just what this will be is impossible to tell. It is, of course, a moral machine. Down by the lake an immense upright wheel has been erected. This will revolve, carrying little cars, to be filled evidently with desperate persons, around and around, up and down.[23]

Crane's explanation of the machine's morality is somewhat gratuitous, for the desperate persons going round and round, up and down, on the machines and in Asbury Park in general, provide the authoritative bite without help from the comment. Because the

[22] See Joseph J. Kwiat, 'Stephen Crane and Painting', *American Quarterly*, IV (Winter 1952), 333–4.

[23] 'Crowding into Asbury Park', New York *Tribune*, 3 July 1892, p. 28. See also 'Joys of Seaside Life', in which Crane says of the 'razzle-dazzle': 'Many people are supposed to enjoy this thing, for a reason which is not evident. Solemn circles of more or less sensible-looking people sit in it and "go 'round".' The observation wheel 'goes around carrying little cars filled with maniacs, up and down, over and over' (New York *Tribune*, 17 July 1892, p. 18). Crane describes the typical patron of these moral machines in 'On The Boardwalk', New York *Tribune*, 14 Aug. 1892, p. 17.

resort prospers by making it possible for such people to believe they are enjoying themselves, Crane's articles glance wryly at a wide variety of machines and fakirs—Hindu silk merchants, the frankfurter man, the mobile tintype gallery ('Babies and pug dogs furnish most of the victims for these people'), the camera obscura, a sleight-of-hand Italian who 'manoeuvres with a quarter of a dollar and a pack of playing cards' and is able to pride himself in his ability merely because no one cares enough about the trick to ask or figure out how it is done, transient entertainers, street singers, gentlemanly prize-fighters. These are the Asbury Park 'professionals' who provide 'very mild' amusement for the innocents abroad at the seaside. On one wonderful day Crane was even able to loose a broadside upon both communities at once: Ocean Grove orthodoxy complained of the din necessary to Asbury Park respectability.

The big 'Observation Wheel' on Lake-ave. has got into a great deal of trouble, and it is feared that the awe-stricken visitor will be unable to see the 'wheel go 'round' hereafter. Complaints were made by the hotel-owners in the neighborhood that the engine connected with the machine distributed ashes and sparks over their counterpanes. Also, residents of Ocean Grove came and said that the steam organ disturbed their pious meditations on the evils of the world. Thereupon the minions of the law violently suppressed the wheel and its attendants.[24]

By August, however, Crane's aim in Asbury Park was narrowed upon the wealthy founder of the resort, James A. Bradley; and he was then able to perform a worthwhile organizational feat, which he apparently kept strictly to himself—the alignment of his attacks upon both communities into a recognizable ironic parallel suggestive of some of the better uses of this technical device in *Maggie*. 'Founder' Bradley, as Crane sees him, wears a 'white sun-umbrella with a green lining and has very fierce and passionate whiskers':

He is noted for his wealth, his whiskers and his eccentricities. He is a great seeker after the curious. When he perceives it he buys it. Then he takes it down to the beach and puts it on the boardwalk with a little

[24] 'On The New-Jersey Coast', New York *Tribune*, 24 July 1892, p. 22.

sign over it, informing the traveller of its history, its value and its virtues.

On the boardwalk now are some old boats, an ancient ship's bell, a hand fire engine of antique design, an iron anchor, a marble bathtub and various articles of interest to everybody. It is his boardwalk, and if he wants to put 7,000 fire engines and bathtubs on it he will do so. It is his privilege. No man should object to everybody doing as he pleases with his own fire engines and bathtubs.

'Founder' Bradley has lots of sport with his ocean front and boardwalk. It amuses him and he likes it. It warms his heart to see the thousands of people tramping over his boards, helter-skeltering in his sand and diving into that ocean of the Lord's which is adjacent to the beach of James A. Bradley.[25]

Because the coincidence of wealth and proprietorship enables him to carry his desires into action, Bradley becomes for Crane, in effect, the focus of Asbury Park's values, just as the sombre-hued preacher is the focus of Ocean Grove's values. Instead of a professionally distinctive valise, Bradley's eccentric badge is a white umbrella with green lining; instead of rebukes to frivolity in his eyes, Bradley sports fierce and passionate whiskers in his pursuit of 'the curious'. Just as the preacher imposes his traditional doctrines upon the Ocean Grove worshippers, Bradley imposes his fire engines and bathtubs—appropriately antique, outworn items —upon his Asbury Park 'worshippers' who recognize him as the titular head of the local social hierarchy. Bradley's junk disfigures the boardwalk and distracts attention from the ocean in the same way that the orthodox black valises disfigure a sincere moral quest and distract the mind from a realistic moral attitude. Both Bradley and the preacher, like the vain Italian with his cards and quarter, are able to foist their outworn specialties upon a gullible audience under the illusion that such antiquities arc significant, 'of interest to everybody', merely because the innocent worshippers accept them without question. Thus, the holiday-maker who comes to the seaside at Asbury Park is in the same position as the worshipper

---

[25] 'On The Boardwalk', p. 17. Bradley was also on Pennington's Board of Trustees and 'a faithful member of the Ocean Grove Camp Meeting Association' (Gullason, 'Cranes at Pennington', p. 540).

who comes to Ocean Grove: the one ignores the sea for the various machines and Bradley's exhibits, and the other ignores a moral reality for the mechanical ceremonies and professional orthodoxies.

But the strongest evidence of the ironic analogy between Bradley and the preacher is found in Crane's preoccupation with Bradley's own semi-professional efforts at prohibitive moral legislation:

> He likes to edit signs and have them tacked up around. There is probably no man in the world that can beat 'Founder' Bradley in writing signs. His work has an air of philosophic thought about it which ... may devote four lines to telling the public what happened in 1869 and draw from that a one-line lesson as to what they may not do at that moment. He has made sign-painting a fine art, and he is a master. His work, sprinkled broadcast over the boardwalk, delights the critics and incidentally warns the unwary. Strangers need no guide-book nor policemen. They have signs confronting them at all points, under their feet, over their heads and before their noses. 'Thou shalt not' do this, nor that, nor the other.[26]

Frivolity in Asbury Park meets with the same orthodox rebuke as frivolity in Ocean Grove. Bradley's signs are external accoutrements, like the professional's sombre-hued suit, deliberately manufactured and then delivered to the accepting public. Also, as Crane stresses the great number of signs, these prohibitive commandments are identified with the other junk which defaces the boardwalk. Hence, society in both communities is morally and aesthetically out of touch with reality: reality is hidden from view by an impenetrable warp and woof of forbidding signs, antique trash, and black valises, as innocence panders to innocence. And if it seems incredible that such irony as this apparently failed even to disturb the benign complacency of either community, the fact merely implies the density of the innocence which made such complacency invulnerable.

---

[26] Ibid. Crane returned to Asbury Park in 1896, after fame had come, and spoke so plainly that even local readers must have understood: 'there are a number of restrictions here which are ingeniously silly and are not sanctioned by nature's plan nor by any of the creeds of men, save those which define virtue as a physical inertia and a mental death' ('Asbury Park as Seen by Stephen Crane', New York *Journal*, 16 Aug. 1896, p. 33).

A week after the study of Bradley the parade story appeared and Crane was fired.[27] Although in his article he obviously aligns himself with the 'tan-colored, sun-beaten honesty' of the marchers 'who possessed principles', and reserves his barbed lash for the smug onlookers, his own moral commitment is not allowed to becloud his vision. These honest, principled marchers are also 'the most awkward, ungainly, uncut and uncarved procession that ever raised clouds of dust on sun-beaten streets'. They are 'slope-shouldered, uncouth and begrimed with dust. Their clothes fitted them illy, for the most part, and they had no ideas of marching. They merely plodded along, not seeming quite to understand, stolid, unconcerned . . . an assemblage of the spraddle-legged men of the middle class, whose hands were bent and shoulders stooped from delving and constructing.' In short, Crane looked at these men with the same eyes he had turned upon his mother and his university life: the moral principle is distinguished from the personal character, and both principle and person are accepted, without illusion, for what they are as Crane perceives them. Hence, the fact that the marchers themselves objected to this report should cause no great surprise. In mere quantity of newsprint the simple recognition of their honesty and principle is all but submerged beneath the uncomplimentary passages.

However, the importance of this article as a whole is easily exaggerated. Apart from excluding Crane permanently from the pages of the *Tribune*, it merely confirmed a bent to which he was already committed. Compared with the death of Agnes, the storm raised by this story could not have been much of a personal crisis. Compared with his success in imposing form upon his Asbury Park and Ocean Grove material, the anticlimactic parade article could not have been much of a personal triumph. Crane had already enjoyed the hand-to-mouth independence of an unknown free-lance writer in New York during part of the previous winter,

---

[27] The parade article is reprinted and expertly discussed by Schoberlin, *Sullivan County Sketches*, Introduction, pp. 5–11. See also Victor A. Elconin, 'Stephen Crane at Asbury Park', *American Literature*, XX (Nov. 1948), 275–89; Joseph J. Kwiat, 'The Newspaper Experience: Crane, Norris, and Dreiser', *Nineteenth-Century Fiction*, VIII (Sept. 1953), 99–117.

and the summer job was merely a temporary expedient. The loss of this job did not in itself even turn him from reporting to fiction: his reporting thereafter certainly had one less market, but *Maggie* had already been written and the *Tribune* had already published most of the Sullivan County tales.

These unsigned pieces divide clearly into two groups: the fictional tales concerning the adventures of four campers, i.e., the so-called *Sullivan County Sketches* collected in Schoberlin's 1949 edition, and a recently discovered group of nine sketches which appeared in the *Tribune* from February to July 1892.[28] There seems little reason for doubting that Crane wrote these pieces in the latter group. Lew Boyd of 'Hunting Wild Hogs' anticipates Jim Boyd's house in 'The Mesmeric Mountain'; long-dead Nelson Crocker of 'The Last Panther' may have been a forebear of Jim Crocker who dies in 'The Black Dog'; in 'Two Men and a Bear' a man receives 'a nice contusion that fitted the side of his head like a hat', and the tramp in 'Billy Atkins Went to Omaha' (New York *Press*, 20 May 1894, part 4, p. 3) acquires 'a contusion that fitted like a new derby'. Crane's characteristically angular imagery is everywhere present. Yet they are critically less important than those of the other group because they lack the sort of imaginary plot which struggles to assert itself in the adventures of the four campers. Instead, most of these pieces take the form of folk tales or reminiscences recorded by a wryly sceptical intelligence who simultaneously enjoys the anecdote and suspects that it has been distorted and embellished by oral tradition. 'Not Much of a Hero', perhaps the best example,

---

[28] 'The Last of the Mohicans', 21 Feb., p. 12, 'Hunting Wild Hogs', 28 Feb., p. 17, 'The Last Panther', 3 Apr., p. 17, 'Not Much of a Hero', 1 May, p. 15, 'Sullivan County Bears', 1 May, p. 16, 'The Way in Sullivan County', 8 May, p. 15, 'Bear and Panther', 17 July, p. 18, 'Two Men and a Bear', 24 July, p. 17, 'A Reminiscence of Indian War', 26 June, p. 17; see Thomas A. Gullason, 'A Stephen Crane Find: Nine Newspaper Sketches', *Southern Humanities Review*, II (Winter 1968), 1–37; *Stephen Crane: Sullivan County Tales and Sketches*, ed. R. W. Stallman (Ames, Iowa, 1968). Young Crane often had more than one piece published in the same issue of the *Tribune*: two items appear on 1 May (pp. 15, 16), 3 July (pp. 14, 28), 10 July (pp. 8, 17); on two occasions he triumphantly had *three* pieces in the same paper: 17 July, 'A Ghoul's Accountant' (p. 17), 'Bear and Panther' (p. 18), 'Joys of Seaside Life' (p. 18); and 24 July, 'Two Men and a Bear' (p. 17), 'The Black Dog' (p. 19), 'On the New-Jersey Coast' (p. 22).

examines the activities of Tom Quick, a local hero who hated Indians in the manner of Nathan Slaughter or Colonel John Moredock, and concludes that he was not the heroic 'Indian fighter' of tradition:

He was merely an Indian killer. There are three views to be taken of 'Tom' Quick. The deeds which are accredited to him may be fiction ones and he may have been one of those sturdy and bronzed woodsmen who cleared the path of civilization. Or the accounts may be true and he a monomaniac upon the subject of Indians.... Or the accounts may be true and he a man whose hands were stained with unoffending blood, purely and simply a murderer.

In 'A Reminiscence of Indian War' Crane suggests that the cowardly failure of fifty men to fight at the battle of the Minisink was due to their being led by a man who made a 'valorous oration' before the fight began: 'as for the man with the high aims and things', he later told Nellie Crouse, 'I shouldn't care to live in the same house with him if he was at all in the habit of talking about them' (*Letters*, p. 116). And 'The Last of the Mohicans' compares Cooper's romantic figure with a drunken derelict who lived out his old age and died in Sullivan County. But the other six pieces all retell local hunting yarns. Crane's prose is comparatively relaxed, his irony eases in the direction of humour, and there is little hint of any concealed meanings lurking beneath the surface. Thus, these minor pieces anticipate a comparatively large group of New York sketches, written between late 1892 and late 1896, which— as will be seen—share the same general characteristics.[29]

The other Sullivan County tales, however, are more interesting.[30] According to Louis Senger, the 'tall man' of these sketches,

[29] 'Travels in New York: The Broken-Down Van', the first of these New York sketches, appeared with those of Sullivan County: New York *Tribune*, 10 July 1892, p. 8. 'Across the Covered Pit' belongs with the lesser Sullivan County group: see R. W. Stallman, 'Stephen Crane: Some New Stories', *Bulletin of the New York Public Library*, LXI (Jan. 1957), 39–41.

[30] For publication dates, see Schoberlin, pp. 5–6. For their original acceptance and appearance in the *Tribune*, see W. F. Johnson, 'The Launching of Stephen Crane', *Literary Digest and International Book Review*, IV (Apr. 1926), 288–9. Stallman, *Crane*, p. 485, states that 'The Mesmeric Mountain' was written in late 1899, even though earlier (p. 42) he implies that it was written with the others. Crane's style affirms the earlier date.

Crane himself is the 'quiet man' (Schoberlin, p. 18); and according to C. K. Linson, Crane is the 'little man'.[31] Such confusion provides an admirable port of entry into the intense world of Crane's art because, if he is an ironist, then *both* Senger and Linson are entirely correct. Crane as the quiet man, who is always superfluous in the action of the sketches, is the detached, ironic observer of the external facts of the protagonist's adventures—the same ironic observer who enjoyed the summer antics at the Jersey shore. But because the most crucial actions of these adventures really take place within the protagonist's own mind, Crane also assumes the little man's position in order to examine, to analyse for the reader, the mental and emotional turmoil resulting from the juxtaposition of a particular personality and a specific situation; that is, Crane as the little man is the ironic vision turned inward upon his own mental machinery. As will be seen, these two views of reality —the quiet man as ironic observer and the little man as unheroic and all-too-human protagonist, the ironically detached perception of factual event and the acute awareness of what goes on within a typical mind labouring under emotional stress, 'the involved, self-deluded character and the detached ironic narrator'—are present in all Crane's work from the *Sullivan County Sketches* to 'The Upturned Face'.[32] They represent the double vision of the ironist as it functions in his art; and, as might be expected, a rough division of Crane's writings into newspaper realism, fiction, and poetry aligns itself with the three major emphases inherent in this double vision. In Crane's newspaper work and minor fiction, in general the work he himself dismissed as 'any sort of stuff that would sell', the emphasis is upon the detached observation of external event: Crane's world apart from man is godless, amoral, 'flatly indifferent' to man and his moral and emotional life, and therefore dramatically unprofitable except as the inexorable setting in which human life has to be lived—'There can be little of dramatic import in environment', Crane states in 'The Blue Hotel'.

[31] Corwin Knapp Linson, *My Stephen Crane*, ed. Edwin H. Cady (Syracuse, 1958), p. 40.

[32] Joseph X. Brennan, 'Stephen Crane and the Limits of Irony', *Criticism*, XI (Spring 1969), 184.

'Any room can present a tragic front; any room can be comic.' Thus, it follows that in his important fiction, the 'matter that pleased himself' which he wrote 'very slowly', the emphasis falls upon the interior life of the mind because the meaningful or significant in Crane's world is strictly a human property, a moral dimension not available outside man. The difference in the quality of work resulting from these two emphases is most obvious in the newspaper sketches because these pieces range from the trivial— hack writing as in 'Evening on the Roof'—to the intense artistry of Crane's finest work—as in 'An Experiment in Misery' and 'War Memories'—: in so far as a sketch approaches the level of art, the emphasis shifts from external fact to internal action. Crane's poems (and a few of his letters, particularly those written to Nellie Crouse), distinct from either the fiction or the news reporting but related to both, are best approached as the comparatively direct revelation of his personal philosophy, the all-important moral norm by means of which Crane is able to transcend and control his own vision and thus prevent the two views from merging towards a pointless blur of ambiguity.

At this point, however, it is merely necessary to suggest that Crane's fiction begins with his projecting his own imagined responses to a situation into his protagonist. When he examined Bradley he understood the man's mind, and judged it, but he expressed only the results it produced to imply the mentality which would concern itself with such accomplishments. This implication of his subject's state of mind makes the early newspaper work valuable and distinguishes it from the flat reports of other correspondents; it implies that Crane from the beginning was more interested in the interior reality of the mind than in the comparatively inert factual results it produced; and it suggests that in his fiction he would attempt to catch the weak mental machinery in the very act that produced the sort of result he reported for the *Tribune*. Arthur Oliver's memoir of a conversation with Crane that summer reveals that the ironic vision had analysed the craft of fiction as it was then practised and, as usual, had rejected everything except what it perceived as essential:

'Somehow I can't get down to the real thing,' I said. 'I know I have something unusual to tell, but I get all tangled up with different notions of how it ought to be told.'

'Stevie' scooped up a handful of sand and tossed it to the brisk sea breeze.

'Treat your notions like that,' he said. 'Forget what you think about it and tell how you feel about it. Make the other fellow realize you are just as human as he is. That's the big secret of story-telling. Away with literary cads [*sic*] and canons. Be yourself!'[33]

Although this dialogue was obviously written by Oliver there is nothing wrong with the doctrine. To apply it to the *Sullivan County Sketches* one has to realize only that the little man is no Henry Fleming.

The little man's mind is an oversimplified exaggeration in which the qualities that signify his humanity—primarily his ego, his fear, and his imagination—are isolated through Crane's selection and emphasis, as if to make the first try at catching the weak mental machinery in action that much easier. Simply because the little man's mind is not an ordinary one 'the whole ordinary world of intercourse is unable . . . to make its way into the Sullivan County Sketches' (Berryman, p. 40). The reader is allowed a glimpse of the ordinary world at the end of the better sketches when the cause of the protagonist's fear is revealed as trivial, so prosaic that it cannot begin to justify the terror preceding this unmasking. Before such revelation, however, the simple fact is either misunderstood or unknown—a count reveals that Crane specifically calls the cause of the characters' fear 'the unknown' ten times in these sketches— and thus the important cause of terror has to lie within the mind, during the action before the denouement, has to be the horrible illusions evoked by the imagination. These illusory images, of course, can never be part of the ordinary world because they are created by, and only exist in, the imagination itself. The little man's ego usually puts him into the position of confronting the unknown, a normal human apprehension of the unknown stimulates his imagination into running riot, his fear immediately trans-

---

[33] 'Jersey Memories—Stephen Crane', *New Jersey Historical Society Proceedings*, n.s. XVI (Oct. 1931), 454–5.

fers itself from the unknown reality to the terrifying images evoked by his imagination, and once this process has been triggered into action Crane calmly sits back and ironically contemplates the protagonist's frantic stuggles towards awareness.

'Four Men in a Cave', neither the best nor the worst of the sketches, begins when the little man's ego prompts him to explore a cave—to confront the unknown—as vengeance upon this hole in the ground which, he imagines, had 'gaped at him'. Because he is afraid, he has been persuading his three companions to accompany him, and the only part of his 'orations' that the reader hears—'We can tell a great tale when we get back to the city if we investigate this thing'—may or may not be true because, until the unknown is experienced, there is no way of knowing whether the adventure will make such a tale possible. However, when a man is afraid he has to argue himself into action, and this specious argument persuades all four men—the scared orator as well as the others—to enter the cave and confront the unknown. Until they fall down the slippery incline into the mad hermit's chamber they are always free to turn round or back out, and the little man twice suggests it as he is first in line; but they push on because none wishes to acknowledge such cowardice. The darkness in the cave having spurred their imaginations to greater activity, the men have to override their fear by channelling its energy into the substitute emotion of anger, and again the little man reveals his position in line by being the most vehemently angry of the four. Their anger in this context, as pointless as the 'reasoning' the devil offers Goodman Brown in a similar context, masks their fear and allows them to continue. Their quarrelling rises to a climax when the little man stops, and then all four fall down 'to the unknown in darkness', the little man, a poor candidate for the crew of an open boat, biting and scratching 'at his companions, for he was satisfied that it was their fault'.

When the men confront Tom Gardner, Crane makes the technical blunder which often disfigures these sketches. Although his diction in the portrait of the hermit implies the harmless, recognized eccentric of the guide's offhand comment—the guide does not even bother to remove his pipe—when first encountered Gardner is given a couple of dogs and a 'long, thin knife' to make him terrible.[34] The two aspects of the portrait do not merge very well, the reader is fooled as well as the four campers, and the focus which should remain upon the minds of characters—particularly that of the little man—becomes blurred. Nevertheless, the men's imaginations still outstrip reality:

> 'A vampire!' said one.
> 'A ghoul!' said another.
> 'A Druid before the sacrifice,' murmured another.
> 'The shade of an Aztec witch doctor,' said the little man.

Whatever the hermit may be, he is none of these, even when first encountered. Thus, in spite of the blunder, the greater part of the men's terror still springs from their imagined illusions. Because of their fright they neither see the 'wide crack' in the cave wall nor unite to defend themselves. Instead, the little man's 'quaking companions' push him into the absurd poker game, and once the hermit wins all his money the four men are ordered out of the cave. The unknown has now been experienced, but it is not yet fully understood.

Understanding comes only with the guide's explanation of the hermit's harmless reality. When they acquire this knowledge two reactions necessarily take place within the minds of the men: they realize that their fears—now dissipated—were without reasonable basis, and they suffer chagrin at the recollection of them and the wild illusions which accompanied them. The little man reveals this humiliating deflation, which reality always works upon the over-heated imagination, by interrupting the guide with a shrill 'seething sentence' irrelevant to the reality of the hermit. And the pudgy man reveals the same deflation by his sneering repetition of the little man's original oration: no great tale back in the city is

---

[34] The imagery of the 'great, gray stone, cut squarely like an altar' beneath 'three candles' and before which stood a man 'with what seemed to be a small volume clasped in his yellow fingers' should not be lost on readers familiar with Crane's background or the Ocean Grove professionals. Gardner is another innocent who went to the city, wandered into 'one of them there dens', and became converted.

possible because the teller would have to include his own absurd fears, his own lurid illusions, and his own shame and disgust at himself which came with understanding.

The same flaw of appearance which takes in both reader and character occurs in 'A Ghoul's Accountant'. The 'ghoul' carries a 'three-pronged pickerel-spear' as he approaches the sleeping camp, where only nature is awake to react—and thus to establish the reader's response before the little man is awakened. But once the 'ghoul' is revealed as a gruff, illiterate farmer, the little man is released and the sketch ends. 'A Ghoul's Accountant' is a good story in terms of its kind, but because there are more chills than contemplation in its terror it is not exactly Crane's kind of story. In rather the same way, the denouement of 'An Explosion of Seven Babies' accounts for what has happened but does not otherwise qualify the actions of either the 'giantess' or the little man. The typical Crane twist is the ending: the irrationality of the little man's kicking the salesman in the stomach balances the irrationality of the assault the woman has just made upon him.[35] In 'The Octopush' the fishermen marooned on four stumps are happy until darkness makes each feel 'that he was alone, separated from humanity by impassable gulfs'. Their fears swiftly increase once their imaginations begin to work: 'The little man started up and shrieked that all creeping things were inside his stump. Then he tried to sit facing four ways, because dread objects were approaching at his back.' Crane then shifts to the drunken guide's illusion that his stump has actually turned into an 'octopush' which he perceives with 'eyes that saw the unknown'. But this sketch deteriorates in the ending. The guide remains drunk and the four men, reunited round a 'great fire of pine sticks' on the shore, have their imaginations calmed by light and companionship. And the irony of the little man's kicking the guide—his own fears and illusions, even without the aid of alcohol, are as absurd as those of the man

[35] As A. W. Hart argues, the woman did not really mistake the little man for the salesman; if she had, she would not have left him to attack his companion: 'Stephen Crane's Social Outlook as Revealed in His Writings', unpublished Ph.D. thesis (Michigan State, 1955), p. 74.

he kicks—is not clearly communicated because his anger is partly justified by the guide's previous conduct.

The main issue is obscured by chance in three sketches. In 'A Tent in Agony' the little man, alone in camp, frantically climbs a tree to evade an intruding bear. When the bear by chance gets entangled in the tent and rolls down a hill toward the three returning campers, the little man scrambles down, lights his pipe, and allows the others to infer that he has personally vanquished the bear: 'There's only one of me—and the devil made a twin.' 'The Holler Tree' begins with a squabble between the little man and the pudgy man over a basket of eggs carried by the latter, and it ends when the little man's struggles inside the tree topple it, by chance, upon these eggs. The little man accepts this chance event as a personal triumph over the pudgy man and, as in 'An Explosion of Seven Babies', the absurdity of this illusion balances the absurdity of the little man's earlier illusion that the pudgy man was responsible for his falling into the hollow tree. Within this framework the little man talks himself into a position from which he must either climb the hollow tree or admit that he is afraid to do so (a plot device later put to excellent use in 'A Mystery of Heroism'). And once he has climbed it, he himself also suggests that he might slide down inside. He is reluctant because 'something' might be down in the hole; but while he argues, the rotten wood breaks and, the situation finally beyond his control, he falls inside, angrily blames the pudgy man for his plight, and struggles until he topples the tree. Chance is everywhere in 'The Black Dog'. By chance, the men are lost and they blunder upon a house in which, by chance, an old man is near death; by chance, a starving dog is within range of the smell of beef tea; and perhaps by chance, if he is not scared to death, the old man dies while the dog howls beneath his open window. Still, the pattern of fear, illusion, crisis, and deflation is present. The little man's imagination awakens with the first hint that the old man will not die until the impending appearance of the black dog occurs. He and the pudgy man quarrel to mask their fear as they wait in increasing suspense, and when the dog does appear he blindly hurls everything he can find—including, by chance, the bowl of beef tea—through the window at the 'phantom'. When this ghost diminishes to a mere hungry dog, he is again able to 'triumph' over the pudgy man; and again his triumph is illusory because he responded to the situation exactly as the pudgy man did, and a chance combination of events—not the intelligence or courage of the little man—resolved this situation.

The three sketches remaining seem the best of the lot because, in each, the emphasis is securely placed upon contemplation. In 'The Cry of a Huckleberry Pudding' the little man's cries, from where he has wandered away from camp in the darkness, terrify his three companions. Their imaginations instantly leap into frenzied activity, and at the climax all three are suddenly deflated when they learn that all this 'tangled chaos' of sound came from a little man with a stomach-ache. The reader is not misled; there are no ghoulish farmers with long knives or pickerel spears in this sketch, and Crane's comic exaggeration should reassure the most innocent: 'The group, waiting in the silence that followed their awakening, wriggled their legs in the agony of fright. There was a pause which extended through space. Comets hung and worlds waited.' Also, after the ironic deflation the reaction of the terrified men is carefully stated: 'The three men contemplating him suddenly felt themselves swell with wrath. They had been terrorized to no purpose. They had expected to be eaten. They were not. The fact maddened them.'[36] The cause of this reaction cannot reasonably be their fear, because at this point all fear has been done away with. But the horrible illusions evoked by their imaginations are not so easily dissipated. The simple fact exposes the absurdity of these illusions, the men are ashamed of themselves for having conceived them, and by means of anger at the little man they relieve their shame by wrongly transferring to him the blame for their own weakness.

In 'Killing His Bear', unique among the sketches because the only fear in it is the implicit fear of the little man that he may fail to make the kill, the act of killing the animal is seen from within

---

[36] Crane uses this same reversal later in 'The Duel that Was not Fought', 'Five White Mice', and most effectively in 'The Bride Comes to Yellow Sky'.

the mind of the hunter, and thus the whole sketch is given to the contemplation of what takes place within a mind under the stress of intense excitement. As in 'The Black Dog' the little man is forced to remain totally inactive during an interval when he knows the bear is continuously approaching. Under such pressure the imagination, excited to anticipation, conceives countless images of what is about to happen: 'Swift pictures of himself in a thousand attitudes under a thousand combinations of circumstances, killing a thousand bears, passed panoramically through him.' When the bear finally appears, 'the little man, with nerves tingling and blood throbbing', experiences a climax of emotional intensity which prepares for the final ironic comment:

The little man saw swirling fur over his gun barrel. The earth faded to nothing. Only space and the game, the aim and the hunter. Mad emotions, powerful to rock worlds, hurled through the little man, but did not shake his tiniest nerve.

When the rifle cracked, it shook his soul to a profound depth. Creation rocked and the bear stumbled.

Thus, the anticipated experience is undergone, and then follows the rest of the usual pattern: a deflation to prosaic, illusionless reality. The accomplished fact of 'a dead bear with his nose in the snow' is presented flatly in language devoid of the excitement which colours the prose preceding the kill. And the final ironic sentence— 'Upon his face was the smile of the successful lover'—underscores the vast distinction between excited anticipation and the emotional emptiness of achievement. The lover's achievement, like the little man's kill, destroys anticipation by fulfilling it; the result is an emotional stasis, however pleasant, in which neither anticipation nor the images it evokes in the imagination are present—in which creation does not rock, the earth does not fade, and only one of a thousand illusory images of a man killing a bear will apply, perhaps not even this single one.[37] However, in this sketch reality does in a sense measure up to illusion in so far as illusion is dissipated

[37] This sketch, in its structure, subject-matter, imagery, and careful pacing of the prose, strongly implies that by 1892 Crane had acquired a normal and healthy understanding of sexual experience from the male point of view.

through fulfilment; Crane did not again resolve a situation in this manner until he wrote 'The Blue Hotel'.

'The Mesmeric Mountain', much like 'Four Men in a Cave', begins with the little man 'muttering to himself with his eyes fixed on an irregular black opening in the green wall of forest'. His imagination aroused by the unknown lying beyond the opening, he refuses the pudgy man's fact—'it leads to ol' Jim Boyd's over on the Lumberland Pike'—in favour of his own imaginings: 'I don't know just what, but I'm sure it leads to something great or something. It looks like it.' Then, after staring at the hole for another hour, he walks into it alone and begins his adventure with the mountain which affects him in the same way that this hole in the woods has, though more violently. When he first sees the mountain in the distance, after getting lost and climbing a tree, he utters an 'ejaculation' and falls to the ground, apparently in surprise, not fright, for he recognizes the peak as Jones's Mountain 'about six miles' from camp, and he is shocked to learn he has travelled so far. The mountain here is no more than a landmark. The little man orients himself by means of it, fixes his course away from it, but then again gets lost and travels in a circle, for after hiking till he is exhausted 'he dived at a clump of tag-alders and, emerging, confronted Jones's Mountain'. At this point the important sequence of action begins.

The tired little man, surprised at coming to the mountain after believing he had been hiking away from it, 'sat down in a clear space and fixed his eyes on the summit' which is as unknown to him as the hole in the forest was, and his imagination immediately beings to work: 'His mouth opened widely, and his body swayed at times. The little man and the peak stared in silence.' But as the peak no more 'stares' than Gardner's cave had 'gaped' at him, the little man's illusions assume control of his mind as he gradually becomes mesmerized by his own imagination, not by the mountain. Crane implies the change occurring within the man by presenting the trance-like hush of external nature at twilight; and both trances are broken by the simultaneous leap of a pickerel in a lake and the leap of the little man into furious action based on his illusions.

'For the love of Mike, there's eyes in this mountain! I feel 'em! Eyes!'

> He fell flat on his face.
> When he looked again, he immediately sprang erect and ran.
> 'It's comin'!'
> The mountain was approaching.

The little man flees in terror, but again travels in a circle and returns to the foot of the mountain: ' "God!" he howled, "it's been follerin' me." ' Finally, after even a handful of pebbles thrown at it fails to stop its hostilities, he desperately runs straight up the mountain which 'swayed and tottered, and was ever about to smite him with a granite arm'. Once the unknown summit is experienced, his illusion of the mountain's attempt to kill him collapses, and he shifts instantly from absurd terror to a sense of triumph just as absurd, as illusory, as his terror had been:

> Immediately, he swaggered with valor to the edge of the cliff. His hands were scornfully in his pockets.
> He gazed at the western horizon, edged sharply against a yellow sky. 'Ho!' he said. 'There's Boyd's house and the Lumberland Pike' [as the pudgy man had told him before he left camp].
> The mountain under his feet was motionless.

The little man's adventure with the mountain—perhaps the best example of the psychological sequence which appears imperfectly throughout these sketches—clearly outlines the basic pattern of most of Crane's later work. The later work differs from the Sullivan County tales partly because the later protagonists, except for poor Maggie, have better mental machinery than the little man has. The little man does not even know enough to recognize his own illusions for what they are and to be ashamed of them; like his real-life kinsmen and contemporaries, Founder Bradley and the Ocean Grove minister, he therefore learns nothing from experience and remains the prisoner of his own limitations.

If one were to set forth the pattern of action imperfectly employed in these sketches, it would have to take the form of a psychological progression to awareness of reality: a character is faced with an unknown quality or situation which, for some reason, he soon has to experience; because he is apprehensive about what he does not yet understand, his imagination, in anticipation of the coming experience, becomes excited to the creation of terrifying illusions; these illusions become the immediate cause of fear, and both fear and illusions increase in intensity until the moment when the unknown becomes experienced; then, as reality never measures up to the imagination, the prosaic fact both dissipates fear and reveals illusion for what it is; only the remembrance of both fear and illusion is left, and *ideally* this remembrance should make the protagonist ashamed of himself. The obvious implication of the final step is that if a man is sufficiently honest and intelligent to be ashamed of his own weaknesses he will eventually be able to understand himself and accept his place in a world full of other fallible human beings. The psychological basis of this whole pattern is explicitly stated in 'The Cry of a Huckleberry Pudding':

The cry of the unknown . . . is mightier than the war yell of the dreadful, because the dreadful may be definite. But this whoop strikes greater fear from hearts because it tells of formidable mouths and great, grasping claws that live in impossibility. It is the chant of a phantom force which imagination declares invincible, and awful to the sight. (Schoberlin, p. 67)

More generally, Crane had discovered the role of the imagination in a situation of intense emotional stress, and from this discovery he was able to forge that element of his craft which he most needed: the pattern of psychological action which allowed him to take direct advantage of his ironic vision in fiction—his 'one trump'.[38]

The employment of the pattern may be faulty in the *Sullivan County Sketches*, but the better ones reveal that Crane had his

[38] This crucial pattern in Crane's work has been well examined by Max R. Westbrook, 'Stephen Crane and the Revolt-Search Motif', unpublished Ph.D. thesis (Texas, 1960), pp. 147–9; and by James B. Colvert, 'Structure and Theme in Stephen Crane's Fiction', *Modern Fiction Studies*, V (Autumn 1959), 202–7. The pattern is implicit in Berryman's statement: 'A Crane creation, or character, normally is *pretentious* and *scared*—the human condition; fitted by the second for pathos, by the first for irony' (*Crane*, p. 280). And Berryman was anticipated by Jean Whitehead Lang, 'The Art of Stephen Crane', unpublished Ph.D. thesis (Cornell, 1944), pp. 66, 73–4, 91, 122–3.

essential subject firmly in hand by the summer of 1892.[39] The
parade story came at a good time. By August, Crane was ready to
enter upon the next stage of his literary life.

[39] Two other concepts introduced in these sketches crop up importantly in
the later work. First, in Crane's world, no matter how ashamed a man's illusory
fears may make him feel, such a man is better off than the one who never suffers
such an experience; the first has imagination, and the other—endowed with
'merely a stomach and no soul'—does not. Second, the sketches argue that any
man, no matter what his illusions or how great his fright, will eventually reach
a point at which he will stand and fight back (see Schoberlin, pp. 49, 57, 68, 85).

II

CRANE UNDERGROUND

CRANE'S Bowery work is difficult to interpret, partly because in writing it he is experimenting and learning his craft—he later inscribed a copy of *Maggie* for H. P. Taber, editor of the *Philistine*, with 'I wrote this book when I was very young; so if you don't like it, shut up' (quoted by Stallman, *Crane*, p. 214)—and partly because he left a couple of critical comments about it which can point readers in the wrong direction. For example, he wrote to an editor of *Leslie's Weekly* late in 1895 that 'the nearer a writer gets to life the greater he becomes as an artist, and most of my prose writings have been toward the goal partially described by that misunderstood and abused word, realism' (*Letters*, p. 78). When critics add to this statement Linson's recollection of Crane waiting with the Bowery tramps—as ill-clad and hungry as any of them—before writing 'The Men in the Storm', his implicit position as the youth of 'An Experiment in Misery', the events preceding the writing of 'The Open Boat', and his frantic efforts to get to the Spanish-American War, it becomes only too easy to identify him with the writers of the cult of experience. Certainly the Bowery, in 1892 'the most famous centre of poverty and crime in America',[1] must originally have appealed to Crane as the exact opposite of Asbury Park and Ocean Grove. But *Maggie, George's Mother*, and the better Bowery sketches all reveal that the ironist found in the Bowery merely a more violent form of the same sham respectability, innocence, and evasion of responsibility he had found at the Jersey shore. Moreover, Crane's actual Bowery experience is somewhat remote from either *The Red Badge* or *The Black Riders*, easily the two best works written during his Bowery years. Whatever Crane

---

[1] Carl Van Doren, *Twenty Stories by Stephen Crane* (New York, 1940), Introduction, p. vi.

may have believed about the value of experience to a realistic writer, his work—both early and late—reveals that experience, or reality, or 'life' was, for him, mental and moral:

What makes Crane's realism remarkable is his search for the truth about what goes on inside a mind, given a certain set of circumstances. The circumstances did not matter to Crane as much as what they produced; and he was always willing to accept suggestions as to where he should go in search of material. His interest lay in . . . recording how the thoughts flowed through the mind of the sufferer.[2]

'Realism' certainly applies to Crane's work, but it is a psychological realism, and thus his writings do not belong with the cult of experience: the point of 'The Open Boat' is not that three men escaped from the sea, but that in the process of undergoing this experience they have become 'interpreters'.

However, if Crane eludes this pigeon-hole, his inscription in presentation copies of *Maggie* has allowed him—or at least this one novel—to be filed securely under naturalism:

It is inevitable that you will be greatly shocked by this book but continue please with all possible courage to the end. For it tries to show that environment is a tremendous thing in the world and frequently shapes lives regardless. If one proves that theory one makes room in Heaven for all sorts of souls (notably an occasional street girl) who are not confidently expected to be there by many excellent people. (*Letters*, p. 14)

This inscription brings up the whole thorny problem of naturalism, a critical ogre which has bedevilled Crane scholarship ever since innocent Hamlin Garland tried to do a young author a favour by reviewing the first edition of *Maggie* in B. O. Flower's crusading *Arena* (VIII [June 1893], xi–xii). In order to be a useful critical term distinct from either 'realism' or 'romanticism', literary 'naturalism' has to signify

a manner and method of composition by which the author portrays *life as it is in accordance with the philosophic theory of determinism*

---

[2] Lang, 'Art of Stephen Crane', p. 119. 'I know what the psychologists say,' Crane writes, 'that a fellow can't comprehend a condition that he has never experienced, and I argued that many times with the Professor' (*Letters*, p. 158).

(exemplified in Zola's *L'Assommoir*). In contrast to a realist, a naturalist believes that man is fundamentally an animal without free will. To a naturalist man can be explained in terms of the forces, usually heredity and environment, which operate upon him.

This excellent definition by Lars Åhnebrink will, of course, not satisfy anyone who wishes to define a genus on the basis of occasional characteristics—such as setting, tonality, character, animal imagery—instead of the definitive philosophic determinism. The ideal naturalistic setting, presumably, should be found in Dante's *Inferno*, for this tale is set in literally a hell of a place; there are plenty of primitive, 'tough' characters from the lower classes in the Old Testament; and Shakespeare's *Richard III* abounds with animal imagery; yet none of these works is considered naturalistic because none portrays human life as being primarily determined by external forces. Crane's tone, in all his important Bowery writings, is inevitably ironic—never more so than in *Maggie*—and thus the author is always present as an ordering, discriminating, judging intelligence, a tone which is as far removed from the anonymous reportage of *Sister Carrie*, on the one hand, as it is from Edward Townsend's sentimental Chimmie Fadden on the other. Moreover, Charles Child Walcutt, as eminent an authority as Åhnebrink, has stated categorically that any or all of the occasional characteristics of naturalism can be present in a work that is not naturalistic, and that a given work is properly termed naturalistic only when it contains philosophic determinism. Also, Donald Pizer has admitted that Crane's 'primary goal [in *Maggie*] was not to show the effects of environment but to distinguish between moral appearance and reality, to attack the sactimonious self-deception and sentimental emotional gratification of moral poses'.[3] Yet *Maggie*, traditionally considered 'par excellence the

---

[3] Åhnebrink, *The Beginnings of Naturalism in American Fiction* (Upsala, 1950), pp. vi-vii; Walcutt, 'Harold Frederic and American Naturalism', *American Literature*, XI (Mar. 1939), 11; Pizer, 'Stephen Crane's "Maggie" and American Naturalism', *Criticism*, VII (Spring 1965), 174—a good discussion of *Maggie*'s 'characteristics which clash with its neat categorization as naturalistic fiction' (p. 168). Another such study is William T. Lenehan, 'The Failure of Naturalistic Techniques in Stephen Crane's *Maggie*', *Stephen Crane's* Maggie: *Text and Context*, ed. Maurice Bassan (Belmont, California, 1966), pp. 166–73;

exemplar of literary naturalism', remains exhibit A for anyone who hopes to enrol Crane beneath this banner.[4]

Readers who find the above definition of naturalism acceptable, however, are apt to invoke Lawrence's dictum—'Never trust the artist. Trust the tale'—and then state the obvious: the work, including *Maggie*, belies the inscription. If 'environment' means external living conditions, *Maggie* in no way proves that environment is a tremendous force which 'frequently shapes lives regardless'. All the characters in this novel, including Maggie herself, are free to choose their own course of action within the usual limitations provided by the particular situation, or else Crane's intense irony is gratuitous. Maggie cannot be determined by heredity because she in no way resembles her mother, brother, or what little is shown of her father. And she cannot be determined by her external environment simply because the novel's structure places her *and* her slum environment in exactly the same position relative to the other characters: both are alike passive, inert, acted upon, actually shaped by the twisted values and hypocritical actions of Mrs. Johnson, Jimmie, and Pete; and Maggie's downfall at the hands of Pete, as predictable as the fate of a roomful of new furniture in the hands of drunken Mrs. Johnson because Maggie chooses to resist Pete about as much as the furniture resists her mother, 'is inevitable only under the precondition of human irresponsibility'.[5] But again Crane's irony, in all the Bowery work, proclaims that he does not believe human irresponsibility is ever inevitable or determined by anything other than the wilful dishonesty of human

---

still better is Milne Holton, 'The Sparrow's Fall and the Sparrow's Eye: Crane's *Maggie*', *Studia Neophilologica*, XLI (1969), 115–29.

[4] R. W. Stallman, 'Crane's "Maggie": A Reassessment', *Modern Fiction Studies*, V (Autumn 1959), 258; cf. any literary history. For a late example which borders upon parody, see David Fitelson, 'Stephen Crane's *Maggie* and Darwinism', *American Quarterly*, XVI (Summer 1964), 182–94: because Jimmie is 'soundly reared in a climate of familial antagonism, he enters manhood with a clear understanding of the nature of reality' (p. 189); 'there is also a possible botanical association: "The girl, Maggie, blossomed in a mud-puddle" ' (p. 188); 'survival' in this novel, whose heroine commits suicide, is 'the absolute value' (p. 193).

[5] Max R. Westbrook, 'Stephen Crane: The Pattern of Affirmation', *Nineteenth-Century Fiction*, XIV (Dec. 1959), 220–1.

beings. The Mrs. Johnsons, George Kelceys, and professional tramps of Crane's world are held fully responsible for their quality of personal honesty, and they are lashed unmercifully when they fail to uphold it.

Yet Crane's comments are more often trustworthy than not, if his irony is taken into account. His inscription, taken strictly at face value, is obviously persuasion addressed to a genteel, mildly sentimental reader—or to someone who thought no more deeply about the slums than Garland did—to induce him to read the book and thereby honour Crane's implicitly distinguishing him from those 'many excellent people'. But all this sentimental pulpit rhetoric about making room in Heaven for 'street girls', coming from the ironist who already had aligned Founder Bradley with the Ocean Grove minister and had written 'Killing His Bear', sounds a bit too pat; set against the extremely tough-minded Bowery writings, it rings like a lead coin dropped carefully in the hope that it will pass scrutiny. In short, I suggest that this inscription may be an ironic equivocation—perhaps another ironic private joke comparable to the coupling of Bradley and the minister—that Crane's use of 'environment' meant one thing to the innocent reader interested in the appalling conditions of slum life and something entirely different to Crane himself. In Crane's day the word 'Bowery' implied a specific *moral* condition, well-defined and locally recognized, in addition to what the word now means:

> It is probably the most brilliantly lighted thoroughfare on this planet. . . . But the method adopted for this lighting is cheap and vulgar, and emphasizes the popular meaning which the word 'Bowery' has taken on. . . . Whatever has the Bowery stamp is not merely an imitation, but it is a loud and offensive falsity. In New York, when the people see a great glass stud, cut to look like a diamond worth $10,000, and worn on the shirt of a store clerk, they call it a Bowery jewel, and they say of the man that he looks very Bowery.[6]

All Crane's Bowery writings seem to me primarily concerned with

[6] Julian Ralph, 'The Bowery', *Century*, XLIII (Dec. 1891), 234 (Crane mentions such a Bowery jewel, *Letters*, pp. 129–30). Edward Marshall, Crane's good friend, also noted this moral reality in 'New York Tenements', *North American Review*, CLVII (Dec. 1893), 755.

this aspect of the local 'environment' which stems from moral cowardice rather than lack of grocery money; and if such a view is correct, the real scene of struggle in all of these writings, as in the Sullivan County tales, should lie within the mind of the protagonist rather than outside in the street, saloon, or tenement. *Maggie*, in other words, quite reasonably proves the theory that so sacrosanct a quality as innocence is fatally incompetent to cope with a moral environment which is 'very Bowery'. If this interpretation of environment is acceptable—not the physical conditions of slum life, but a *moral* force which is a loud and offensive falsity because of the dishonesty of the inhabitants—then Crane's inscription obviously makes sense in terms of his ironic presentation of Pete, Jimmie, and Mrs. Johnson. Such a moral environment, as Jacob Riis argued, is indeed a 'tremendous thing in the world' and it frequently shapes the lives of children who grow up in it; but it is not to be excused by any appeal to philosophic determinism.

Ironic joke or not, the apparent meaning of the inscription is flatly contradicted, and the private meaning suggested above is affirmed, by Crane's best-known comment on the Bowery. Here he is not trying to persuade anyone to read anything, and the angry prose permits little doubt of his sincerity. Hence, it seems to me that all Crane's Bowery work is best approached through an examination of the excellent sketch which was written specifically to define the basis of Bowery life. Too often overlooked is the fact that Crane suggested this sketch to his reader in order to prompt an intelligent view of *Maggie*:

Mrs. Howells was right in telling you that I have spent a great deal of time on the East Side and that I have no opinion of missions. That— to you—may not be a valid answer since perhaps you have been informed that I am not very friendly to Christianity as seen around town. I do not think that much can be done with the Bowery as long as the [*word blurred*] are in their present state of conceit. A person who thinks himself superior to the rest of us because he has no job and no pride and no clean clothes is as badly conceited as Lillian Russell. In a story of mine called 'An Experiment in Misery' I tried to make plain that the root of Bowery life is a sort of cowardice. Perhaps I mean a lack of ambition or to willingly be knocked flat and accept the licking. . . . I had no other purpose in writing 'Maggie' than to show people to people as they seem to me. If that be evil, make the most of it. (*Letters*, p. 133)

This comment was written late in 1896, and thus it is possible that Crane's view of Bowery life might have changed from what he believed earlier; but the 'Experiment' appeared in the New York *Press* on 22 April 1894 (part 3, p. 2), and it implies most strongly that Crane's unsentimental attitude toward the Bowery denizen in 1896 was to be no different from what it was when he created Mrs. Johnson.

'An Experiment in Misery' begins and ends with a conversation between the young man of the sketch and an unnamed friend. Editors err when they reprint the sketch without this enclosing frame because the opening conversation states plainly that the young man is conducting a deliberate experiment with the carefully specified purpose of discovering not the tramp's physical or economic environment, but 'his point of view or something near it'. The concluding passage reaffirms this purpose and suggests that the experiment has been successful:

'Well,' said the friend, 'did you discover his point of view?'
'I don't know that I did,' replied the young man; 'but at any rate I think mine own has undergone a considerable alteration.'[7]

This enclosing dialogue implies that the young man began his experiment with the conventional feeling of mere pity without any understanding of the outcast, and that the awareness acquired through his experiment led him to adopt a more realistic attitude——one necessarily closer to Crane's own view of the Bowery tramps. Both the experience itself and the careful ordering of it as the experiment progresses should bring any intelligent observer from innocent pity to awareness.

Structurally, the enclosed portion of the sketch progresses from night to morning, darkness to light, innocence to understanding; and the division occurs roughly two-thirds of the way through

[7] *The New York City Sketches of Stephen Crane and Related Pieces*, ed. R. W. Stallman and E. R. Hagemann (New York, 1966), pp. 34, 43. Subsequent page numbers in the text refer to this edition.

with 'Finally a long lance point of gray light shot through the dusty panes of the window' (p. 39). The young man largely observes during the first part, and understanding, the meaning behind his observations, is acquired during the second part.

However, Crane's irony undermines the uninformed view from the very beginning because the youth assumes the conventional attributes of the outcast with all the earnest innocence of the amateur blacking himself all over to play Othello. He chooses to begin his experiment 'late at night', taunts from small boys reduce him to 'profound dejection', and a convenient rain helps his attempt to make himself feel miserable. Moved by these deliberately cultivated feelings of self-pity—he is not, after all, really a tramp at any point in the sketch—he searches for 'an outcast of high degree that the two might share miseries', and thus associates himself with the tramps in Chatham Square. At this point he considers the 'pageantry of the street' from what he *assumes* is the tramp's point of view in a paragraph stressing the movement and power in the crowds, lights, streetcars—all the life in which the outcast does not participate because, the youth believes, this life has rejected the tramp. Then, after revealing his amateur status by refusing a second helping of free soup in a saloon, the youth meets the drunken professional whose appearance should shake anyone's innocence: 'His head was a fuddle of bushy hair and whiskers from which his eyes peered with a guilty slant. In a close scrutiny it was possible to distinguish the cruel lines of a mouth, which looked as if its lips had just closed with satisfaction over some tender and piteous morsel. He appeared like an assassin steeped in crime performed awkwardly' (pp. 35–6). Such moral attributes hardly fit the sentimental image of a poor downtrodden unfortunate because this bum is the real thing, so obviously a parody of a 'respecterble gentlem'n' that when he sings 'a little melody for charity' even this innocent young man feels real 'astonishment'. But they immediately proceed to the flophouse; and the youth, still intent upon the unfamiliar externalities, progresses no further towards enlightenment until morning comes.

Instead, the reader is overwhelmed with the powerful imagery which makes the flophouse seem like 'a graveyard, where bodies were merely flung'. These images are so effective that readers easily forget about dramatic propriety. In context they cannot present an objective portrait of the external reality, or Crane's own view of this particular flophouse; they are strictly a property of the youth's mind, and their function—implied by the fact that in the morning he sees the same external reality quite differently— is to show that he is still immersed in the darkness of the conventional point of view. This function is heavily reinforced by the passage which ends the first part of the sketch. The youth innocently interprets the wails of a sleeping tramp as

an utterance of the meaning of the room and its occupants. It was to him the protest of the wretch who feels the touch of the imperturbably granite wheels and who then cries with an impersonal eloquence, with a strength not from him, giving voice to the wail of a whole section, a class, a people. This, weaving into the young man's brain and mingling with his views of these vast and somber shadows that like mighty black fingers curled around the naked bodies, made the young man so that he did not sleep, but lay carving biographies for these men from his meager experience. (p. 39)

In his innocence the youth lumps all these men together and considers them, as a class, forced into their situation by external 'granite wheels'—an obviously naturalistic judgement which Crane specifically associates with the shadows that shroud the men from the youth's eyes. Also, his constructing imaginary biographies for them from his extremely 'meager experience' prepares the ground for the bit of real biography which the assassin soon reveals to him.

When the light comes, the first action the youth notes is, significantly, a bald-headed bum pulling up his blanket to hide from this light. The young man then sleeps, to awaken to the cursing of the assassin (who is merely scratching flea-bites), and he immediately sees that the lurid graveyard of the night before has vanished: 'daylight had made the room comparatively commonplace and uninteresting'. This deflating experience, comparable to those of the little man in the *Sullivan County Sketches*, signifies that illusion is about to give way to reality, that the youth's education can now begin.

He soon realizes that these men are not to be lumped indiscriminately into a single class. Their nakedness reveals that 'here and there were men of brawn, whose skins shone clear and ruddy. They took splendid poses, standing massively, like chiefs', and only after donning tramp clothing do they look like the others with 'bumps and deficiencies of all kinds'. But the youth first suspects that he has outgrown his amateur standing as he leaves the building:

When he reached the street the young man experienced no sudden relief from unholy atmospheres. He had forgotten all about them, and had been breathing naturally and with no sensation of discomfort or distress.

He was thinking of these things as he walked along the street . . . (p. 40)

Then, after buying 'breakfast' for the assassin (who would have preferred a drink) his companion's biography reveals that the real professional is not created by any external 'granite wheels'. This tramp had, for three days, a 'great job out'n Orange,' but there he had to hustle; the South, in spite of easy living and 'good grub', also required a man to hustle; and he had 'lived high' while working in Toledo, but found it too cold in the winter. The professional tramp's point of view is summed up in the last of the assassin's biography:

I was raised in northern N'York. O-o-o-oh, yeh jest oughto live there. No beer ner whisky, though, way off in the woods. But all th' good hot grub yeh can eat. B'gawd, I hung around there long as I could till th' ol' man fired me. 'Git t'hell outa here, yeh wuthless skunk, git t'hell outa here an' go die,' he ses. 'You're a fine father,' I ses, 'you are,' an' I quit 'im. (p. 42)

The structure of the sketch implies that this real biography differs radically from the imaginary biographies the youth had constructed in the darkness of the previous night. This tramp is no unfortunate outcast rejected first by his own father and then by the rest of society: he is a shiftless lout with the typical moral coward's urge to get something for nothing. As such, he is the one who has rejected his father just as he rejected his 'great job in Orange', just as he continues to reject normal life—because he is too shiftless to be anything but a parasite. He is the moral coward utterly willing to be knocked flat and to accept the licking rather than make any effort of his own to fight back. Thus, his real biography establishes the moral posture behind the most obviously absurd statement in the sketch: 'B'gawd, we've been livin' like kings.'

The enclosed portion of the sketch ends with both the external forces and the failure of the will presented side by side. The externalities, emblematic of the life and energy in which the tramp *chooses* not to participate, are presented first; and as these forces have remained constant throughout the experiment—just as the mesmeric mountain remains constant throughout the little man's adventure, as the character of Pete remains constant throughout *Maggie*—their presentation should recall the youth's earlier view of them from Chatham Square:

The people of the street hurrying hither and thither made a blend of black figures, changing, yet frieze like. They walked in their good clothes as upon important missions, giving no gaze to the two wanderers seated upon the benches. They expressed to the young man his infinite distance from all that he valued. Social position, comfort, the pleasures of living, were unconquerable kingdoms. He felt a sudden awe.

And in the background a multitude of buildings, of pitiless hues and sternly high, were to him emblematic of a nation forcing its regal head into the clouds, throwing no downward glances; in the sublimity of its aspirations ignoring the wretches who may flounder at its feet. The roar of the city in his ear was to him the confusion of strange tongues, babbling heedlessly; it was the clink of coin, the voice of the city's hopes which were to him no hopes. (pp. 42–3)

But at this point such external forces, such 'granite wheels', no longer account for the outcasts because the youth now understands the tramp's 'point of view'. He has, after all, just heard one of the 'wretches' describe his flounderings as 'livin' like kings'. Hence, the moral failure ends the enclosed body of the sketch, and Crane chooses his words carefully to emphasize the active role of the will: 'He confessed himself an outcast, and his eyes from under the lowered rim of his hat began to glance guiltily, wearing the criminal expression that comes with certain convictions.'[8] Any given external conditions of life—the blizzard in 'The Blue Hotel', the sea in 'The Open Boat', the desert in certain poems, the physical slum environment in *Maggie* and *George's Mother*—are merely externalities, nothing more, and all men must eternally cope with them; when a man is willing to be knocked flat by them and to accept the licking, he reveals a failure of the will, and such moral cowardice inevitably distinguishes the professional bum from the honest man temporarily reduced to sleeping in Bowery flophouses.[9]

In his 1896 letter to the reader unable to understand *Maggie* Crane unfortunately could not refer to a still more explicit piece written early the previous year, while he was in Mexico for the Bacheller and Johnson syndicate, because this article did not get published. In it Crane considers the lowest class of Indians in Mexico and, after observing ironically that a man must not attempt 'psychological perception' unless he is willing to have his preconceptions overturned, he again distinguishes sharply between his subjects' external circumstance and their inner or moral reality. Externally, their condition is terrible: 'At first it seemed to me the

[8] Crane finds the extreme form of the tramp's moral cowardice in Sing Sing's executed convicts—men 'who died black souled, whose glances in life fled sidewise with a kind of ferocity, a cowardice and a hatred that could perhaps embrace the entire world' ('The Devil's Acre', *New York City Sketches*, p. 300); cf. *George's Mother*, ch. 14, where George brutally defies his mother's helplessness: 'He regarded her then with an unaltering scowl, albeit his mien was as dark and cowering as that of a condemned criminal.'

[9] Jacob Riis describes the moral failure as 'pauperism' in *How the Other Half Lives* (New York, 1890), ch. 21:

> The great mass of the tenements are shown to be harboring almsseekers. They might almost as safely harbor the small-pox. That scourge is not more contagious than the alms-seeker's complaint.... A moral distemper, like crime, ... where once it has taken root it is harder to dislodge than the most virulent of physical diseases. The thief is infinitely easier to deal with than the pauper, because the very fact of his being a thief presupposes some bottom to the man.... To the pauper there is none. He is as hopeless as his own poverty. I speak of the *pauper*, not of the honestly poor. There is a sharp line between the two.

most extraordinary thing that the lower classes of Indians in this country should insist upon existence at all. Their squalor, their ignorance seemed so absolute that death—no matter what it has in store—would appear as freedom, joy.'[10] Then Crane immediately compares them with the American slum dwellers, whose ignorance is not so dense, and whose moral condition is painted on their faces:

The people of the slums of our own cities fill a man with awe. That vast army with it's [sic] countless faces immovably cynical, that vast army that silently confronts eternal defeat, it makes one afraid. One listens for the first thunder of the rebellion, the moment when this silence shall be broken by a roar of war. Meanwhile one fears this class, their numbers, their wickedness, their might—even their laughter. . . . They are becoming more and more capable of defining their condition and this increase of knowledge evinces itself in the deepening of those savage and scornful lines which extend from near the nostrils to the corners of the mouth.

The poverty-ridden Indian with all his ignorance, however, is not morally poor, not a cynic, not wicked, and he sports no savage and scornful lines about his mouth. Crane does not believe that an increase in material goods will improve his moral condition:

It is so human to be envious that of course even these Indians have envied everything from the stars of the sky to the birds, but you cannot ascertain that they feel at all the modern desperate rage at the accident of birth. Of course the Indian can imagine himself a king but he does not apparently feel that there is an injustice in the fact that he was not born a king any more than there is in his not being born a giraffe. . . . He is born, he works, he worships, he dies, all on less money than would buy a thoroughbred Newfoundland dog and who dares to enlighten him? Who dares cry out to him that there are plums, plums, plums in the world which belong to him? . . . I would remember that there really was no comfort in the plums after all as far as I had seen them and I would esteem no orations concerning the glitter of plums.

These Indians, in short, are quite content in their poverty, not at

[10] All quotations from R. W. Stallman, 'Stephen Crane: Some New Sketches', *Bulletin of the New York Public Library*, LXXI (1967), 560–2.

all the moral kin of the Bowery cynic. Having established this truth,
Crane proceeds to generalize:

A man is at liberty to be virtuous in almost any position in life. . . .
These Indians are by far the most poverty-stricken class with which I
have met but they are not morally the lowest by any means. Indeed,
as far as the mere form of religion goes, they are one of the highest.
They are exceedingly devout. . . . But . . . I measure their morality by
what evidences of peace and contentment I can detect in the average
countenance.
    If a man is not given a fair opportunity to be *virtuous*, if his environ-
ment chokes his *moral* aspirations, I say that he has got the one important cause of complaint and rebellion against society. . . . Inversely
then, if he possesses this fair opportunity, he cannot rebel, he has no
complaint. I am of the opinion that poverty of itself is no cause. It is
something above and beyond [my italics].

No external environment, that is, no poverty of itself, chokes one's
moral aspirations: Crane clearly implies that if the environment of
these Indians will not do the job, no environment will. Certainly
the assassin's home environment in northern New York, given his
fond recollection of it, could not in itself have thwarted an urge
toward moral manhood; and, of course, there is nothing particularly bad about George Kelcey's environment when the tale of his
degeneration begins. But a vicious *moral* environment created and
sustained by cowards and hypocrites—whether in the Bowery or
in the wealthy home of Senator Cadogan ('The Second Generation')—makes the choice of a wrong action easier for the innocent.
Crane ends his report with a reference to the Indian's face, an
implicit comparison with the face of the American slum cynic:

I refuse to commit judgment upon these lower classes of Mexico. I
even refuse to pity them. It is true that at night many of them sleep
in heaps in doorways, and spend their days squatting upon the pave-
ments. It is true that their clotheing [*sic*] is scant and thin. All manner of
things of this kind is true but yet their faces have almost always a
certain smoothness, a certain lack of pain, a serene faith. I can feel the
superiority of their contentment.

Crane implies above that he *has* encountered a 'lowest class' of people morally far beneath the poor Indians of Mexico. His Bowery writings show that this claim is not a mere figure of speech.

The moral cowardice of the assassin, in the more loud and offensive form embodied by Pete, Jimmie, and Mrs. Johnson, is also the root of the cynical Bowery life in *Maggie*. (Except for the old beggar-woman with the musical box, there is no character in the novel comparable to the professional pauper: Pete and Jimmie both work to earn the money they squander, and the real tramp never works; Mrs. Johnson is always actively destructive, and the tramp never acts, even to destroy, if action can be avoided by passive acceptance.) Yet even this skeleton key will not unlock the novel's structure. It will not account for the brief glimpse (in chapter 17) of Maggie as a successful prostitute, for Crane's insistent use of parallel scenes, for the highly untypical sentimental overtones of the plot, or for Maggie's incredible lack of awareness. Such problems as these have to be referred to the way in which the novel was put together.

W. F. Johnson recalled that he had read a 'first draft' of *Maggie* in the summer of 1891.[11] We need not rely absolutely upon Johnson's memory because numerous phrases, images, even scenes in *Maggie* are also present in the *Sullivan County Sketches*—Mrs. Johnson recalls the 'giantess' of 'An Explosion of Seven Babies', in chapter 11 there appears 'a quiet stranger' who is about as artistically necessary as the quiet man is to the sketches, and *Maggie* requires the sustained clash between illusion and reality as interpreted by the protagonist just as the sketches do. Yet this date is important because Crane had no great opportunity to study the Bowery until after the summer of 1891; and *Maggie*, therefore, at least in its original conception, is exactly like *The Red Badge*, strictly a creation of Crane's imagination. If this assumption is correct we should be able to find, somewhere in *Maggie*, this

[11] Johnson, 'Launching', p. 289; cf. Frank W. Noxon, 'The Real Stephen Crane', *Step Ladder*, XIV (Jan. 1928), 4–9. *Maggie: A Girl of the Streets*, by 'Johnston Smith', was first published at Crane's expense in February or March 1893 (see *Letters*, p. 15); the second edition appeared, after *The Red Badge*, in June 1896. For the 'more than three hundred variants between the 1893 and 1896 editions', see Joseph Katz, 'The *Maggie* Nobody Knows', *Modern Fiction Studies*, XII (Summer 1966), 200–12. My quotations are from the 1893 edition.

distinctive imaginary construction which provided the foundation
for the novel.

The *Maggie* we read, however, was certainly written after
Crane had studied the Bowery.[12] His own observation and experience lie behind the excellent dialect of his characters—with its
contractions, repetitions, its rhythmic use of 'see'—and much of
the specific detail with which the book abounds: the policeman
beating the noses of a team of horses, Jimmie's life as a truck driver,
the soup-kitchen evangelist who says 'you' instead of 'we', the
terrific crash of a fire engine into a tangle of trucks, the pauper's
musical box 'capable of one tune', the children mocking the
drunken mother as she is ejected from the saloon. But all such
journalistic etchings from actual experience have nothing to do
with determinism and little enough to do with *Maggie*'s structure.
They are merely the physical properties which clothe the conflicts
of the plot with versimilitude and thereby invest the story with its
aura of realistic authority, what Howells admired as its fidelity to
observed fact.

However, to get beneath this obvious surface realism is to
encounter yet another element which intervenes between it and
Crane's specifically imaginary construction. This aspect of *Maggie*
is conventional, sentimental, and superficially moralistic; and thus
it tends to undermine the very realism which the factual physical
properties seek to establish. Maggie is an innocent lamb created
only for slaughter, seduced and abandoned by a wicked man,
rejected by her 'righteous' family, and cast out upon the streets to
the sensational horrors of prostitution and suicide—death being
the conventionally acceptable wages of sin. Considered from this
point of view, the novel is 'amoral only in the sense that it is not
conventionally moral; actually it is as moral as a tract. It is an
indictment, prepared with the fervor of an evangelist.'[13] And this

[12] 'It is faithful; no newspaper man in New York, no one who is familiar with
the life of the tenements, can deny the accuracy of the picture' ('Holland'
[Elisha Jay Edwards], 'Society Leaders' Suffrage Crusade', Philadelphia *Press*,
22 Apr. 1894, p. 5). Cf. Kwiat, 'Crane and Painting', p. 335.

[13] John C. Bushman, 'The Fiction of Stephen Crane and Its Critics',
unpublished Ph.D. thesis (Illinois, 1943), p. 32.

sort of tale is in no way characteristic of either the *Sullivan County Sketches* or the early news reporting. The most reasonable explanation for its appearance in *Maggie* is that Crane found this sentimentally moralistic pattern recurring again and again in the abundant slum literature of the early 1890s and decided to go to work on it.[14]

Crane's irony forces this sentimental plot to function as a means of exposing the dishonesty of his characters. The wayward girl, forlorn and repentant, returns to her dear old mother, and is thrown out of the house. Her brother is affected by her fall, but he quickly recovers. The mother bears her appointed cross with appropriately Christian phrases, but they sound rather odd in the foul mouth of this merciless hypocrite and career drunkard. When Jimmie suggests the parable of the prodigal son, his mother easily 'refutes' his argument by pointing out that the parable was not about a prodigal daughter. The superb tableau which ends the story—Mrs. Johnson wallowing in self-pity, the audience of neighbours, Miss Smith performing as lay evangelist—is a ghastly parody of the stock finale appropriate to the sentimental plot: we have the bereaved mourner, the 'sympathetic' friends and comforters, the consoling scriptural clichés spoken responsively, and Miss Smith's role as the innocent leader of this chorus of hypocrites is a travesty of the protestant minister's function in the sentimental version. Crane's irony, in short, largely redirects whatever shaping force these conventional materials might have exerted on the novel, and thereby reduces Christianity in this Bowery world to the level of Maggie's own ineffectual innocence. 'It is as though the church, too, were a sentimental theatre which encouraged moral poses but which ignored the essential nature of itself and of its audience' (Pizer, ' "Maggie" and American Naturalism', p. 172). Instead of actively coping with an entrenched Bowery morality, Christianity, again like Maggie herself, like the Bowery theatre, merely provides temporary gratification for the

[14] The best study is Marcus Cunliffe, 'Stephen Crane and the American Background of *Maggie*', *American Quarterly*, VII (Spring 1955), 31–44. Eric Solomon, *Stephen Crane: From Parody to Realism* (Cambridge, Mass., 1966), pp. 23–44, notes Crane's parody of these materials.

moral weaknesses of the hypocrites who are willing and able to use it for this end in 'a world in which religion is inoperable' (Katz, '*Maggie* Nobody Knows', p. 206).

Thus, both the realistic details drawn from experience and the conventional properties from slum literature can be identified with sources exterior to Crane's imagination. All such gleanings seem related to the rest of *Maggie* roughly as the records of Chancellorsville are related to the rest of *The Red Badge*, as 'Stephen Crane's Own Story' is related to the rest of 'The Open Boat.'

If we assume that Crane's first thoughts about the novel most probably would have taken some form of the psychological pattern which recurs in the *Sullivan County Sketches*, and that Maggie is the protagonist comparable to the little man, then it should be evident that the analogous unknown which Maggie both fears and, as it happens, cannot avoid is prostitution. The threat of prostitution is introduced, as one of only two possibilities, the moment Maggie is seen out of her childhood: ' "Mag, I'll tel yeh dis! See? Yeh've edder got teh go teh hell or go teh work!" Whereupon she went to work, having the feminine aversion of going to hell.' And this threat remains implicit throughout the novel. It looms as the authority behind Maggie's tearful insistence upon being assured that Pete loves her, after she has been seduced, and in chapter 12 it dictates her shrinking from contact with obvious prostitutes. But given this much of the pattern, the protagonist and the feared unknown, it is possible to reconstruct the story that Johnson and some of Crane's fraternity brothers at Syracuse may have read— it seems to me that he did write it—a version of *Maggie* that even young Crane would not have tried to publish.

If the psychological progression had been worked out as it is in the sketches, Maggie's fear of prostitution would have evoked in her imagination all sorts of terrifying illusions concerning it, lurid notions that Crane could hardly have published in the 1890s. The final step in this pattern would have made Maggie realize, through some climactic encounter, that the reality of prostitution, once experienced, was not nearly as bad as her illusions about it had led her to fear it would be; and the author certainly could not have found a legitimate publisher for such an implication. The *Maggie* we have, therefore, is quite different. Nevertheless, the ghostly outline of this discarded plot constantly lurks just beneath the surface of the story Crane finally published. Two outstanding clues betray its presence. The first is found at the beginning of chapter 17 when Maggie appears briefly as an entirely reconciled and successful prostitute with her 'handsome cloak' and 'well-shod feet'. Nothing whatsoever in the novel we read prepares us for this scene—which may explain why Crane presents an impression-istic telescoping of the career of a generalized prostitute not specifically identified as Maggie. We are prepared for the *fact* of prostitution, even for Maggie's suicide as the last desperate means of avoiding it, but not for this view of her, apparently content and prosperous in her vocation, quite at home as she crosses the rainy street.[15] This image, of course, presents precisely the logical result of the working-out of the pattern which recurs in the sketches. The other clue is the fact that the centre of this novel, or at least of Maggie's own part in it, is the protagonist's psychological pro-gression to awareness just as it is in *The Red Badge* or 'The Open Boat'. Maggie's journey begins in chapter 5 with her illusory view of Pete's character; it ends in chapter 14 when she becomes aware of what he really is; and this progression to awareness is the essential part of the novel so far as Maggie herself is concerned.

Yet Maggie as a person is not at all the sort of character required by this discarded plot: her nature is just the opposite—innocent gentle, decent—a nature so violently opposed to life as a prostitute that she commits suicide as a release. Also, the book contains much more than Maggie's progression to awareness: no one, apparently, has been troubled by the fact that virtually half the novel (nine chapters out of the nineteen) has comparatively little to do with Maggie's personal story. Maggie's tale takes place in chapters 5 through 9, 12, and 14 through 17. The remaining chapters, given to Jimmie, Mrs. Johnson, and Pete, are not concerned with any

---

[15] Cf. Cunliffe, pp. 36–7; Joseph X. Brennan, 'Ironic and Symbolic Struc-ture in Crane's *Maggie*', *Nineteenth-Century Fiction*, XVI (Mar. 1962), 308.

progression because these characters, like the assassin of the experiment, do not progress in any way. The first four chapters focus upon Jimmie; chapter 10 presents Jimmie's moral crisis which he shirks by means of the superb fight in Pete's saloon in chapter 11; chapter 13 is a conversation between Jimmie and his mother in which Jimmie finally abandons compassion for his sister; chapter 18 is given to Pete's drunken purification rite before an audience of prostitutes; and the final chapter presents Mrs. Johnson's orgiastic indulgence of self-pity before the neighbours. This half of the novel, in which Jimmie is most often on stage, diverts attention from Maggie's personal movement toward awareness and, as will be seen, does so for good reason. Thus we are presented with a mutual opposition more fundamental to the structure of the story than is the clash between journalistic realism and the conventional-sentimental seduction plot. As a result, the critic is more or less forced to choose one of two possibilities: that this novel was flawed in its original conception—that, in fact, the mutual opposition arises from bifurcation and Crane's own uncertainty about what he wants to say—or that it was flawed in its execution, for flawed it certainly is. Although a good argument could be made for the former possibility, and probably far easier with *Maggie* than with any other work in the canon, the evidence favours the latter, in my view at least. For one reason, any appeal to bifurcation opens the door to environmental determinism, and determinism tends to excuse those moral weaknesses—in Pete, Jimmie, and Mrs. Johnson—which Crane so obviously condemns in *both* parts of the novel. For another reason, Crane works hard to cover up the flaws in his own story, a deliberate effort which does not imply a confused conception. In short, it seems reasonable to argue that *Maggie* began with Crane's established psychological progression to awareness, and slowly developed away from it through replotting, rewriting, and the additions from research and experience, as a very young author laboured to reshape intractable material into a publishable form which would still convey some of the psychological 'truth' of his original imaginary conception. The evidence becomes more convincing when we examine the novel's crucial relationship between Maggie and Pete. This relationship, assuming that Crane began as outlined above, became shaped by a fundamental shift in the plot which must have occurred quite early in the revision: the unknown was changed from prostitution to the character of Pete who, whatever else he may be, is clearly seen by Maggie as the protecting bulwark between herself and prostitution. This change by itself allowed Crane to write a marketable story based on the protagonist's journey to awareness, fixed Maggie's essential nature as we now have it, and made the logical ending of suicide aesthetically reasonable. Also, the relationship between Maggie and Pete, once moulded in this fashion, in turn shapes the functions of Mrs. Johnson and Jimmie. The Bowery world of this novel has two faces, the tenement and the saloon—the two institutions which Riis found at the heart of slum life. Pete dominates the saloon side of this world just as Mrs. Johnson dominates the tenement side;[16] and Jimmie, as Pete's friend and Mrs. Johnson's son, equally at home in saloon or tenement, is the bridge uniting these two faces of a single reality. (The sentimental Bowery theatre is an extension of the values embodied in the saloon, and is thus an appropriate medium for Pete to use in entertaining Maggie.) We have to assume that Maggie is familiar with the tenement and her own mother and brother, at least so far as she is capable; but Pete is an unknown to her, and she sees him in the illusory light of her wildly romantic day-dreams.[17] Thus, with implicit help

[16] Pete and Mrs. Johnson are coupled with their respective institutions by parallel presentations in chapters 2 and 11: the place is first portrayed, then the character in typical action within it. Both characters have the same moral qualities; both are shown drunk and contemptuously treated. 'Like Mrs. Johnson, Pete desires to maintain the respectability of his "home", the bar in which he works. Like her, he theatrically purifies himself of guilt and responsibility for Maggie's fall as he drunkenly sobs . . . to an audience of prostitutes' (Pizer, '"Maggie" and American Naturalism', pp. 173–4). Jimmie becomes morally indistinguishable from the rest of the Bowery world by the end of chapter 13.
[17] See Marion L. Shane, 'The Theme of Spiritual Poverty in Selected Works of Four American Novelists: Twain, Crane, Fitzgerald, and Dreiser', unpublished Ph.D. thesis (Syracuse, 1953), pp. 80–103. 'It is perhaps more accurate to say that her thought coils around her mental image of Pete' (Gordon O. Taylor, *The Passages of Thought* [New York, 1969], p. 115).

from Mrs. Johnson and the tenement, Pete becomes initially, in Maggie's mind, the idealized Galahad which he certainly is not.

Maggie's vision is badly distorted by innocence and adolescent love; and this distortion, fed by the cheap offerings of the Bowery theatre, is immensely increased by her desire to escape from the tenement world with its alternatives of sweat-shop or prostitution. Because Pete really embodies all the sham glitter and cheap sophistication of the saloon over which he presides, he lures Maggie with the illusion of happiness just as the saloon lures the tenement dweller—Maggie's own father in chapter 3—with the illusion of escape. Crane thus emphasizes Pete's 'manners', his dandy's clothes and patent-leather shoes, the superficial toughness which makes him seem unique to Maggie, far above the rest of her world. Because Mrs. Johnson and the tenement world which she embodies are actively negative forces in Maggie's life, her illusions about Pete are the more understandable, like those of the little man in 'Killing His Bear', if we associate them with anticipation or wishful thinking. For Maggie, in other words, a conflict is set up which places Pete and the illusion of escape into happiness on one side and her mother and the tenement world on the other. This is the basic conflict which is worked out in the novel. But as Pete, like the saloon, is thoroughly a part of the Bowery world of Mrs. Johnson and the tenement, this conflict is in itself entirely illusory: it exists only within Maggie's mind, and it can be sustained only as long as her illusions of Pete's character remain unchallenged. Because of this, Maggie's illusory world does not collapse with her seduction, the event which would provide the climax in the tractarian's version of the plot: her seduction is merely incidental in her progress to awareness because Crane has shifted the focus of her attention from the fact of seduction to the character of her seducer. Awareness, the climax of Crane's pattern so far as his protagonist is concerned, finally comes when her illusory image of her lover is destroyed by experience in chapter 14 (well after the fact of seduction) as she watches Pete collapse beneath the blandishments of Nell. At the end of this chapter, when Maggie says 'I'm going home', her eyes are open, her illusions shattered, and she is as much a forlorn waif as she ever will be. Once Pete reveals the emptiness behind the sham, there is nothing left for Maggie to do but 'timidly accost' a series of persons—including her mother, brother, and Pete himself—who disown her. Pete's 'respectability', the hypocritical self-righteousness of Mrs. Johnson and Jimmie, and the adjectival use of 'Bowery' all define the same loud and offensive falsity of weaklings not brave enough to face up to the dishonesty of their own actions, the consequence of that moral cowardice which Crane specified as the root of Bowery life. Once Maggie becomes aware of this, once her illusions are revealed for what they are, she has completed much the same psychological journey to awareness that the little man of the sketches made several times before her.

Mrs. Johnson's function is to make retreat and acceptance of the tenement world extremely undesirable for Maggie. Thus, although the full force of the physical slum reality probably strengthens Mrs. Johnson's role, this drunken hypocrite needs no aesthetic reinforcement from her environment. She is never seen as a merely passive creature, a non-assertive woman whose life is determined by her environment; she is always presented as actively destructive, and as such she assuredly determines her environment herself. No matter how bad her environment, either physical or moral, may be at any given point in the novel, Mrs. Johnson inevitably acts to make it worse. The tenement home is merely squalid before she is turned loose in it, and she reduces it to chaos by smashing everything too heavy to pawn. The father, indifferent and irresponsible, is at least at home and sober until his wife's actions excuse his leaving to get drunk at the saloon. The children can know hunger and cold from their environment, but with their mother present they also know fear and pain. Most damning of all, when Maggie returns home after being seduced she is not yet either a prostitute or a suicide, and she becomes both only after being driven from home by her own mother. No environment could long endure the assaults of Mrs. Johnson because she is consistently destructive, physically through her aimless and drunken rage, morally through her egregious hypocrisy.[18] Even Pete is, in appearance, a cut above this woman: he is at least forced to maintain neatness and order in the saloon to promote the illusion of respectability which makes his position in the Bowery world profitable.

A closer look at Maggie herself will reveal the importance of Jimmie's role in the novel; for Maggie is an anomaly in this Bowery world and the suspension of disbelief she requires of the reader is somewhat unwillingly mustered. Although her eyes see very little she remains true to her personal honesty and acts morally in terms of the values that we are told she is able to perceive. Thus, Crane never presents her ironically, as he consistently presents her mother, brother, and Pete; his irony in Maggie's portrayal is always directed at her innocence, never at Maggie herself as a person. Yet even her innocence seems unreasonable:

> her tastes and mental perceptions are sometimes absurd to the point of exasperation. When, for example, Pete shouts at a waiter, 'Ah, git off d'eart!' and from this evidence Maggie infers that 'Pete brought forth all his elegance and all his knowledge of highclass customs for her benefit,' one might well wonder whether any kind of moral light could pierce such density. (Brennan, 'Structure in *Maggie*', p. 314.)

Maggie's density and the critical difficulties it brings to the novel follow quite reasonably if we assume that Crane began with his psychological progression, as outlined above, and then shifted Maggie's attention from prostitution to Pete. This revision made the novel as we know it possible, but it also led its author into a formidable technical trap. In order for this pattern to deliver an ironic jolt at the end of the sequence the protagonist finally has to

---

[18] Mrs. Johnson's destructive *consistency* stems from the illusion that she is wreaking vengeance upon the universe: 'It seems that the world had treated this woman very badly, and she took a deep revenge upon such portions of it as came within her reach. She broke furniture as if she were at last getting her rights. She swelled with virtuous indignation as she carried the lighter articles of household use, one by one under the shadows of the three gilt balls' (chapter 8). Unaware of even the most elementary fact of life in Crane's world—that the universe is "flatly indifferent" to her existence—her whole mental and moral being rests upon a non sequitur; therefore, her rage can only be pointless, and any action arising from it can only be destructive (cf. Westbrook, 'Pattern of Affirmation', pp. 224–8).

become aware of a reality which has remained unchanged throughout the story: Tom Gardner in his Sullivan County cave does not change in any way, and the professional pauper studied by the youth is at the end of the experiment exactly what he was when the youth first met him. Thus, when Crane changed the unknown, which Maggie has to learn to perceive correctly, from an abstract condition of life to a character within the world of the novel, he assumed a technical burden which was new to him: an interrelationship of characters having different levels of awareness of a common reality. In other words, the reality of Pete's character, which Maggie is unable to grasp until the end of chapter 14, is a reality which all the other characters, as well as the reader, have fully understood since the beginning. Hence, even though Pete, Jimmie, and Mrs. Johnson are no more than dimly aware of a severely limited area of reality, Maggie has to be even less aware than they are if Crane is to make her the protagonist of his revised pattern. She has to perceive an unbelievably limited range of values *within* the already narrow Bowery reality understood by the other characters.

Crane struggles hard with this problem. He begins with explicit statement: Maggie 'blossomed in a mud puddle. . . . None of the dirt of Rum Alley seemed to be in her veins'. But he soon forces us to believe that she missed more than dirt. It is unreasonable to suppose any girl old enough to be seduced could be so completely blind to the wholesale hypocrisy of the world she has grown up in, particularly when two of the most obvious hypocrites in it are her own mother and brother. She also missed the fact that 'Sadie MacMallister next door to us was sent teh deh devil by dat feller what worked in deh soap-factory', even though, according to her mother, this instructive incident was called to her attention as a warning. Finally, when Crane felt compelled to write that 'She did not feel like a bad woman. To her knowledge she had never seen any better', he must have known he was stacking the cards. A fallen woman, in the idiom of the Bowery reality surrounding Maggie, is still a fallen woman; otherwise the sham respectability of the hypocrites and the taking advantage of such a woman—as

Jimmie takes advantage of Hattie—would be impossible. Thus, the difficulty remains. For Maggie to progress through her illusions to an understanding of Pete—and by implication, of Jimmie, her mother, and the entire Bowery world—she has to begin at a level of awareness so low that the favourable connotations of her innocence also sink dangerously towards mere stupidity.[19]

Hence, one of the two main functions of Jimmie's part of the novel is to divert our attention from this necessary density of his sister. Jimmie is the most complex character in the novel, he is the child who introduces us to the casual brutality of the Bowery world, he has an entire chapter devoted to his growing up and the formation of his Bowery attitudes, he becomes the head of the family after his father's death, and he obtrusively usurps the stage from Maggie at crucial points in the story. Because Maggie's struggle to awareness is more a matter of ontology than morality, Jimmie's other important function is to embody the only significant moral struggle in the novel. Whatever moral crisis Maggie undergoes as a result of her seduction takes place off stage, between the end of chapter 9 and her reappearance at the beginning of chapter 12. We are occupied with Jimmie's reaction to this event, and are never given Maggie's immediate reaction at all. Jimmie reacts by hiding the demands of moral responsibility beneath the cheap relief of anger, just as the Sullivan County campers use anger to mask their fear.

Jimmie's handling of his moral crisis is given three times (in chapters 10 and 13) to ensure that we understand that his failure is, like the professional tramp's 'point of view', a failure of the will. He may perceive his moral duty as through a 'blurred glass'

---

[19] For Crane's view of innocence, see 'A Detail' (*New York City Sketches*, p. 177). A character in *Active Service* says, 'I've never seen any full-grown person in this world who got experience any too quick for his own good' (*The Work of Stephen Crane*, ed. Wilson S. Follett [New York, 1925–7], IV, 160). The logical extreme obtains when one is dishonest for so long that the intellect loses its power to distinguish right from wrong: this is the 'successful man' (*The Poems of Stephen Crane*, ed. Joseph Katz [New York, 1966], p. 98). In *Maggie*, the fat clergyman who 'gave a convulsive movement and saved his respectability by a vigorous side-step' (chapter 16) suggests this unholy 'innocence'.

darkly, but he does perceive it:

> It occurred to him to vaguely wonder, for an instant, if some of the women of his acquaintance had brothers.
>   Suddenly, however, he ... fumed about the room, his anger gradually rising to the furious pitch.

When this emotional ascent is interrupted by the entrance of his mother, he tells her the news; Mrs. Johnson quietly sits down long enough to determine her response, then jumps up cursing her daughter (later Jimmie tells her of Maggie's death; she quietly finishes her dinner while she determines her response, then begins to 'mourn' her lost daughter). But Jimmie again hesitates:

> He was trying to formulate a theory that he had always unconsciously held, that all sisters, excepting his own, could advisedly be ruined.
>   He suddenly broke out again. ... In a fury he plunged out of the doorway.

This response is that of Pete telling Maggie to 'go teh hell' at the first threat to his respectability, that of Mrs. Johnson cursing her daughter in order to avoid facing up to her own blatant failure as a mother: all three Bowery natives react alike to the same stimulus, and the illusory value of their response is shown by means of the excellent fight in Pete's saloon and the comment which closes both chapters 10 and 11: 'What deh hell?' But the superb irony of Jimmie's shirking moral responsibility in this context—through his lack of compassion for his sister, through continuing his own dishonest dealings with women—is that his response here presents precisely that moral attitude which, in Pete, is responsible for the very seduction of innocence to which he is responding. Once Jimmie commits himself, the last possibility of a morally significant stance in this Bowery world is abandoned, and whatever energy the situation has evoked is merely dissipated in pointless rage.

The parallel actions or scenes, omnipresent to a surprising degree in so short a novel, have already received critical attention; and I would add only that, if this reading is acceptable, Crane's use of this device—except for his parallel equation of Mrs. Johnson with the tenement and Pete with the saloon—can hardly be called structural in the sense of plot. Crane's psychological pattern stands apart, not in itself dependent upon any ironic parallel. Nevertheless, this device does serve two important functions in *Maggie*. It functions structurally in the sense of a craftsman's means of ordering and controlling the specific ironies called forth by the plot: whenever a scene or action reappears in its parallel treatment the irony inevitably is heightened, and thus the ironic tone mounts gradually throughout the novel to the summit achieved by the intensely bitter ending.[20] Also, Crane's use of this device in this novel is so insistent that, in itself, it suggests an essentially static world which is 'very Bowery': morally, this world has become a meaningless round of temporary gratifications by hypocrites too stupid and too dishonest even to desire an escape from the cycle of their own moral cowardice; and thus Pete, Jimmie, and Mrs. Johnson embody, again, the pointless flounderings of Crane's archetypal Bowery character, the assassin.

Because the moral ground such characters create and sustain is too barren even to receive the seed of Christianity *Maggie* implies that Crane's ethical orientation, even this early in his career, is a common-sense stoicism, not the faith and moral code of his parents —a distinction which seems to me crucial to an understanding of both the man and his work in general and his poems in particular. Christianity is dead in Crane's Bowery and, by extension, in any world that is Bowery in character: the hypocrites wilfully destroy it, the professional paupers are too shiftless to make the effort required for any sort of moral commitment, the innocents have no effect, and innocence itself in such a moral context only hastens one's own destruction. If Christianity is ever to take root a certain minimal intelligence, some indication of a willingness to learn (if only from one's own experience), and sufficient moral strength at least to desire to be personally honest are all absolutely

---

[20] See Brennan, 'Structure in *Maggie*', p. 307; and Janet Overmyer, 'The Structure of Crane's *Maggie*', *University of Kansas City Review*, XXIX (Autumn 1962), 72. Crane's use of this device continues into his later work with far greater artistry, as will be seen in 'War Memories' and 'The Bride Comes to Yellow Sky'.

necessary. But Jimmie

> studied human nature in the gutter, and found it no worse than he
> thought he had reason to believe it. He never conceived a respect for
> the world, because he had begun with no idols that it had smashed. . . .
> He menaced mankind at the intersections of streets. . . . Above all
> things he despised obvious Christians and . . . his sneer grew so that
> it turned its glare upon all things. He became so sharp that he believed
> in nothing. (chapter 4)

Caritas in such a world as Jimmie's Bowery requires stoic brotherhood—in the sense of shared understanding and acceptance of
man's place in the universe, the sort of brotherhood that is shared
by four men in an open boat adrift on an amoral sea—as a precondition to its very existence. Maggie cannot act significantly
until she has attained a certain level of awareness, the assassin is a
mere parasite because he has chosen to live a life devoid of purpose,
and even the hypocrites such as Mrs. Johnson cannot improve
until they at least learn to accept with tranquillity that over
which they can have no control—Jimmie, for example, has no
power to alter the moral truth he perceives, that 'what is wrong
for Pete cannot be right for him',[21] but he is too weak to affirm
any kind of maxim that might interfere with his own selfishness.
All these people, in short, need primarily an understanding of the
reality in which they live: they require an empirical body of
knowledge, not a revealed one. Such matters, however, can be
examined more conveniently in conjunction with Crane's poems;
here it is merely necessary to recall that his sympathy toward
Christianity 'cooled off . . . when I was thirteen or about that'.
Maggie offers no evidence for any hope of its revival.

This novel remains a major document in the study of Crane.
The evidence implies that it grew slowly, through intense thought
and labour by an author who had to replot, revise, rewrite no one
knows how many times. None of the other Bowery works suggests
anything approaching the effort that went into this one. Such a
view should help considerably in accounting for Crane's 'meteoric

---

[21] Max R. Westbrook, 'Stephen Crane's Social Ethic', *American Quarterly*,
XIV (Winter 1962), 590.

rise' to competency in the principal area of his craft: a great deal
of wrestling with the specific problems peculiar to Crane's best
work, the problems of expressing his own ironic vision in terms of
marketable material, went into the gradual evolvement of *Maggie*.
And from Crane's own point of view as a budding writer he must
have emerged victorious from these struggles, no matter what the
commercial success of his book; technically, that is, *Maggie* in
several ways and in spite of glaring flaws is a fine piece of work, an
accomplishment which provides reasonable justification for the
high hopes Crane had for it. The failure of the 1893 edition is not
difficult to explain: with no access to established channels of
distribution, Crane himself had to get the book before the public
on the news-stands where it 'was supposed to sell for fifty cents a
copy. This was high for a day when the newsstands were thick
with novels in wrappers at twenty-five and ten cents each—novels
much longer than "Maggie," and written by men and women much
better known than Johnston Smith.'[22] This edition brought Crane
no money, but it earned him the admiration and support of
Howells and others such as Garland, E. J. Edwards, and Edward
Marshall. To account for the comparatively lukewarm reception of
the 1896 *Maggie* one has only to make the comparison drawn by
the 1890s—with *The Red Badge*. The realistic view of a shooting
war seen from within the lively mind of Henry Fleming was new,
wonderfully fresh, and believable. By comparison, Maggie's
innocence and sparsely furnished mind were hardly believable,
and the journalistic surface realism of yet another look at the
slums of New York was neither new nor fresh: as Cunliffe argues
(p. 43), 'it was *fiction*, which contained nothing that the reader
could not find in . . . such books as *Darkness and Daylight in New
York*. Why bother to print research that had already been done
more fully and factually by others?' Crane's privately won
victories in *Maggie* had to be carried forward into other writings.

   Even winners have to eat, however, and Crane, from the
beginning of his stay in New York until he was exiled late in 1896

[22] John T. Winterich, 'Romantic Stories of Books: *The Red Badge of Courage*',
Publisher's Weekly, CXVIII (20 Sept. 1930), 1305.

by the persecution of the police after the Dora Clark incident,[23] maintained a casual connection between body and soul by writing sketches and articles for any editor who would publish them. Although the place of these short pieces in the canon is extremely ill-defined—largely because the few scholars who have not ignored them have tended to treat them as little parables of naturalism— Crane himself did not want them to be consigned to the oblivion of old newspaper files: 'Some of my best work', he wrote to his brother Will, 'is contained in short things which I have written for various publications, principally the New York *Press* in 1893 [1894] or thereabouts. There are some 15 or 20 short sketches of New York street life and so on which I intended to have published in book form under the title of "Midnight Sketches" ' (*Letters*, p. 135). Crane's main error here concerns the number of these sketches: as collected by Stallman and Hagemann, there are about forty of them.[24] But the main error of editors who have reprinted them seems to be a perennial urge to arrange them in some sort of order based upon common subject-matter, common setting, or date of composition; the result, so far as critical evaluation is concerned, has been less than satisfactory. These editorial approaches provide no means of making qualitative judgements because they ignore the critical demands of Crane's irony; and they provide no means of placing these pieces in the context provided by the rest of Crane's work because they ignore the possibility that a young ironist might have had private literary reasons for writing them, the possibility, that is, that even the least of these sketches might have served some purpose other than the obvious one of so

[23] The definitive study of this incident is Olov W. Fryckstedt, 'Stephen Crane in the Tenderloin', *Studia Neophilologica*, XXXIV (1962), 135–63. The relevant newspaper articles are reprinted in *New York City Sketches*, pp. 217–60.

[24] *The New York City Sketches* (New York, 1966). Page references in the text will be to this edition. The Midnight Sketches, for purposes of this discussion, are those pieces which Crane wrote between the summer of 1892 and late 1896. Hence, I omit everything written before or after this period. I also exclude interviews, fables, reviews, 'A Prologue', fragments, the Dora Clark news articles (including the one Crane wrote himself, pp. 226–31), and the eight pieces (pp. 185–214) which the editors leave undated. Forty-three pieces remain. Crane's letter to his brother excludes the pieces written for the Bacheller and Johnson syndicate during his trip west in 1895.

many words dashed off in hope of so much grocery money.

The implication of Crane's private purpose is unavoidable, given his literary and economic situation while most of these pieces were written. When he came to New York he had published only the Sullivan County tales; and, even without the evidence of his struggles with *Maggie*, it can only be absurd to argue that his precocious awareness would have allowed him to believe that the sort of prose these tales contain was sufficient to support a lifetime in which writing was to be the sole means of income. Crane needed flexibility of craftsmanship, enough both to say what he wanted to say and to gain him a decent living from his pen, and he was especially weak where most hack-writers competing for the available dollars probably were strong—in handling the conventional and the sentimental. His economic station was on the near frontier of poverty, at least until the Spring of 1894 (see *Letters*, p. 37); and during these lean years he never held a regular job with a newspaper. Because the local editors, apart from the guardians of the *Tribune*, respected his work and bought it whenever they could,[25] and because he had already functioned capably as a reporter at the Jersey shore, Crane's failure to hold a steady newspaper job in New York has to be ascribed primarily to his own choice (food and lodgings were always available to him, at a pinch, at the homes of his brothers). The Midnight Sketches justify this conclusion because they suggest Crane's comparative lack of interest in the factual level of reality which still constitutes the average news reporter's view of the world, and his great interest in improving his own literary situation by broadening his competence in his craft. Hence, these pieces imply their importance to the canon by the manner in which they fit into the context provided by the later work. The general characteristics of Crane's ironic vision (see above, pp. 24–5) provide the means for judging the quality of the individual sketch: whenever Crane's main emphasis falls upon the detached observation of external fact or event the resulting sketch can be associated with some area of his minor fiction; in so far as Crane's main emphasis shifts from the external

[25] See Curtis Brown, *Contacts* (London, 1935), p. 260.

fact—no matter how superbly the externals may be portrayed—to the internal or moral reality beyond the fact, the resulting sketch rises above the banality of mere newspaper realism to approach the sort of art found in his best fiction.

Given such an approach, the Midnight Sketches fall quite easily into four general categories: parody, the humorous presentation of the conventional, the sentimental presentation of the conventional, and those more important sketches which artistically portray some sort of implicit moral reality beyond the facts presented. As the labels imply, these categories are not based upon the facts which Crane offers in any group of sketches, upon common settings, or upon dates of composition; they are determined solely by the manner in which Crane presents his facts or uses his setting.[26] The moral posture of Billie Atkins, for example, does not differ appreciably from that of the assassin, but because of the differences in the presentation of these two studies of the tramp's point of view, 'Billy Atkins Went to Omaha' obviously falls within the second category above, and the 'Experiment' belongs with Crane's best work. None of the sketches in the first three categories is greatly concerned with any hidden moral reality, although moral comment is often present either implicitly, as in 'Coney Island's Failing Days', or explicitly, as in 'Opium's Varied Dreams'. All these sketches offer comparatively relaxed prose without the characteristic intensity of Crane's more serious work because the writer here does not seem primarily intent upon *what* is being communicated. Crane's private purpose in writing these pieces seems rather to have been, in general, the development of a frankly conventional, and therefore commercial, means of presenting

[26] Three of the forty-three sketches defy all reasonable attempts to include them within these four categories; but even this defiance results from the manner of Crane's presentation, not from settings or facts in themselves. 'Heard on the Street Election Night' is an obvious experiment, an attempt to communicate a specific scene and mood solely by means of an impressionistic juxtaposition of unconnected comments from a crowd reading news bulletins. 'A Tale of Mere Chance' is an uncharacteristic Crane story which seems a deliberate sally into Poe territory. And if 'When Every One Is Panic Stricken' is the hoax the editors claim, then Crane's purpose is again frankly experimental—an attempt to create imaginatively a piece which would pass as typical realistic news reporting.

external facts or events which, in themselves, were worthy of no great attention from anyone. 'In a Park Row Restaurant', for example, reveals absolutely nothing new about rush hours in restaurants, but the reader is carried effortlessly from beginning to end by the Westerner's jocular appraisal of the thoroughly familiar. Critically speaking, therefore, the sketches in the first three categories belong with Crane's minor fiction. The pieces in the final category do communicate a moral reality beyond the fact, Crane's prose is more characteristically intense (with variations in degree from sketch to sketch), and his private purpose in writing them is never limited to the development of a conventional presentation. The writer of these sketches is the excellent craftsman with something important to say and a delight in using all the literary resources at his command to say it in a manner which 'pleased himself'. Thus, these few pieces deserve the same close critical attention that scholars have awarded his major fiction.

Crane's competence as a parodist has been thoroughly examined by Eric Solomon,[27] and we need note only that, of all four classes of writing, the light pieces written for *Truth* probably required the least effort. An ironist at large in the New York of the 1890s would have had to make an effort to avoid parody, and Crane's tendencies toward the outrageous lampoon had already revealed themselves in his early news reporting. 'Why Did the Young Clerk Swear?' seems the most interesting example, at least for critics, because it parodies the typical style of the naturalistic novel—the accretion of apparently pointless details into some sort of mosaic while the reader is kept awake by promises, seldom fulfilled, of erotic scenes to come. Crane returned to parody later in his career: it crops up occasionally in *Active Service*, it turns *The O'Ruddy* into a hilarious romp, and (as Solomon argues, pp. 252–74) his best use of parodistic techniques is encountered in 'The Blue Hotel' and 'The Bride Comes to Yellow Sky'.

Crane's struggles to portray the conventional in a palatable

---

[27] Stallman and Hagemann reprint four obvious parodies: 'Why Did the Young Clerk Swear?', 'At Clancy's Wake', 'Some Hints for Play-Makers', and 'A Night at the Millionaire's Club'.

manner seem more meaningful than his parodies because, if his view of life was naturally ironic, the smooth presentation of the conventional, in the terms of the 1890s, must have been a profitable skill which did not come easily for him. In most of his attempts his irony gives way to humour rather in the fashion of a painfully aware parent refusing to restrain a happy step-child: that is, Crane's humour seldom leaves any doubt about the mature aware-ness behind it, there are plenty of sardonic little flicks of the whip, and it ranges from the easy laughter of 'A Lovely Jag in a Crowded Car' to the dry bite of 'Yen-Nock Bill and His Sweetheart'; but his humour is usually its own excuse for being and, as such, it lacks the energy, the controlled, purposive drive which informs his irony. Like the lately discovered Sullivan County pieces, the sketches in this category are not apt to attract much attention, all use humour as an excuse for noticing the ordinary, and almost any one will serve as well as any other to illustrate the fairly obvious characteristics shared by all of them.[28]

'Billy Atkins Went to Omaha', which has some significance for Crane's view of Bowery life, features a professional bum of sixteen years' standing, 'mellow with drink and in the eloquent stage' at a Bowery flophouse where he tells of a past journey from Denver to Omaha; and Crane plays happily with the various adventures Billie endures *en route*, adventures which are quite predictable because the professional refuses to work long enough even to earn the price of a railway ticket. Billie's only approach to life is to make a 'great sneak' upon whatever he desires, and he has to employ this talent continually:

Billie boarded trains and got thrown off on his head, on his left shoulder, on his right shoulder, on his hands and knees. He struck the ground

---

[28] I would place fifteen sketches in this largest of the four categories: 'Travels in New York', 'Billy Atkins Went to Omaha' (original prints 'Billy' in title and 'Billie' throughout text), 'Coney Island's Failing Days', 'Stories Told by an Artist', 'In a Park Row Restaurant', 'The Duel that Was not Fought', 'A Lovely Jag in a Crowded Car', 'New York's Bicycle Speedway', 'Evening on the Roof', 'Yellow Undersized Dog', 'The "Tenderloin" as It Really Is', 'In the "Tenderloin" ', 'A Tenderloin Story: Yen-Nock Bill and His Sweetheart', 'Diamonds and Diamonds', and 'Stephen Crane at Asbury Park'.

slanting, straight from above and full sideways. His clothes were shred-
ded and torn like the sails of a gale blown brig. His skin was tattooed
with bloody lines, crosses, triangles, and all the devices known to
geometry. But he wouldn't walk, and he was bound to reach Omaha.
So he let the trainmen use him as a projectile with which to bombard
the picturesque Western landscape. (p. 56)

As Crane's diction implies, Billie's sufferings are ridiculous because
they are entirely pointless: he has absolutely no reason for going to
Omaha, and any human being who would choose to accept such
treatment as this to avoid earning a trivial rail-fare clearly deserves
everything he gets. Crane's prose laughs as it ridicules: 'He
repaired to a coal car and cuddled among the coal. He buried his
body completely, and . . . snug in his bed, smiled without dis-
arranging the coal that covered his mouth' (p. 55). 'They discovered an east-bound freight car that was empty save for one
tramp and seven cans of peaches' (p. 55). While a fellow-hobo
shines shoes for some food that Billie desperately needs, the professional 'stood around and watched'; and on arrival in Omaha he
begs accommodation in the jail rather than earn the cheapest bed
available. The sketch ends with Billie saying just before he falls
asleep, 'Hully mack'rel. I mus' start back fer Denver in th'
mornin' ' (p. 57). Crane's ironic contempt has to be deserved—by
the moronic viciousness of Mrs. Johnson, the dishonesty of Pete
and Jimmie—but Billie is, by his own choice, so completely
worthless that he is even beneath contempt. His self-willed and
pointless suffering deserves only laughter, from any man, and
Crane makes the most of it.

Crane's lighter fiction occasionally reveals his humour capably
supporting a story which will never cause much critical excitement.
It can be found in 'His Majestic Lie', in some of the less important
Whilomville Stories such as 'Lynx Hunting', and a full measure is
laced into *The O'Ruddy*. It can be appreciated at its best in 'The
Wise Men', which tells of a foot-race between two bar tenders in
Mexico City. This story may be slight enough, but it is one of
Crane's happiest, it sustains the warmest tone to be found in his
work, and—as H. G. Wells said—'I cannot imagine how it could

possibly have been better told.'²⁹ In terms of mere literary mileage, however, Crane's ability to combine conventional material with a humorous presentation served him best in *Active Service*. No one would rank this long novel with Crane's best work, but it is competently written without excessive irony, and it is better than *The Third Violet* largely because it is funnier and less sentimental.

Conventional material tinted with a sentimental colouring was even more in demand than humour, as a look at the newspapers and the magazine fiction of the 1890s will reveal.³⁰ Crane's sentimental failures are painfully obvious—because of dreary characters such as Hawker and Miss Fanhall, dialogue which bores the reader ('The Landlady's Daughter'), and self-consciously elaborate prose too precious to bear the weight of reality (see portions of his letter to Lily Brandon Monroe, *Letters*, pp. 21–2). But this should not obscure the fact that he more often succeeded. Also, critics should be aware of a more startling fact: that an *ironist's* successful handling of mauve-decade sentimentality is a feat roughly comparable to shingling a roof after having deliberately thrown away one's hammer; the normal and far easier technique would be to retain the irony, as Crane did in *Maggie*, and hammer the sentimentality to death with it. Nevertheless, 'A Christmas Dinner Won in Battle' graced the pages of the *Plumber's Trade Journal* with a thoroughly competent manipulation of plot, character, and dialogue which must have been sentimentally banal long before Crane was born. 'The Art Students League Building' is a nostalgic celebration of the wild life of young artists who could have doubled as lay ministers whenever they were not in residence.

---

²⁹ 'Stephen Crane from an English Standpoint', *North American Review*, CLXXI (Aug. 1900), 239.

³⁰ 'The Landlady's Daughter' may well be Crane's first fragmentary experiment in the sentimental line. I would place twelve sketches in this category: 'The Art Students League Building', 'The Gratitude of a Nation', 'An Ominous Baby', 'Mr. Binks' Day Off', 'The Silver Pageant', 'A Christmas Dinner Won in Battle', 'A Great Mistake', 'Sailing Day Scenes', 'In the Tenderloin: A Duel Between an Alarm Clock and a Suicidal Purpose', 'The Devil's Acre', 'Minetta Lane', and 'Opium's Varied Dreams'. The last four pieces, a third of the category, suggest that the sentimental shudder was a minor Crane speciality. I have placed 'An Experiment in Luxury' with the major sketches, after some hesitation, but it could almost as reasonably be included here.

The prose style suggests Alice Brown instead of Stephen Crane: 'Everyone was gay, joyous, and youthful in those blithe days and the very atmosphere of the old place cut the austere and decorous elements out of a man's heart' (p. 15). Crane admits that upon rare occasion they did drink beer, but even this lapse is made harmless by an unimpeachable reference to *Trilby*. And 'Mr. Binks' Day Off' is an extremely well-written account of a banal Saturday-afternoon outing taken by a clerk and his family, a trip from their Harlem flat to visit 'Aunt Sarah' in rural New Jersey. Absolutely nothing memorable happens, Mr. and Mrs. Binks are so typically urban lower middle class that they tend to become invisible, Aunt Sarah and Uncle Daniel would be quite at home in a Whittier poem, and the sketch exploits the sentimental cliché of a city man's renewing himself through temporary contact with a rural environment: 'They were purified, chastened by this sermon, this voice calling to them from the sky. The hills had spoken and the trees had crooned their song' (p. 70). It seems to me an error to dismiss such pieces as mere trivia so far as Crane himself is concerned. They are too carefully written, and the diction and tone imply an author who is checking every word to make sure his irony is not showing.

'An Ominous Baby' and 'A Great Mistake' belong with the travels of Mr. Binks. These pieces are not grimly naturalistic parables of poverty forcing the deprived to lawlessness: the main character is not only too young to be held morally responsible, but even too young to realize that he is deprived. This baby, in his rags and dirt, is perfectly happy playing with his piece of rope until he sees the fire engine of the other child and, naturally, wants to play with it—a response which would hardly differ if the rich baby had the rope and the poor one the fire engine. He does not wish to steal the toy. He only wants to play with it and, in fact, he asks four times to be allowed to play with it. But when his repeated request is denied he does not accept his rebuff in the manner of Billie Atkins: he immediately sets to work to get what he wants. His overt action is wrong, of course, in terms of the adult moral world, but his motivation is healthy enough and he is too young to know how to channel it in any other way: 'le triomphe de l'enfant pauvre est moins un symbole social qu'une allegorie de l'histoire humaine depuis ses origines. C'est l'homme des cavernes que reparaît en nous dans les conflits de propriété.'[31] If anything in this sketch could be called morally ominous it has to be the rich child's selfishness which, not unreasonably in this context, provokes the violent reaction from the other one. In 'A Great Mistake' the baby cautiously steals a lemon from a fruit stand, but his caution is not caused by any awareness that it is wrong to steal; he believes the fruit vendor is 'undoubtedly a man who would eat babes that provoked him' (p. 131). Both stories show an infant who, much like Maggie, is ready and willing to act, and yet too innocent to direct his action properly; the opposite is the morally weak adult, such as Jimmie or the professional tramp, who realizes how his action should be directed and then deliberately refuses to act. However, the tone of both pieces is light in comparison with that of 'A Dark-Brown Dog'. Except for their Bowery setting, they strongly anticipate—in their elementary plot, relaxed mood, and faithful portrayal of the child's point of view—the later *Whilomville Stories*.

In much the same way the sketches in this category, in general, can be seen as Crane's explorations in that area of his craft which suddenly blossomed in 1896 with 'An Indiana Campaign', 'A Grey Sleeve', 'The Little Regiment', and 'Three Miraculous Soldiers'—all published in *The Little Regiment*.[32] As one scholar has claimed, these mildly sentimental tales 'could have as easily been written by Richard Harding Davis; they are merely competent and conventional'.[33] But this is precisely the point that needs to be stressed. By 1896 half of Crane's years as a writer were already behind him; and before this date his competent stories, such as the Sullivan County tales, were not at all conventional, and

---

[31] Jean Cazemajou, 'Stephen Crane et ses esquisses de vie new-yorkaise', *Caliban*, no. 1 (janvier 1964), 17–18.

[32] 'A Grey Sleeve' appeared in the Philadelphia *Press* in October 1895, but the others did not achieve even magazine publication until 1896.

[33] Will C. Jumper, 'Tragic Irony as Form: Structural Problems in the Prose of Stephen Crane', unpublished Ph.D. thesis (Stanford, 1958), p. 252.

his conventional stories, such as 'The Reluctant Voyagers', were hardly competent. One of the more subtle ironies of Crane's career may well be that he had to work long and hard to acquire the capability of producing stories so competent and conventional that scholars can safely ignore them.

In each of the nine remaining sketches Crane stalks a moral reality beyond the fact, and uses the fact artistically to trap this reality and communicate it to the reader. [34] 'The Pace of Youth' presents commonplace facts—two young people fall in love, and in running away to get married they escape pursuit by the girl's father—but Crane's imagery endows this simple tale with moral reverberations which thrust well beyond these facts. The central image is the merry-go-round, and Crane expands this image to include life in general by working it into three areas which together encompass practically the whole story: the physical environment, the emotional life of the lovers, and the analogous relationships between the children on the merry-go-round and the lovers and between the lovers and Stimson. Crane carefully sketches two portraits of the shore environment surrounding the merry-go-round: one presents it during the day (pp. 274–5), the other at night (pp. 278–9), and both versions reproduce the essential attributes of the intervening portrait of the merry-go-round (p. 275)—motion, colour, sound, an overhead source of light. But the identification with the merry-go-round is most strongly implied by a certain sense of artificiality in the external environment: 'In the mighty angle, a girl in a red dress was crawling slowly like some kind of a spider on the fabric of nature. . . . Upon the edge of the sea stood a ship with its shadowy sails painted dimly upon the sky' (pp. 274–5). 'Sometimes people unable to hear the music, glanced up at the pavilion and were reassured upon beholding the distant leader still gesticulating and bobbing, and the other members of the band with their lips glued to their instruments' (p. 279).

[34] 'An Experiment in Misery', 'An Experiment in Luxury', 'The Men in the Storm', 'When Man Falls', 'A Dark-Brown Dog', 'A Detail', 'An Eloquence of Grief', 'The Pace of Youth', and 'In the Depths of a Coal Mine', 'A Dark-Brown Dog' may have been written later; Stallman suggests January 1900 (*Crane*, pp. 480, 497).

The young lovers are on a private merry-go-round of their own emotions:

They fell and soared, and soared and fell in this manner until they knew that to live without each other would be a wandering in deserts. They had grown so intent upon the uncertainties, the variations, the guessings of their affair that the world had become but a huge immaterial background. . . . They were the victims of the dread angel of affectionate speculation that forces the brain endlessly on roads that lead nowhere. (p. 277)

And because they tend to view external nature in terms of their own emotions (p. 280), their love also reinforces the image of the external world as an immense merry-go-round. Stimson is to the lovers (he considers them 'children' [pp. 281–2]) as the ticket-seller and ring-handler are to the children who ride the merry-go-round, the figure of authority who appears to regulate, within certain limits, the actions of those beneath him.[35] All three means of expanding the central image merge in the climactic chase which ends the story. The young lovers have seized the brass ring of the moral world—a feat which Stimson and his wife seem to have missed (p. 281)—and the supervisory older generation is obliged to let Frank and Lizzie assume their rightful place on the larger merry-go-round. Hence, the image patterns in this story are developed by means of the sort of parallel constructions found in *Maggie*; and, again as in *Maggie*, they are superimposed firmly upon a central character's psychological progression to awareness. Stimson has the illusion that he can control young love in Frank and Lizzie; at the first threat to this control he reacts with rage, and both his rage and the illusion which it sustains direct his actions until the moment of the lovers' elopement; he then experiences the deflating truth that he cannot control the moral force of love in

[35] The parallel relationships imply a further analogy: Stimson is to his merry-go-round as the creator is to the macrocosmic merry-go-round. Stimson's pomposity and obvious limitations are given to the god external to man in several poems; and in such a context the further analogy is especially suggested by both Stimson's complacent admiration of 'Stimson's Mammoth Merry-Go-Round' and his final gesture which 'meant that at any rate he was not responsible' (p. 282).

other human beings, his former rage is revealed as futile because its object was the protection of the illusion which experience has just shattered, and his final capitulation suggests that eventually he will be able to live with this new reality which has been forced upon his awareness. The literary result is Crane's finest treatment of romantic love. All the remaining sketches are concerned with less agreeable realities.

'An Experiment in Luxury' masquerades as a companion piece for the 'Experiment in Misery', but a reading of almost any paragraph from 'Luxury' after almost any paragraph from 'Misery' will suggest that Crane was immensely interested in the professional tramp's point of view and as immensely bored with the millionaire and his family. This sketch occasionally lapses into wordy passages which fill up space but accomplish little else. Crane fulfilled his assignment and made his point, but the point has been missed and the sketch overestimated because of its nominal association with the much greater one. The naïve youth who conducts the experiment is placed in an absurd position occasioned partly by his own innocence and partly by his conversation with an 'old friend who could only see one thing at a time' (p. 43). The friend suggests that the youth make a 'social study' of the millionaire, and thus implies that there is some relation between wealth and a man's social condition—although he does not accept the religious cliché which equates misery with wealth and happiness with poverty. Then the youth misunderstands a remark by his friend and leaps 'with warmth' to defend the son of the family he is about to visit. Although the friend denies having made any accusation, the implication is plain that the youth begins his 'social study' somewhat on the defensive. However, the millionaire's son proves to be a conventional young man home from college, the beautiful daughters are all but ignored, the wife is both vain and stupid but quite harmless because of the artificiality of the sphere in which she operates, and the great man himself is placed 'in a far land where mechanics and bricklayers go, a mystic land of little, universal emotions, and he had been guided to it by the quaint gestures of a kitten's furry paws' (p. 48). Socially, the portrait presents an utterly banal family who happen to be rich. This millionaire is neither a fool, a hypocrite, a moral coward, nor a mind distinguished by anything more meaningful than making money and enjoying it; and thus the youth's defensiveness gradually starves to death, there being absolutely nothing for it to feed upon except the snobbery of the footman. This morally innocuous family implies that all prating about the 'mystery of social condition' —like the religious rationalization of the unequal distribution of wealth—rests upon a precious illusion which erroneously associates the human qualities of man's social dimension with his economic status. This family is exactly like their house:

It had an inanity of expression, an absolute lack of artistic strength . . . a homely pile of stone, rugged, grimly self reliant, asserting its quality as a fine thing when in reality the beholder usually wondered why so much money had been spent to obtain a complete negation. Then from another point of view [that which worships wealth] it was important and mighty because it stood as a fetich, formidable because of traditions of worship. (p. 45)

And the only victim of this fetishism in the family, apparently, is the wife who reveals that 'kind of pride which, mistaking the form for the real thing, worships itself because of its devotion to the form' (p. 49). According to this sketch, if Crane could have heard Fitzgerald argue that 'the very rich are different from you and me', he too would have given Hemingway's reply: 'Yes, they have more money.' But by 1894 this whole matter was drearily familiar to the man who had been surrounded by such families every summer at Asbury Park.[36]

'A Detail', is Crane's cameo-portrait of innocence and its probable fate in his world. The central character 'made one marvel that in that face the wrinkles showed no trace of experience, knowledge; they were simply little, soft, innocent creases. As for her glance, it had the trustfulness of ignorance and the candour of

[36] Crane's ironic contempt reappears when he considers millionaires who are not thus morally undistinguished (*Poems*, ed. Katz, pp. 98, 101), but again the mere fact of wealth is irrelevant. Crane remained unimpressed: 'The virtue of the rich is not so superior to the virtue of the poor that we can say that the rich have a great advantage' (Stallman, 'Some New Sketches', p. 561).

babyhood' (p. 177). This innocent old lady, alone and penniless, has come to the city to seek work, and will soon be overwhelmed:

she suddenly came into the tempest of the Sixth Avenue shopping district, where from the streams of people and vehicles went up a roar like that from headlong mountain torrents.

She seemed then like a chip that catches, recoils, turns and wheels, a reluctant thing in the clutch of the impetuous river. . . . Meanwhile the torrent jostled her, swung her this and that way. (pp. 176–7)

The two girls she meets 'look like full-rigged ships with all sails set' (p. 177), and are thus able to stay afloat in this maelstrom of experience. Immediately after her futile request for work the sketch ends as the two girls watch this 'aged figure' walk away from them. 'At last, the crowd, the innumerable wagons, intermingling and changing with uproar and riot, suddenly engulfed it' (p. 178).

Like 'A Detail', the remaining sketches are all concerned in one way or another with the Bowery world ('In the Depths of a Coal Mine' can reasonably be included even though the setting changes, because the human flaws Crane finds in Pennsylvania are precisely those he found in New York); and they are best approached as examinations of particular moral failings which fall within Crane's general assessment of Bowery life which, in itself, did not change. His view of the Bowery as primarily a moral reality is essentially repeated in his judgement of another local jungle: like the Bowery, the Tenderloin is not at all

a certain condition of affairs in a metropolitan district. But probably it is in truth something more dim, an essence, an emotion—something superior to the influences of politics or geographies, a thing unchangeable. It represents a certain wild impulse, . . . the spirit that flings beer bottles, jumps debts and makes havoc for the unwary; also sings in a hoarse voice at 3 a.m. (p. 163)

Hence, these sketches are no more naturalistic than the others are. As in *Maggie*, the people they portray are free to choose their own actions, and Crane's irony holds them responsible for their choices.

Both 'When Man Falls a Crowd Gathers' and 'An Eloquence of Grief' contain the same ironic barb. An Italian collapses in the street and thus attracts a 'dodging, pushing, peering group . . . satisfied that there was a horror to be seen and apparently insane to get a view of it' (pp. 107–9). Even after the man has been taken away some of this crowd

continued to stare at the ambulance on its banging, clanging return journey until it vanished into the golden haze. It was as if they had been cheated. Their eyes expressed discontent at this curtain which had been rung down in the midst of the drama. And this impenetrable fabric, suddenly intervening between a suffering creature and their curiosity, seemed to appear to them as an injustice. (p. 111)

The other sketch is of a police court 'crowded with people who sloped back comfortably in their chairs, regarding with undeviating glances the procession'. These spectators, secure from the misery they witness like those who stare at the Italian, have 'come for curiosity's sweet sake', and thus they reveal 'an air of being in wait for a cry of anguish, some loud painful protestation that would bring the proper thrill to their jaded, world-weary nerves' (p. 262).[37] Both sketches stress this brutish curiosity of spectators who can see nothing in suffering except their own cheap gratification; the contemplation of human misery enables them to feel comfortably superior to the sufferer—a feeling which logically is about as justifiable as Mrs. Johnson's 'virtuous indignation' on her way to the pawnshop.

A different view of casual brutality is offered in 'A Dark-Brown Dog'. The love which grows between a baby and a stray dog is crushed when the drunken father flings the dog through a fifth-storey tenement window. This man's action is in no way determined by forces exterior to himself. Crane's statement is explicit: 'the father was in a mood for having fun, and it occurred to him that it would be a fine thing to throw the dog out of the window' (p. 136). Given this capricious cruelty—for which the reader is well

[37] Crane's imagery in this sketch sardonically implies an analogy between police court and church to suggest that these spectators would still be only spectators, even at a church service.

prepared by Crane's making the whole family, including the baby, beat this dog just for the fun of it—the dog is to the father as furniture is to Mrs. Johnson, as Maggie is to Pete, as Hattie is to Jimmie: merely something to be used irresponsibly to provide a momentary amusement for the destroyer. But the considerable impact of this sketch is implicit because it derives from the baby's love for the dog: the father's brutality towards the dog strikes his own child, and suggests that he cares no more for the one than he does for the other.

During the summer of 1894 'In the Depths of a Coal Mine' took Crane and Linson on a field trip to view a way life more desperate than anything even the Bowery could offer. Linson has recalled how profoundly shaken Crane was at the sight of children 'yet at the spanking period' working as slate-pickers, in appalling sur-roundings, for fifty-five cents a day. But there is no overt expression of pity anywhere in the sketch, and the children are considered strictly from a detached point of view. Crane's response is a controlled rage which vents itself equally upon the moral failure which has victimized these children and upon the victims' own innocence. His condemnation of their innocence is explicit and sharp, an ironic portrayal of the mindless way in which these young slate-pickers swagger in their anteroom to hell (p. 291); but his anger at the grown-up greed which also is responsible for their plight is expressed more artistically. A single image dominates this sketch from the beginning, the coal breakers which squat 'upon the hillsides and in the valley like enormous preying monsters, eating of the sunshine, the grass, the green leaves' (p. 289). And the real monster is summoned forth at the end (editorially toned down from the ending Crane had written); here the breaker is identified as the 'imperturbably cruel and insatiate, black emblem of greed, and of the gods of this labor' (p. 297). This animalized machine thus symbolizes coal-mining only so far as this industry dominates the physical landscape; it is also, and more importantly, the black emblem of the human greed which dominates a moral landscape where children are casually enslaved. Hence, every comment Crane has made throughout the sketch about the physical machine 'eating of the sunshine' implies an analogous moral reference.

'The Men in the Storm', which seems to me the artistic companion piece to 'An Experiment in Misery', is a work of considerable subtlety behind its mask of newspaper realism. Crane begins the sketch with the blizzard and immediately opposes this natural force to the moral world of human beings (just as he was later to do with the blizzard in 'The Blue Hotel'): 'All the clatter of the street was softened by the masses that lay upon the cobbles until, even to one who looked from a window, it became important music, a melody of life made necessary to the ear by the dreariness of the pitiless beat and sweep of the storm' (p. 91). He also opposes the storm to the moral world by portraying men who react to this storm as real men should—the streetcar drivers who, 'muffled to the eyes, stood erect and facing the wind, models of grim philosophy', and others who are out 'busily shovelling the white drifts from the walks' (p. 91). Such men as these provide the basis for distinguishing between two classes in the crowd waiting before the lodging-house door. Part of this crowd are 'strong, healthy, clear-skinned fellows with that stamp of countenance which is not frequently seen upon seekers after charity', and these men, like the stoical drivers, 'remained silent and impassive in the blizzard, their eyes fixed on the windows of the house, statues of patience' (p. 93). But the other class, the complainers and rumour-mongers, approach by 'slouching along with the characteristic hopeless gait of professional strays' (p. 92), and thus reveal themselves as members of 'the shifting, Bowery lodging-house element who were used to paying ten cents for a place to sleep, but who now came here because it was cheaper' (p. 93). This distinction, carefully drawn at the beginning, gradually disintegrates as the sketch proceeds until, with the rout of the dry-goods merchant, it disappears entirely.

This fat and prosperous merchant, who regards the crowd from across the street, indulges in the same illusory superiority that Crane found in the onlookers at the police station and around the fallen Italian:

He stood in an attitude of magnificent reflection. He slowly stroked his moustache with a certain grandeur of manner, and looked down at the snow-encrusted mob. From below, there was denoted a supreme complacence in him. It seemed that the sight operated inversely, and enabled him to more clearly regard his own environment, delightful relatively. (p. 95)

But immediately the mob falls into exactly the same illusion. They jeer at the merchant until he flees, and upon this success 'the mob chuckled ferociously like ogres who had just devoured something' (p. 95). This conquest, although only a momentary amusement like the drunken father's throwing the dog out of the window, ironically reveals the force of brotherhood and co-operation available to these men for responsible use if they so desire, and if, as a precondition to such a desire, the 'professional strays' would reassume the moral energy of the better class in the crowd. Instead, the incident merely solidifies the mob by merging the better class with the jeering professionals; and the remainder of the sketch shows that these men are not going to struggle against anything except each other.[38] The professional pauper's attitude towards life is highly contagious, as Riis warned; it quickly infects those who do not stay morally braced to resist it. And the sketch ends as the men, now merely one undistinguished mob, fight among themselves to pass through a doorway that none of them will ever own to temporary respite from the natural forces which, inevitably, will confront them again in the morning. *George's Mother* is Crane's detailed analysis of the gradual degeneration which occurs when an honest man succumbs to the lure of professional pauperism.

No one knows just when *George's Mother* was written. It was published in May 1896, but Howells claimed in July that it was 'two years, now, since' he had seen the novel in manuscript; Jeanette L. Gilder said it 'was written before he wrote "The Red Badge of Courage," and lay in a publisher's safe until the author called for it and took it elsewhere'; an anonymous interview of May 1895 stated that it was then 'in the publisher's hands' under its original title of *A Woman Without Weapons*; and an amazingly

[38] Cf. A. W. Hart, 'Social Outlook', p. 95.

imperceptive review by Harry Thurston Peck implied that it had been written even before *Maggie*. Although the only manuscript evidence we have is a draft of five paragraphs from chapter 2 written on two pages which also bear 'The Holler Tree', a posthumously published Sullivan County sketch, the critical consensus—established by Berryman, Stallman, Colvert, Jumper, and others—is that *George's Mother* was begun before *The Red Badge*, laid aside, and finished after it.[39] The evidence for this opinion seems remarkably good, and to explore it is to specify the place of this novel in the context of Crane's development.

Crane left an appropriate statement with an interviewer shortly after *George's Mother* appeared: 'the first chapter is immaterial; but, once written, it determines the rest of the book. He grinds it out . . . forcing himself to follow "that fearful logical conclusion"; writing what his knowledge of human nature tells him would be the inescapable outcome of those characters placed in those circumstances.'[40] But, as Jumper argues (p. 169), the exposition of 'those characters placed in those circumstances' requires, in this novel, about the first five chapters. The point of view does not establish itself before the fifth or sixth chapter, and this first part of the novel is in style and narrative technique more reminiscent of *Maggie* than the rest of it is; see, for example, the presentation of Jones (*Work*, X, 20–3), and compare the effect George's attention

[39] Howells, 'New York Low Life in Fiction', New York *World*, 26 July 1896, p. 18; Gilder, 'Romance by Swinburne and Realism by Crane', New York *World*, 31 May 1896, p. 20; anon., 'Stephen Crane', *Bookman*, I (May 1895), 230; Peck, '*George's Mother*', *Bookman*, III (July 1896), 446–7; Maurice Bassan, 'An Early Draft of *George's Mother*', *American Literature*, XXXVI (Jan. 1965), 518–22; Berryman, *Crane*, pp. 65, 85; *Stephen Crane: An Omnibus*, ed. R. W. Stallman (New York, 1952), p. 15; James B. Colvert, 'Stephen Crane: The Development of His Art', unpublished Ph.D. thesis (Louisiana, 1953), pp. 127–8; Jumper, pp. 74–5, 169. Crane obviously refers to *George's Mother* in his letters of 9 May 1894—'I am content and am writing another novel which is a bird'—and 15 November when he has 'just completed a New York book that leaves Maggie at the post' (*Letters*, pp. 36, 41). However, when Crane names his works and tells, not always correctly, when each was written, *George's Mother* is conspicuously absent from the list (*Letters*, pp. 95, 117)—possibly because it would have been awkward to state in the context of these letters that the novel had been written in two stages.

[40] Herbert P. Williams, 'Mr. Crane as Literary Artist', *Illustrated American*, XX (18 July 1896), 126.

has upon Bleecker (X, 32) with the effect Maggie's attention has upon Pete. But after about the fifth chapter the point of view takes more or less permanent lodgings within the mind of George, the third-person limited narrative technique of *The Red Badge* replaces the omniscient narration of *Maggie*, and the story finally gets under way as a straightforward analysis of a man's moral degeneration which, given George's vanity and laziness, never falters or suggests any real hope of recovery.

When seen in this light *George's Mother* is about as much a companion piece to *Maggie* as 'An Experiment in Luxury' is to 'An Experiment in Misery'. The relationship between the two novels is a superficial one of materials and setting; but the reader has to admit that on the surface there appears to be plentiful evidence of kinship. The Kelceys and Johnsons live in the same tenement, Maggie and Pete appear in both stories, George and his mother are as gulled by illusions as Maggie is, and all three characters are ironically affected by a moribund religion. The 'drinking in *George's Mother* is an elaboration of the saloon function which Crane put in *Maggie* . . . The saloon is a jolly place where the wounds of life are licked' (Shane, p. 89); and hence, the brotherhood, courtesy, and fraternal warmth of the saloon society that George encounters through Jones and Bleecker are illusory— as George learns when he attempts to borrow money from members of this club—just as Maggie's view of Pete was illusory. 'If there ever has been in a New York cafe an impulse from the really Bohemian religion of fraternity,' Crane later wrote, 'it has probably been frozen to death' (*New York City Sketches*, p. 167). The church is as repulsive to George as the tenement is to Maggie, and for the same reason: the moral failings of those entrusted with the keeping of these institutions, Mrs. Johnson, Mrs. Kelcey, the plump young minister, have destroyed them. The pointless formalism of Mrs. Kelcey and her kind strangles all spirit and leaves only 'dreary blackness arranged in solemn rows . . . made by people who tilted their heads at a prescribed angle of devotion'. The analogy is strengthened by Mrs. Kelcey's being about as far out of touch with reality as Mrs. Johnson is: 'at the same point in life that Mrs. Johnson escapes from reality by taking to drink, Mrs. Kelcey escapes from reality by taking to dreams about George' (Shane, p. 85), and these wishful illusions are coloured by her empty religion: George will 'become a white and looming king among men' if only he will work hard, eschew alcohol, and go regularly to prayer meeting—the Horatio Alger myth (see Solomon, *Parody to Realism*, pp. 49–67).

But the original title implies a closer analogy between Mrs. Kelcey and Maggie, and enough of it remains to suggest what Crane's first intentions for this novel may have been. Both Maggie and Mrs. Kelcey are women without weapons in their respective situations. Just as Pete becomes the barrier between Maggie and prostitution, George, whose father and brothers are dead, becomes the barrier between his mother and despair. Both women thus place their faith in young men who are vain, selfish, morally weak; partly because of their complete dependence each sees her young man in terms of what she desires him to be; and both women are helpless to do anything but accept the inevitable when their men fail them and their illusions are shattered. If the central focus of the novel had remained on the mother, as either title suggests, and if this pattern had been developed as it is in the Sullivan County tales, Mrs. Kelcey's illusions would have been pierced by some climactic encounter with reality (instead of merely eroding away as they do in the novel we have), and her despair, when actually experienced, would have been much less fearsome than it had appeared to be in her imagination. But while such a pattern is everywhere visible in *Maggie*, it is hardly even suggested by *George's Mother*.

It is at this point, just beneath the surface concerns of material and setting, that any companion-piece relationship between these two novels disintegrates. Maggie's illusions arise from fear, innocence, and romantic love, but George's arise from vanity and the rationalization needed to preserve this vanity from the consequences of his own laziness. Because George's dominant weakness is vanity he is psychologically distinct from Maggie. Prostitution is a reality which exists outside the mind, no matter how the apprehensive imagination may consider it, but George's discontent with his situation is not suggested to his mind by the external situation itself—youth, health, a steady job under a lenient foreman with fellow workers who seem pleasant enough, a clean and orderly home kept by a parent who loves him and tends to his needs as best she can. His vanity rules his judgement and makes this comparatively decent situation seem undesirable. With Maggie's fear, an external cause triggers a response which manifests itself as a state of mind; but with George's vanity, a state of mind causes a response which manifests itself as a qualitative judgement of an external reality. Thus, Maggie can be personally honest in a way that is almost impossible for George, and after about chapter 5 George as a person is consistently treated ironically, as Maggie never is, because he is personally dishonest. As such a basic distinction between these two protagonists should suggest, the plots of these novels are also mutually distinct: the plot of *Maggie* is based on the conceptual pattern of the *Sullivan County Sketches;* but the pattern embodied by George Kelcey, as both Colvert and Westbrook have noted, 'is identical with that of "the assassin" in the earlier story, "An Experiment in Misery," in that both characters bring themselves to the utter depths of degradation through their own lack of moral courage'.[41]

Like the professional tramp, George is entirely aware of that which he does not have the moral strength to face. He may be foolish enough to believe that knowledge of a city is to be gauged by the number of bar tenders one knows, but he realizes that his moral responsibility requires him to stay sober and hold a steady job, both for his own sake and to provide for his mother. The scene of his awakening after Bleecker's drunken party reveals his awareness, his laziness, and shows that he is unfit for life in precisely the same way that the assassin is:

As he lay pondering, his bodily condition created for him a bitter philosophy, and he perceived all the futility of a red existence. He saw his life problems confronting him like granite giants, and he was no

[41] Colvert, 'Development of His Art', p. 65; cf. Westbrook, 'Revolt-Search', p. 112.

longer erect to meet them. He had made a calamitous retrogression in his war. Spectres were to him now as large as clouds.

Inspired by the pitiless ache in his head, he was prepared to reform and live a white life. His stomach informed him that a good man was the only being who was wise. But his perception of his future was hopeless. He was aghast at the prospect of the old routine. It was impossible. He trembled before its exactions.

Turning toward the other way, he saw that the gold portals of vice no longer enticed him. . . . Upon reflection, he saw, therefore, that he was perfectly willing to be virtuous if somebody would come and make it easy for him.[42]

Unlike the youth who concludes his experiment and returns to manhood with his new awareness, George chooses, with the same awareness, to sink deeper into futility.

However, as George knows very well what he is doing, his powers of rationalization become increasingly overworked in order to sustain his vain opinion of himself in the face of his degeneration. His vanity, which began to rear its head as soon as he outgrew seeing himself only 'as a stern general pointing a sword at the nervous and abashed horizon', now places his own ego squarely at the centre of the universe. Sentimental novels have told him a goddess exists solely for his own emotional purposes, and George is quite convinced that he is worth every moment of her prolonged wait: 'He believed that the commonplace lot was the sentence, the doom, of certain people who did not know how to feel.' Thus, when Pete takes Maggie from beneath his nose because he has been too weak even to speak to her, he suffers 'his first gloomy conviction that the earth was not grateful to him for his presence upon it', and *therefore* he eagerly accepts Jones's invitation to Bleecker's party: 'As he walked home he thought that he was a very grim

---

[42] *Work*, X, 58–9. This passage in particular recalls the sketch because the progression from darkness to light, from the drunken illusions of ideal felicity to the bitter awareness of the morning after, is used to reveal George to himself as it was used to reveal the tramp's point of view to the youth. Also, there are George's 'red existence' and the assassin's 'red grin', George's temporary inclination towards a 'white life' and the 'hully white nightshirt' which amazes the assassin, George's life problems as 'granite giants' and the youth's sentimental conception of 'imperturbably granite wheels'; and the entrance of light in both scenes is used to indicate the change from illusion to reality.

figure. He was about to taste the delicious revenge of a partial
self-destruction. The universe would regret its position when it
saw him drunk' (X, 48–9). And such 'reasoning' again duplicates
the abortive mental processes behind Mrs. Johnson's 'virtuous
indignation'. George never grows up. Psychologically and morally
he is still a child jousting with a child's vanity at what he wishes to
believe is a nervous and abashed horizon; and the moment he
suspects a pot of gold is not about to drop into his lap of its own
accord, he is ready to give up.

But if the pattern of George's degeneration is the same as that
of the assassin's, the *presentation* of it is much the same as that of
Henry Fleming's development. Once Crane begins to use the
third-person limited narrative technique in this novel, George's
moral decay becomes the opposite of Henry's moral growth:
Henry progresses from innocent vanity through experience of
reality to the threshold of responsible manhood; George, in spite
of his inadequacies, has assumed the pose of manhood before the
novel opens, and he regresses from this position through a wilful
withdrawal from reality to the vanity of the professional pauper.
Both George and Henry are young men who suffer from vanity and
its attendant day-dreams, both are adept at rationalizing their
failures, both are treated ironically by the author, both seek
recognition from their peers, both undergo a moral crisis of sorts
in a secluded sanctuary—Henry in the forest chapel and George
in the Bowery church—and, with each as protagonist, the inner
life of the mind becomes the centre of the novel in a manner which
will not apply to *Maggie*. Even the function of the wafer-like sun
as the image of external nature undisturbed by human suffering
reappears, in its customary place at the end of a chapter (14), in
George's Mother: 'A pale flood of sunlight, imperturbable at its
vocation, streamed upon the little old woman, bowed with pain,
forlorn in her chair.' Also, both novels reveal the same general
pattern in their use of two broad categories of recurring imagery.
Henry is immensely troubled by his imaginary notions of the
horrors of war, and his progress to an awareness that 'the great
death is, after all, but the great death' is constantly impeded

by his attributing moral qualities to external nature.[43] George accepts the values of the saloon as his own index of reality, and his mother accepts the formalism of the church for the same purpose. In short, both novels contain running patterns of two groups of images signifying illusions, and the two illusory notions that they represent are in each novel constantly contrasted with the reality which is distinct from either. In *George's Mother* the reality of life is implied, just as it is in 'An Experiment in Misery', by the roar of the city, the movement and purpose of the normal people; thus, both the saloon and the church represent withdrawals from this active life, and the empty rituals of fraternity practised by Bleecker and his group are emphasized to mock the equally empty rituals which conquer Mrs. Kelcey. While this double strand of running imagery should recall the patterns of saloon and tenement in *Maggie*, the *use* of these image clusters in the later novel is again quite different: the saloon and tenement represent the reality in which Maggie is immersed, but for George and his mother the saloon and church represent futile retreats from reality; and Crane is careful to observe the artistic decorum demanded by the way in which he has patterned his imagery—he shows us that Mrs. Kelcey is as personally dishonest, as wilful in her withdrawal from reality, as George is. She deliberately refuses to accept what her eyes reveal to her because she knows that her vain and lazy son is no king among men, that if her dreams of his greatness were 'worded, they would be ridiculous'. When she saw him loafing with the street-corner louts by the saloon door, 'she slunk away, for she understood that it would be a terrible thing to confront him and his pride there with youths who were superior to mothers' (X, 76). She refuses to see what everyone else in the tenement sees, that she has 'a wild son'.

Perhaps the most telling resemblance between this novel and

---

[43] Most of Henry's struggles to perceive correctly 'the machinery of the universe' were excised by Crane in his revisions, but the original weight given to this theme can be gauged from the surviving manuscripts. See Olov W. Fryckstedt, 'Henry Fleming's Tupenny Fury: Cosmic Pessimism in Stephen Crane's *The Red Badge of Courage*', *Studia Neophilologica*, XXXIII (1961), 265–81.

The Red Badge, however, is that one of the principal means of showing change of character in both is the relationship of the protagonist to the group. Just as Henry leaves the dullness of the farm to join the army, George leaves the dull reality of his job and home to join the wastrels led by Bleecker, but each—Henry because he believes he is unique in his fear, George because he is not yet an accomplished drunkard—is unable to feel himself a real part of the group he joins. Henry cannot very well distinguish himself in his group so long as the regiment merely waits to go into action, and George cannot distinguish himself within Bleecker's group because these drunkards do nothing at all. Compared with Bleecker's club, the street-corner gang to which George turns is roughly as different as the army to which Henry returns is from the army he deserts: even though it is the same regiment, Henry returns to a group of experienced veterans who know for certain that they will fight again when morning comes. Moreover, the entrance of the protagonist into the 'second' group is in both novels accomplished under much the same ambiguous circumstances: Henry, with his head wound, reaches his regiment, and when he is recognized (chapter 13), he thinks 'he must hasten to produce his tale to protect him from the missiles already at the lips of his redoubtable comrades'; George, 'livid from fear', runs with Fidsey Corcoran to where the rest of the gang waits, and when he is recognized (X, 76), he recites a tale in which he allows himself 'to appear prominent and redoubtable'. Each is accepted, each distinguishes himself in the group activity—Henry in combat, George in drinking, fighting, and being too clever to work—and thus, each eventually finds his real place in life—Henry as a man, George as a professional pauper.[44] While none of these relationships absolutely proves that the greater part of *George's Mother* was written after *The Red Badge*, the fact that George, rather than his mother, so dominates the novel strongly suggests it. Also, the draft fragment published by Bassan implies, as might be expected,

[44] Cf. A. W. Hart, pp. 104–6. In order to preserve the illusion of Maggie's innocence, such a relationship between protagonist and group is absent from the earlier novel. Maggie lacks even 'a reliable friend' with whom she might discuss her view of Pete.

that the curious use of battle-field imagery in connection with Mrs. Kelcey's house cleaning (chapter 2) is more likely to be an ingenious revision by an author whose head was full of such imagery after having written *The Red Badge* than an original conception by an author fresh from writing *Maggie*.

Hence, *George's Mother* can be considered a compendium of the materials and setting of *Maggie*, the narrative technique of *The Red Badge*, and the conceptual pattern implicit in the assassin of 'An Experiment in Misery'. If such a view is reasonable, the main line of Crane's development seems to run from *Maggie* to *The Red Badge* and on into the later work, and *George's Mother* represents a last return to the Bowery (which Crane soon abandoned for the Tenderloin district) primarily for two purposes: to spell out specifically the moral cowardice at the root of Bowery life by analysing a man's gradual deterioration to moral pauperism, and to accomplish this end by a means which confirmed the technical advances won with *The Red Badge* by using them in a different story, with different materials, based upon a different plot. Technically speaking, *George's Mother* does indeed leave *Maggie* at the post because it neither contains the stylistic excesses of the earlier book nor forces us to accept so unbelievable a condition as Maggie's innocence. There is no cheating in the presentation of George or his mother, and Crane's new proficiency with the third-person limited point of view makes the 'fearful logical conclusion' arise smoothly and inevitably out of the frailties of his characters.

The record of Crane's underground labours is by no means complete because neither *The Red Badge* nor *The Black Riders* has yet been considered. Nevertheless, enough of it is present to show that Crane's eyes function in the same way when examining George or his mother, the assassin, the millionaire, the Mexican Indians, the slate-pickers, Maggie or her mother and brother, Pete, the little man, Founder Bradley, or the Ocean Grove professional with his black valise—that the change from life at Asbury Park to life in the Bowery merely confirms the attitudes revealed in the early news articles. When George, through his own moral cowardice, turns his back upon manhood to succumb to the futility of pauperism, he becomes only a more serious version of the Asbury Park holiday-maker who, through his own innocence, turns his back upon the ocean to succumb to Bradley's bathtubs and fire engines. All Crane's characters carry a moral black valise of some sort which they would be much better off without— vanity, laziness, hypocrisy, innocence—and these moral alba- trosses are never determined by external conditions. Externalities —blizzard, tenement, poverty, wealth—are merely the given circumstances in which man must live happily or unhappily, honestly or dishonestly; they may help to reveal a man's character through his reactions, but they do not in themselves wholly determine character or even the specific reactions that they provoke from different kinds of men. The moral failings of man made life comic to Crane's eyes back in Asbury Park and Ocean Grove; the same weaknesses, to the same eyes, made life tragic in the Bowery or the depths of a coal-mine. But Crane the ironist, the aesthetically —and never morally—detached intelligence dissecting its subject, is the constant quality throughout all changes of subject-matter as this ironic vision fights its way to competent craftsmanship in its expression.

Even at this point, therefore, it is probably safe to offer two conclusions: first, that the crucial elements of any good Crane story are three—the protagonist's vision, the protagonist's mental machinery, and the protagonist's personal honesty—all of which lie within the mind; second, that Crane's own pair of eyes, no matter what subject they may henceforth be trained upon, will remain unchanged until the end.

III

PRIVATE FLEMING: HIS VARIOUS BATTLES

THE youth who eventually became Henry Fleming may have existed in Crane's mind as early as 1892 (W. F. Johnson, p. 289), but he was born into a first draft of *The Red Badge of Courage*—most probably in the form of a short story—during ten nights in March 1893 (*Letters*, p. 17). When he was a year old, in February 1894, his various battles had attained sufficient form for Crane to have the manuscript typed—a step which could not have been taken lightly because the author had to borrow the money for the typist's fee (*Letters*, p. 30)—and he finally saw print in December when a condensed version appeared in the Philadelphia *Press* and other American newspapers served by the Bacheller and Johnson syndicate. The whole novel was published in book form, first in America and then in England, during the fall of 1895; and after 'the blaze of the English reviews lighted up January', as Thomas Beer put it, the novel became the runaway best-seller which 'went through fourteen printings within a year at home, and enjoyed immense popularity in England'.[1] The enduring popularity of *The Red Badge* has made it one of only four novels in any way concerned with the Civil War to appear among the 'over-all best sellers of American fiction'; and the value of the first edition (which sold for one dollar in 1895) is such that forged copies are now available to gull the unwary collector.[2] Thus Crane moved

---

[1] For information concerning the composition, growth, and existing manuscripts see Joseph Katz, ed., *The Red Badge of Courage* (Gainesville, 1967), and William L. Howarth, '*The Red Badge of Courage* Manuscript: New Evidence for a Critical Edition', *Studies in Bibliography*, XVIII (1965), 229–47.

[2] See Robert A. Lively, *Fiction Fights the Civil War* (Chapel Hill, 1957), p. 65; Richard H. Wilmer, Jr., 'Collecting Civil War Novels', *Colophon*, n.s., III (Autumn 1938), 515.

from obscurity to international fame shortly after his twenty-fourth birthday with a book conceived and largely written before he was twenty-two.

This continuing popularity has all but buried the novel beneath layer upon layer of commentary which has been accumulating steadily since 1894. Fortunately, the thickest layers of this criticism are easily identified by a generally apologetic argument: the novel is wrenched out of its proper context among Crane's other writings, a different context—either historical or critical—is assumed by the critic, and the argument is developed in order to force the novel to conform to this new mould into which it most stubbornly refuses to fit. The two most popular contexts to be found in this apologetic criticism are the naturalistic and the symbolic, and a brief look at these two critical party lines as they have been applied to *The Red Badge* should help clear the way for a common-sense reading of the novel.

At its most obvious level of error, the assumption of a naturalistic context for *The Red Badge* has led to several studies of 'sources' or 'influences'. This is the literary historian's attempt to identify Crane's literary ancestors as Zola, Tolstoy, Stendhal, or, if the argument is for historical realism and American sources, Bierce and DeForest (source hunters never bother to consider Howells): *The Red Badge* is literary naturalism; so young and ill-educated a man as Crane could hardly have created a major work of literary naturalism intuitively; therefore, he studied authors A, B, or C, and the novel is obviously derivative. But *The Red Badge*, of course, is not literary naturalism at all, and thus Crane had no real need to read any of these authors. He may well have read all of them, among others—most young writers read established practitioners while trying to attain a distinctive style—but Crane's works, even without 'Why Did the Young Clerk Swear?', strongly imply that specifically naturalistic fiction must have bored him.[3] Henry

---

[3] A comic variation of the source-hunter's argument exists: since 1894 altogether too many people have expressed amazement at a 'great Civil War novel' having been written by a mere lad who was not born until half a dozen years after the war ended. In reality 'there is nothing about the Civil War in this book which could not have been learned by a moderately intelligent and

Fleming seems even less affected, let alone determined, by his environment than Crane's Bowery characters are, largely because he is more intelligent. He obviously possesses a will of his own, a sense of responsibility as a soldier, and a conscience which he is unable to ignore; and thus endowed he is remarkably ill-fitted for philosophic determinism. In fact Henry's relations with his environment are often just the reverse of what naturalism assumes they ought to be; instead of the environment determining Henry, Henry's 'weak mental machinery' usually determines his environment, so far as his own view of it is concerned—a matter which can be verified by anyone who reads the chapters in which Henry wanders about in the forest. The better naturalistic critics, who assume the context for purposes of criticism rather than source-hunting, rest their interpretation of the novel largely upon three claims: the prevalence of animal imagery, the 'moving box' episode (and the similar one in which Fleming throws a pine-cone at a squirrel), and the belief that Henry undergoes no change of character and shows no moral development in the course of the action. Each of these claims is easily refuted once the novel is returned to its rightful context. For the moment let us merely have faith that *The Red Badge* was written by an important ironist, not by a Zola or a Dreiser.

But to see Crane as primarily an ironist is in itself a challenge to the literary historian's basic assumptions of historical context and literary antecedents as effective means of approach to such a writer. The ironic vision itself can in no way be explained by a particular historical context (which merely provides the necessary grist for the ironist's mill) or by literary antecedents (which help to account for an individual style). And if we assume that the recurring psychological progression to awareness traced thus far in Crane's work is the basic structure by which his ironic vision expresses itself in fiction, that this pattern is in fact the 'one trump'

---

historically minded high school junior, in a few brief sessions with *Battles and Leaders* or whatever general secondary historical source the student chose.' (MacKinlay Kantor, 'The Historical Novel', in *Three Views of the Novel*, by Irving Howe, John O'Hara, and MacKinlay Kantor [Washington, D.C., 1957], p. 33.)

he mentioned to Willa Cather, then the essential *subject* of his important work comes straight from his ironic perception of the human situation, not from the sort of sources or influences a literary historian can use most effectively in explicating a writer— Emerson, for example—who is not primarily an ironist. Crane's view of the human situation, set forth more clearly in *The Red Badge* than in his earlier work, is that man is born into an amoral universe which is merely the external setting in which human moral life is lived,[4] and that if moral values are to exist and man's life is to be meaningful, morality must be the creation of man's weak mental machinery alone; but even the best of men, the most personally honest, is prone to error and thus liable to bring misery upon himself and others because the mental machinery often distorts that reality which he must perceive correctly if his personal honesty is to result in morally significant commitment. Thus, Crane's essential subject, in *The Red Badge* as in the *Sullivan County Sketches*, *Maggie*, and the 'Experiment in Misery', is man's weak mental machinery as it labours under the stress of some emotion, usually fear, to perceive correctly an area of reality which is not yet within the compass of the perceiver's experience. And if so, *The Red Badge* does have an obvious source which is available to anyone who wishes to investigate it; but the assumption of a naturalistic, a factually realistic, or a specifically literary context leads in the wrong direction. The real source of this novel and any other important Crane work seems to me simply the ironist's incredible awareness of human nature. Our amazement should not be directed at Crane's mastery of the techniques of

---

[4] This view of the universe can reasonably be called naturalistic; but Crane's acceptance of it no more makes his work naturalistic than Matthew Arnold's acceptance of ultimately the same view makes his poetry naturalistic.

If this seems a pessimistic view of nature, it is not only the logical end of Crane's concern with the subject, it is the logical end of America's concern. When Hawthorne and Melville questioned Emerson's view of nature as the benevolent image of the Over-Soul, they revealed an ambiguity in nature that begged closer inspection. Stephen Crane's examination showed nature to be as unmotivated as a machine with which man had come only accidentally in contact. (R. B. West, Jr., 'Stephen Crane: Author in Transition', *American Literature*, XXXIV [May 1962], 227.)

naturalism, or knowledge of the Civil War, or Jamesian grasp of Western literature, but at so young a man's ability to create so superb a psychological portrayal as Henry Fleming.[5]

The attempt to impose a symbolic context upon *The Red Badge*, which apparently originates in the urge to account for Crane's obvious artistry without tampering with the naturalistic interpretation, still lures innocent converts; otherwise it would today be gratuitous to argue against it.[6] The symbolist critic seizes upon those images which provide the key to the conundrum the novel presents in the guise of a story. Once these key 'symbols' are extracted, the rest of the novel—and anything Crane said about it, all Crane's other work (including 'The Veteran'), and everything known of Crane the man—is largely discarded as useless and misleading. This approach can easily be avoided if one merely remembers that 'symbols exist, and exist only, *in context*'.[7] When Crane's red sun is considered in context its wafer-like appearance should not imply the wafer of the Mass. Crane never mentions any dogma, religious ritual, or god external to man except in terms of ironic attack or contempt; and his poems, like *Maggie* and *George's Mother*, do not suggest he was even a Christian, let alone a Catholic. At least five chapters in this novel end with a reference to the sun, as Edward Stone has noted.[8] This fact alone implies—not to Stone, unfortunately—that the sun is used throughout as a general image of external nature, and that one should be extremely wary of making a specific mention bear a symbolic burden which the other examples cannot assume. The mention of this enigmatic sun at the

---

[5] Cf. Colvert, 'Development of His Art', p. 145.

[6] The standard example is R. W. Stallman's widely reprinted interpretation. The best of many opponents are Isaac Rosenfeld, 'Stephen Crane as Symbolist', *Kenyon Review*, XV (Spring 1953), 310–14; Rudolph Von Abele and Walter Havighurst, 'Symbolism and the Student', *College English*, XVI (Apr. 1955), 424–34, 461; Philip Rahv, 'Fiction and the Criticism of Fiction', *Kenyon Review*, XVIII (Spring 1956), 276–99; Stanley B. Greenfield, 'The Unmistakable Stephen Crane', *PMLA*, LXXIII (Dec. 1958), 562–72; Norman Friedman, 'Criticism and the Novel', *Antioch Review*, XVIII (Fall 1958), 356–61; Eric W. Carlson, 'Stephen Crane's *The Red Badge of Courage*', *Explicator*, XV (Mar. 1958), item 34.

[7] Von Abele and Havighurst, p. 429.

[8] 'The Many Suns of *The Red Badge of Courage*', *American Literature*, XXIX (Nov. 1957), 323.

scene of Conklin's death and Fleming's futile rage and grief most obviously suggests the complete separation of man from externals, the total indifference of the heavens to death, war, heroism, blasphemy, and whatever else man may say or do. Given this rather obvious meaning (which is strongly reinforced by the rest of the novel, by Crane's other writings, and by the life of a man who apparently subjected Christianity along with everything else to his own ironic vision), the use of 'wafer' and 'pasted' implies the seal at the end of a legal document and thus suggests completion, finality:[9] the separation of man from externals is absolute, just as death is, and nothing can be done by Fleming to change it.

Similarly Jim Conklin, in spite of his initials and his wound in the side, can hardly be a Christ figure. Initials in American literature can be devil's advocates: for every Joe Christmas there is a Jason Compson, for every Jim Casy a John Claggart. And Conklin received his wound in the side from dramatic necessity: he has to die slowly, remain in his right mind, and retain full use of both arms and legs—that is, he has to wander back from the front, recognize Henry, and dance the hideous hornpipe to make his death so grotesque that it will particularly horrify Henry. Given all these requirements during America's mauve decade when no one would dare be wounded in the groin, the side is really about the only spot available. Throughout his entire canon, Crane inevitably condemns the qualities which Conklin embodies: Conklin is a rumour-monger, a vain, pompous, loud-mouthed, brawling, cursing lout whose greatest joy in life is eating sand-

---

[9] See Scott C. Osborn, 'Stephen Crane's Imagery: "Pasted Like a Wafer," ' *American Literature*, XXIII (Nov. 1951), 362. Crane wrote a parallel scene duplicating Fleming's reaction to Conklin's death, and removed it during revision. After Henry deserts the tattered man his despair and self-loathing vents itself in rage at external nature until at the climax 'He turned in tupenny fury upon the high, tranquil sky. He would have like [*sic*] to have splashed it with a derisive paint' (*Omnibus*, p. 292). Also, the same context, desire, and distinctive image are found in 'The Open Boat': 'When it occurs to a man that nature does not regard him as important, and that she feels she would not maim the universe by disposing of him, he at first wishes to throw bricks at the temple, and he hates deeply the fact that there are no bricks and no temples.' The image of external nature's remoteness, which exactly duplicates the function of the wafer-like sun, is 'a high cold star on a winter's night'.

wiches, who apparently possesses the one virtue of patience in the face of impending danger. And, in view of his other qualities, even this virtue has to be attributed less to calm courage than to mere mindlessness; he is not afraid simply because he does not have enough imagination to frighten himself with. He is one of several Crane characters who 'have merely a stomach and no soul'.[10] If the thought of creating a Christ figure had occurred to Crane he surely could have done better than this.

However, the symbolist approach to *The Red Badge* should immediately be stopped by a consideration of Crane's other work. Nothing in either the earlier or the later work implies a mind which conceives its fiction in terms of conceptual patterns of symbols. (When young Willa Cather asked him 'whether stories were constructed by cabalistic formulae', he replied, 'Where did you get all that rot?') Crane's work obviously abounds with emblematic imagery—the saloon in the Bowery novels, darkness and light in the portrayal of the assassin, the cash register in 'the Blue Hotel', the wounded soldier on the altar in 'War Memories', the fire in 'The Monster'—but all these symbolic images arise out of the process of writing a story *after* it has been imaginatively conceived in terms of a specifically structural plot which in no way depends upon any particular imagery. Hence, Crane's vivid images, in *The Red Badge* as in his other work, result from an artistic labour of craftsmanship, not primarily from the conceiving imagination; and any pattern they may offer will function as an artistic embellishment of an independent plot structure.

Crane's early news articles, the *Sullivan County Sketches*, and *Maggie* provide the only context in which *The Red Badge* may be placed with certainty. And we should add *The Black Riders*, which came immediately after this novel was completed, and *George's Mother*, begun before *The Red Badge* and finished after it. These works surround the novel in the chronology of Crane's development; and a careful reading of them provides the best available approach to an understanding of *The Red Badge* because this novel does not greatly differ from these other works in its essential

[10] *Sullivan County Sketches*, p. 46.

plot, situation, protagonist, and philosophy—even though it differs radically in its technique and resolution.

The little man of the sketches, Maggie Johnson, George Kelcey, and Henry Fleming are all cut from the same bolt: all are young, naïve, untried, subject to fear, troubled by a sense of being unique, given to silly illusions, the environment or society in which they find themselves seems hostile to the ideals they posit for their own lives, and all four protagonists struggle to bridge the gap between their romantically impossible day-dreams and harsh realities.[11] We seldom have much idea of the physical appearance of these characters. None of them can reasonably be called heroic in any traditional sense of the word. Each comes alive only through Crane's acute awareness of human imperfections—vanity, anger, fear, laziness, the capacity for whining self-pity, self-delusion, rationalization—the human limitations which are common to all mankind. Certainly none of these weaknesses is lacking in Henry Fleming. It was the coincidence of this typical Crane protagonist and a war setting that produced the prototype of the modern, anti-romantic treatment of war. Henry Fleming, Dos Passos, three soldiers, Frederic Henry, Robert Jordan, Yossarian possess only 'the common virtues of the ordinary man; their vices [are] those which experience teaches all people to recognize as typical. The significant thing about this modern hero of war literature is that his limitations constitute the essence of his reality.'[12]

Fleming is distinguished from the earlier protagonists only because he is endowed with two new qualities which make the conquest of oneself at least possible. He is given an imagination worthy of Macbeth, and hence he is aware to a degree of sensitivity far beyond that of Maggie or the little man; and he is given a strong conscience, a quality which in Crane's work is inextricably fused with awareness. If awareness permits a man to see what is actually in front of his eyes to be seen, the conscience provides for

[11] See Thomas A. Gullason, 'Some Aspects of the Mind and Art of Stephen Crane', unpublished Ph.D. thesis (Wisconsin, 1953), pp. 21–6. Gullason cites several parallels between the *Sullivan County Sketches* and *The Red Badge*, pp. 101–11.

[12] Sophus K. Winther, *The Realistic War Novel* (Seattle, 1930), p. 15.

the sense of personal honesty through self-criticism. Without awareness a Crane character—such as the militant dogmatists of the poems, who would impose their will upon others by any means—remains unable to acquire the restraint and humility which signify a healthy conscience. However, if a man does have these two qualities, and the strength of will to utilize them, then a knowledge of himself and his place in the world—the only 'salvation' that Crane ever offers—is possible. (No example of such a character can be drawn from Crane's earlier work because Fleming is the first one; examples in his later work are the correspondent in 'The Open Boat', the lieutenant of 'An Episode of War', Manolo Prat, and Dr. Trescott.)

As *The Red Badge* depends so entirely upon the characterization of Henry Fleming, any qualities which Crane introduced for this protagonist should provide the basis for whatever distinctions from his earlier work this novel reveals. The most distinctive innovations in *The Red Badge* are, quite obviously, the technical feats attained through the use of the third-person limited point of view, and the fact that Fleming emerges from his experience with self-knowledge and moral growth. Henry's vivid awareness makes possible the use of the third-person limited narrative technique; the story is tense and exciting only so far as Henry's imagination reacts intensely under the terrific pressures of fear, pride, and the conscience. Actually, in view of the narrative technique used throughout, this awareness of Henry's is *itself* the 'action', the life and force of the entire novel. And the new ending of the story, Henry's success rather than failure, may be attributed to his conscience, that force which makes him turn his awareness upon his own actions, judge them, and thereby learn self-knowledge. The little man of the sketches never does this at all; Maggie tries, but is not intelligent or aware enough to judge properly; George Kelcey has both the conscience and sufficient awareness to judge, but—as with the professional tramps of the Bowery sketches—he lacks the force of will to face and accept his own judgement. Henry Fleming has all three qualities: awareness, conscience, and—more obviously in the latter part of the novel—the necessary strength of will.

However, to call the ending of the novel an innovation is merely to point out that in *The Red Badge*, for the first time in Crane's career, the psychological progression to awareness that has been traced through his earlier work is completed: Henry Fleming does recall his earlier fears and illusions after he experiences the unknown, this remembrance does make him ashamed of his own weaknesses, and the result is his new understanding of himself and his real place in an amoral universe. Otherwise, the structure of the novel is, again, Crane's 'one trump' pattern, this time superbly expanded from short-story to novel length by Crane's excellent method of delaying his protagonist's experience of the feared unknown until the nineteenth chapter; hence, the bulk of the novel is concerned with the first part of the pattern, with what the protagonist reveals of himself during the period of mounting tension until his climactic deflation by actual experience. This structural pattern in itself denies both the naturalistic and the symbolic contexts. Naturalism is rejected because Crane's man always fights his essential battles within himself, and externalities are ultimately of little importance; in *The Red Badge*, as in Crane's other important work, the significant action always takes place within the mind of the protagonist. And any symbols which Crane wrote into this particular rendering of his pattern remain artistic embellishments, wonderfully functional but still separate from the essential plot; as such, they are neither conceptual nor, so far as I can determine, can they legitimately be withdrawn from the story and fitted into any relationship expressive of a 'meaning' which conflicts with Crane's structural psychological progression to awareness.

The novel opens with that sense of uncertainty which plagues Fleming until the last two or three pages. He hears Conklin's rumour that the regiment is about to engage in combat, and immediately withdraws to his hut to think about his own problems —and not at all about Conklin's rumour, by the way; he merely assumes the rumour will prove true (as it does not) and gives his whole attention to worrying about how he will act during his first battle. Thus, Fleming's intensely active imagination is presented at once: the really significant battles in this novel are already raging in full career within Henry's mind long before the first shot is fired in any external skirmish. He had dreamed of 'bloody conflicts that had thrilled him with their sweep and fire'; and, like George Kelcey, his dreams feature great visions of personal glory in which he imagines 'peoples secure in the shadow of his eagle-eyed prowess'.[13] Henry had enlisted, had voluntarily fled his dull farm life, because of these vainglorious desires set in the impossibly romantic picture of war which his imagination has evoked from village gossip and luridly distorted news reports.

The flashback to the farewell scene can serve almost as a structural précis of the novel. Henry had 'primed himself for a beautiful scene. He had prepared certain sentences which he thought could be used with touching effect' (p. 230). But his mother merely peels potatoes and talks tediously of shirts and socks. The result is Crane's usual deflation of vanity, comic here because of Henry's romantic and sentimental foolishness. Nevertheless, buried in his mother's prosaic commonplaces is precisely the view of himself and his duty to which Henry has to inch his way in painful experience throughout the remainder of the novel: 'Yer jest one little feller amongst a hull lot of others, and yeh've got to keep quiet an' do what they tell yeh. . . . Never do no shirking, child, on my account. If so be a time comes when yeh have to be kilt or do a mean thing, why, Henry, don't think of anything 'cept what's right' (p. 231). Fleming is not the undiscovered Achilles of his grand illusions; he is just another lad who has to learn to be a man. And to be a man in Crane's world is to perceive the human situation as it is, accept it, and remain personally honest in fulfilling the commitments such a perception demands of the individual. The fact that Henry has to suffer the experiences of the whole novel even to approach this simple truth merely reveals, again, the most bitterly ironic aspect of Crane's psychological pattern: as in *Maggie* and the Sullivan County tales, the protagonist of *The Red Badge* also has to undergo all his

---

[13] *Omnibus*, p. 229. All further citations of *The Red Badge* in the text refer to this edition, which reprints Crane's deletions from earlier manuscript versions.

suffering in order to perceive, to 'see', a constant reality which is present and available to him before his progression through experience to the perception of it even begins.

Henry's weak mental machinery is at this point so busy with visions of glory and he is so impatient to leave that he hardly hears his mother's advice; but his shame, when he turns to see her praying and weeping among the potato parings, distinguishes him from Crane's earlier protagonists, and implies that eventually he will learn the truth of what he has just been told—that the real hero, in such a world as this, is the quiet, nameless man who can discern what is right and do it, simply because it is right and because he is a man.

Henry's education has already begun before the reader first encounters him. He has experienced the dreariness, boredom, filth, and part of the misery of a soldier's life. The prolonged inaction has left his imagination free to concentrate on that part of his problem which experience has not yet clarified for him, and thus he is first seen lying in his bunk trying 'to mathematically prove to himself that he would not run from a battle' (p. 234). He contemplates the 'lurking menaces of the future', in the only way he can, as these menaces exist within his own mind; and given Henry's imagination, it is no wonder that his thoughts scare him. When Conklin's rumour proves false and still more waiting has to be endured, Henry's tension becomes almost unbearable (p. 239); and his imagination evokes two illusions which Crane exploits throughout the novel: the notion that moral qualities exist in external nature—'The liquid stillness of the night enveloping him made him feel vast pity for himself. There was a caress in the soft winds; and the whole mood of the darkness, he thought, was one of sympathy for himself in his distress' (p. 243)—and the belief that he is unique, separated (at this point by fear) from the other men in the regiment. After timidly broaching the hint of fear to Wilson only to have the conversation end in an abrupt quarrel, Henry 'felt alone in space. . . . No one seemed to be wrestling with such a terrific personal problem' (p. 245). Henry is wrong, of course. The other men are also afraid; but without Henry's imagination they fear only the *fact* of combat, and hence they can play poker while he suffers. Henry no longer fears the actual fact: 'In the darkness he saw visions of a thousand-tongued fear that would babble at his back and cause him to flee, while others were going coolly about their country's business. He admitted that he would not be able to cope with this monster' (p. 245). Such is Henry's state of mind when he is suddenly awakened one morning and sent running towards his first skirmish.

Crane introduces the 'moving box' episode with the flat statement that Henry 'was bewildered'. Barely awake and intensely excited, he has to use 'all his faculties' to keep from falling and being trampled by those running behind him. The passage in question constitutes Henry's *first* reaction to this situation:

he instantly saw that it would be impossible for him to escape from the regiment. It inclosed him. And there were iron laws of tradition and law on four sides. He was in a moving box.

As he perceived this fact it occurred to him that he had never wished to come to the war. He had not enlisted of his free will. He had been dragged by the merciless government. And now they were taking him out to be slaughtered. (p. 248)

This passage is pure rationalization without a hint of naturalism in it. The 'iron laws of tradition and law' are made by men and changed by men. And Henry did enlist of his own free will; he was not dragged to this commitment by any force except his own wish to go to war. All that this passage really reveals is that Henry is so badly frightened he is considering flight even before a shot is fired.

When Henry's curiosity leads him to charge over a rise only to be confronted with still more inaction, Crane unambiguously presents his basic trouble: 'If an intense scene had caught him with its wild swing as he came to the top of the bank, he might have gone roaring on. This advance upon Nature was too calm. He had opportunity to reflect. He had time in which to wonder about himself and to attempt to probe his sensations' (pp. 249–50). Hence, a house acquires an 'ominous look', shadows in a wood are 'formidable', and Henry feels he should advise the generals because 'there was but one pair of eyes ' in the regiment. In the afternoon he tells Conklin the truth when he says, 'I can't stand this much longer' (p. 252). Henry's inner turmoil again obscures his perception: he no more grasps the significance of Wilson giving him the packet than he had heard his mother's advice. He soon witnesses the rout of some troops who run blindly back through his own regimental line, and he intends to wait only long enough to see the 'composite monster' which has frightened these men. But when the charge finally comes, he does not run; he stays and fights.

This episode must have taken considerable thought, for Crane had to find a means of letting Henry engage in battle, an incident to which the four previous chapters have pointed, and still not undergo the unknown experience he fears. In other words, Crane's treatment at this point would commit him one way or the other: if Henry experienced the unknown here the result would be a short story; if this experience could be further delayed the result would be a novel. Crane solved his problem by having Henry fight this skirmish in a trance, a 'battle sleep' induced by fatigue and rage; and because of this Henry later does not accept this combat as that attainment of the experience he has been anticipating.

Thus, Crane in this episode is able to repeat the irony of Henry's farewell scene. When the fight begins, Crane allows Henry to attain the real bearing of responsible manhood at war—for a few moments:

He suddenly lost concern for himself, and forgot to look at a menacing fate. . . . He felt that something of which he was a part—a regiment, an army, or a country—was in a crisis. He was welded into a common personality which was dominated by a single desire. . . .

There was a consciousness always of the presence of his comrades about him. He felt the subtle battle brotherhood more potent even than the cause for which they were fighting. It was a mysterious fraternity born of the smoke and danger of death.

He was at a task. (p. 261)

This is a quiet statement, without any irony, of the ideal which Crane was to honour repeatedly in his writings about the Spanish-

American War. But at this point Henry enters his battle sleep. Then, after the charge has been repulsed, and before Henry emerges from his trance, he feels 'a flash of astonishment at the blue, pure sky and the sun gleamings on the trees and fields. It was surprising that Nature had gone tranquilly on with her golden process in the midst of so much devilment' (p. 265). And this statement implies the mature man's unsentimental view of nature as an amoral external mechanism. But then, when Henry emerges from his trance, his old weaknesses reassert themselves, and he is entirely unable to recall either the achievement or the perception which came to him at either edge of his battle sleep. Once again the reality he is seeking lies within his grasp; and once again his mental turmoil prevents his awareness of it.

This episode also contains some of Crane's famous animal imagery; and, provided it is read correctly, Crane's *use* of this very imagery argues against naturalism. Crane does not use animal images until Henry begins to slip into his battle sleep (p. 261); before this, there is only a single animal image in the three pages of this chapter: 'the colonel . . . began to scold like a wet parrot' (p. 260). And, more important, there is no hint of such imagery in the above description of Henry's moment of manhood before his trance begins. But as Henry descends from full consciousness and becomes something less than a man he abruptly begins to perceive in terms of non-human images: he feels 'the acute exasperation of a pestered animal, a well-meaning cow worried by dogs'; he rages like a 'driven beast'; men 'snarl' and 'howl'; a coward's eyes are 'sheeplike . . . animal-like' (pp. 261–2). And this sort of imagery ends when Henry regains full consciouness. This *use* of imagery is fairly consistent throughout the novel. Hence, the demands of dramatic propriety are as insistent here as they are in the flophouse scene in the 'Experiment in Misery', and for the same reason: the primary function of the imagery in *The Red Badge* is, again, to represent the protagonist's agitated mind as it struggles from lurid distortions to an understanding that reality is, after all, but reality. The imagery in the novel always becomes most vivid when Henry's perception is most distorted, and such a state of mind is the extreme of the condition which Henry labours to transcend by applying his awareness, conscience, and force of will to his experience. Crane's use of such imagery in this novel, in short, strongly implies that he is a humanist, not a naturalist.[14]

When Henry awakens from his battle sleep to find that the charge has been withstood, he becomes vain in complacent admiration of his part in this success; and all his self-congratulation is illusory. Nothing is 'over' for him; no trial has been passed. He uncritically admires actions which were done in a trance; and no Crane character ever feels such pompous self-satisfaction, even for real accomplishment, unless he is a vain fool. Complacency is a delusion in a world where nothing but death is final, where no ideal can ever be possessed because man has to reckon with externalities beyond his control, a stoic's world in which a continuous present poses a continuous demand upon man's moral and physical endurance. The attack is immediately renewed; and this time, after having seen so many others flee that he believes he will be left alone, Henry runs away. One must insist that he runs only nominally from the advancing enemy; what he really runs from is his own imagination. Crane's statement could hardly be more bluntly unambiguous: 'On his face was all the horror of those things which he imagined' (p. 268).[15] Even as he flees, his busy mind rationalizes his flight in terms of his previous feeling of uniqueness (pp. 270–1), and thus he loiters in the rear long enough to learn that the line held and repulsed the charge a second time. Then, miserably ashamed, cringing 'as if discovered in a crime', he moves into the forest.

Henry's journey through this forest, like Marlow's journey up the river into the heart of darkness, charts a pilgrimage within the mind. This moral forest clearly suggests the 'direful thicket'

---

[14] See Max R. Westbrook, 'Stephen Crane and the Personal Universal', *Modern Fiction Studies*, VIII (Winter 1962–3), 353; 'Revolt-Search', p. 183.

[15] See Taylor, *Passages of Thought*, p. 126. There immediately follows a passage which should recall 'The Black Dog' and 'The Cry of a Huckleberry Pudding': 'Since he had turned his back upon the fight his fears had been wondrously magnified. Death about to thrust him between the shoulder blades was far more dreadful than death about to smite him between the eyes . . . it is better to view the appalling than to be merely within hearing' (p. 269).

through which the brave man of the poems has to plunge to find truth, and its 'singular knives'—fear, guilt, shame, hatred of those who remained and fought, vanity, self-pity, rage, his suffering as he sympathetically experiences Conklin's death, the self-loathing evoked by the tattered man—slash at Henry's ego just as the brush and vines entangle his legs. This section of the novel probably required more virtuosity and sheer craftsmanship than any other because, in terms of Crane's structural pattern, no further progress can occur until Henry returns to face his commitment: the unknown experience is thus beautifully delayed while the protagonist undergoes an intense struggle within himself, the outcome of which merely returns him to the position from which he had fled when this section began.

Thus, Crane begins with considerable care. Henry's guilt first evokes rationalization of his cowardice as superior intelligence (p. 272), and from this premise his mind moves through anger at his 'stupid' comrades who had 'betrayed' him, to vanity, self-pity, and finally to a general 'animal-like rebellion against his fellows, war in the abstract, and fate' (p. 273). The adjective is significant because with rationalization Henry was abandoned moral responsibility and again has become less than a man. Such is his state of mind as he enters the metaphorical forest of his inner self and the ensuing scenes portray his struggles to claw his way back up to the human condition again. His terrible journey through this forest can be divided into four parallel scenes or episodes—the craftsman's device of *Maggie* used here with much greater subtlety —which are easily identified: each begins with a specific illusion, a direction of Henry's thought which is followed until the pathway becomes blocked; when the illusion is destroyed, or when the barricade is encountered and Henry has to seek a new direction, the episode ends and the next one begins.

His first illusion arises directly from his attempts to rationalize his cowardice. It begins when he attempts to draw illusory justification from sentimentalized nature, and it expands to include an equally sentimental religious feeling. The 'landscape gave him assurance. A fair field holding life. It was the religion of peace. It

would die if its timid eyes were compelled to see blood. He conceived Nature to be a woman with a deep aversion to tragedy' (p.
274). He throws a pine-cone at a squirrel, and the squirrel, to
Henry's immense satisfaction, runs away: 'There was the law, he
said [conveniently forgetting that a man is not a squirrel]. Nature
had given him a sign' (p. 274). Although he then observes a 'small
animal' pounce into black water and 'emerge directly with a
gleaming fish', Henry needs stronger medicine and, moving 'from
obscurity into promises of a greater obscurity' (p. 275), he soon
gets it. He blunders into the forest 'chapel' with its 'gentle brown
carpet', its 'religious half light'; and the way in which he perceives
this mere hole in the woods should recall his earlier view of death
as a means of getting 'to some place where he would be understood' (p. 253). This sentimental religious feeling is thus equated
with Henry's sentimental view of nature, and both illusions are
brutally shattered when he finds a rotting corpse in the 'chapel'
where one would expect to find the altar. This putrid matter being
eaten by ants does not suggest that death is any gateway to understanding, that nature has any aversion whatsoever to such tragedies,
or that some sort of Christian doctrine is the theme of the novel.[16]
Rationalization which overrides one's personal honesty can only
lead to moral death (as George Kelcey also demonstrates); death
literally blocks Henry's way at this point, and he has to find a new
direction.

His new direction comes when out of curiosity he runs towards
a great roar of battle. This first tentative step towards emerging
from the forest is consciously determined, and Henry is aware that
it is 'an ironical thing for him to be running thus toward that which
he had been at such pains to avoid'; but he now wants 'to come to
the edge of the forest that he might peer out' (p. 277). However,
Henry then meets the tattered man—one of Crane's finest
characters—whose question, 'Where yeh hit, ol' boy?' causes him
to panic; and his guilt and sense of isolation immediately lead him
to another illusion: 'he regarded the wounded soldiers in an

---

[16] The symbolic function of this corpse is spelled out, unnecessarily, in a
passage which Crane wisely cancelled (p. 276, n. 2).

envious way. He conceived persons with torn bodies to be peculiarly happy. He wished that he, too, had a wound' (p. 282). To reveal to Henry the real absurdity of such thoughts, to puncture this insane illusion, Crane lets him witness the appalling death of Jim Conklin. And if this seems too slight an accomplishment for so intensely written a scene, one should remember that this whole section of the novel is, after all, a virtuoso performance in prolonging the delay of Henry's actual experience of combat. Also, Conklin's death is as necessary to Henry's education as his parallel encounter with the corpse was. In its presentation of human suffering considered specifically against the infinite back-drop of the amoral universe this scene is a young author's first attempt at coping with a theme that immensely interested him; hence, as only one critic has noted, there is absolutely no irony in the portrayal of Henry in this passage. 'Although Fleming cuts a rather pitiful figure under the towering sky, Crane's intention is not satirical. In fact this is one point in the book where the author seems to identify himself wholly with his character.'[17] Henry rebels against the universe at this grotesque and meaningless death of a man he has known since boyhood, and his rebellion is simultaneously as futile, as absurd, and as understandable as the belief of the men in an open boat who think that fate will not drown them because they have worked so hard to get within sight of shore. The implicit truth behind the destruction of Henry's illusion is that man's position in this world is bleak enough as it is without wishing for any wounds to make it worse. Finally, it must be stated that the text offers no evidence of Conklin's death accomplishing anything else. Shortly thereafter, Henry commits his greatest sin: he deliberately deserts the tattered man who selflessly worries about others even when he is himself at the edge of the grave.

Because of the importance of the tattered man in Henry's journey to awareness, this episode can reasonably be considered a parallel scene comparable to the two just examined. That is, the desertion of this dying man is in itself Henry's illusion. His bitter and immediate self-loathing—'he now thought that he wished he

[17] Fryckstedt, 'Tupenny Fury', p. 276.

was dead' (p. 290)—foreshadows what Crane makes explicit in the final chapter: the tattered man will always haunt Henry, not because of anything he does to Henry, but because of what Henry does to him. This desertion is the limit of Henry's penetration into the direful thicket of cowardice, selfishness, and immaturity; and as he can go no further, he must once more seek a new direction—metaphorically the only one left to him—a way out of the 'forest' and back to his original commitment.

Henry's subconscious desire to find his way back is revealed by his envying the men of an advancing column so intensely that 'he could have wept in his longings'. He immediately pictures himself as 'a blue desperate figure leading lurid charges with one knee forward and a broken blade high—a blue, determined figure standing before a crimson and steel assault, getting calmly killed' (p. 294). These asinine visions, in this context, are evoked by Henry's desire as a psychological thrust to counteract the opposing force of fear. Thus, Henry begins a debate with himself: he wants to go forward, his fear invents excuses, and his reason overcomes these excuses one by one as they are raised. This debate ends in defeat only because Henry believes there is absolutely no way in which he can return to his regiment with self-respect. And this belief, of course, turns out to be the illusion which forms the basis of his final episode in the forest.

However, Henry's mental debate itself accomplishes two important results: it enables Henry to transcend by an effort of will his most absurd selfishness—his wish for the defeat of his own army—and it sufficiently calms his mind for him to realize, for the first time since his original flight, that his physical condition—hunger, thirst, extreme fatigue—suggests he is actually 'jest one little feller', ordinary, weak, fallible. His inner debate ends when he sees the very men with whom he had lately identified himself flee back through the woods in terror. He leaps into the midst of these panic-stricken men *in an attempt to rally them*, and receives his red badge of courage when one of them clubs him in the head with a rifle butt.

Crane probably seized upon this incident for his final title because of the complex ironies woven into it, because of its centrality to a story about courage and various sorts of wounds, and because Henry has to win his way to manhood by struggle as one wins a badge:

> he does not receive his wound in flight, but in the performance of an act of courage! Henry is struck down (by a coward) while inarticulately striving 'to make a rallying speech, to sing a battle hymn.' He is in a position to suffer such a wound because he has originally fled from his regiment, but he is going against the current of retreating infantry, *towards* the battle, when he gains the red badge.[18]

He has already revealed his intent, his desire to return. The external fact of the wound changes nothing whatsoever within Henry's mind. Chance merely provides the means for which he has already been searching, the means of returning to his regiment secure from outward ridicule. He is guided back by the cheery-voiced soldier, a man who helps others without vanity or even a wish for thanks, exactly as Henry should have helped the tattered man. Henry tells his lie—which ironically proves unnecessary—is nursed by Wilson and, being both physically and emotionally exhausted, is put to bed in his friend's blankets.

In terms of Crane's structural pattern, Henry is now back in his original position and again about to confront the unknown, still untried in battle—so he believes—still afraid. Nevertheless, the short story has become a novel, and within Henry's mind a major battle has been fought and won. Although he still does not know how he will act when he confronts the unknown, the bitter experience of this fantastic day's journey through the moral forest has brought Henry to a secure knowledge of what he can *not* do when the time for this confrontation comes, for him, on the morrow.

His actions the next morning, however, are not reassuring. His vanity returns with his sense of security, he complains loudly, and

---

[18] Eric Solomon, 'The Structure of "The Red Badge of Courage" ', *Modern Fiction Studies*, V (Autumn 1959), 230–1. See also John J. McDermott, 'Symbolism and Psychological Realism in *The Red Badge of Courage*', *Nineteenth-Century Fiction*, XXIII (Dec. 1968), 324–31.

he treats Wilson quite shabbily. This reassertion of the old Henry is demanded by dramatic necessity (if growth of character is contingent upon awareness Crane cannot very well make much of a change in Henry before he experiences actual combat), and Crane justifies it with great care by making it serve at least three functions. Henry's undesirable traits first provide a necessary contrast in order to emphasize the change which has occurred in Wilson, who has already had his baptism of fire:

He seemed no more to be continually regarding the proportions of his personal prowess. . . . He was no more a loud young soldier. There was about him now a fine reliance. He showed a quiet belief in his purposes and his abilities. . . . And the youth saw that ever after it would be easier to live in his friend's neighborhood. (pp. 314–15)

Given Crane's technique of the parallel scene, this passage has to foreshadow the change which Henry will also undergo once he successfully faces up to his own commitment; it can have no other function.[19] Henry's vain foolishness at this point is also important as a contrast with his yesterday's view of himself—yesterday he had seen himself lower than all other men, and mocked by nature; today, like George Kelcey, he imagines himself 'a fine creation . . . the chosen of some gods', and he considers nature 'a fine thing moving with a magnificent justice' (pp. 319–20)—and because these absurdities allow Crane to show that Henry is now capable of perceiving the falseness of his position. His 'pompous and veteranlike' thoughts are just as foolish, of course, as those he revealed during his flight; and neither passage presents Crane's own view of the universe and man's place in it.[20] But no one has noticed that these silly illusions form a carefully wrought sequence in themselves which begins with Henry's smug sense of power over Wilson because of the packet, rises to a climax of loud complaint, and ends suddenly when this swelling pomposity is 'pierced' by a

[19] The precise parallel between Wilson and Fleming is discussed by William P. Safranek, 'Crane's *The Red Badge of Courage*', *Explicator*, XXVI (Nov. 1967), item 21.

[20] Crane uses exactly the same device in a poem: two contrasting views of a morally neutral reality, the sea, are presented, and neither can legitimately be called Crane's own. See *Poems*, ed. Katz, p. 84.

fellow soldier's lazy comment: 'Mebbe yeh think yeh fit th' hull battle yestirday, Fleming.' Henry is *inwardly* 'reduced to an abject pulp by these chance words' (p. 325). Henry, in short, has assumed a vain pose and has been acting out his role as if the external view of himself were all that mattered; the laconic comment pierces this pose by abruptly awakening Henry's conscience, and the whole external pose collapses before this inner voice's inflexible command that Henry view himself as he really is. This whole sequence, finally, helps Henry prepare psychologically to face up to the coming fight.

When the battle comes, Henry turns his reawakened self-loathing and self-hatred upon the enemy, and he chooses to stay and fight rather than run again into that terrible forest: 'He had taken up a first position behind the little tree, with a direct determination to hold it against the world' (p. 330). After making this willed commitment, Henry slips again into the trance of battle sleep, fights like a regular 'war devil', and after the skirmish he emerges from his trance with the praise of his comrades ringing in his ears.

He had fought like a pagan who defends his religion. Regarding it, he saw that it was fine, wild, and, in some ways, easy. He had been a tremendous figure, no doubt. By this struggle he had overcome obstacles which he had admitted to be mountains. They had fallen like paper peaks, and he was now what he called a hero. And he had not been aware of the process. He had slept and, awakening, found himself a knight. (p. 331)

Henry has thus successfully *passed through* the unknown, the feared experience, and *this* time because he has not run he accepts the fact, even though, again because of battle sleep, he has not actually *experienced* the unknown itself. Hence, he has a great deal to ponder about. The excellent irony of this crucial episode is *not* that Henry has become a hero in his battle sleep—Crane never offers the reader such an absurd definition of heroism—but that during this sleep Henry has successfully passed through the very experience upon which his imagination and fear have been intensely centred since the beginning of the novel; the monumental

irony is that Henry has endured all his suffering, all the tortures
of his imagination, over an action which is so easily done that one
can do it superbly while in a trance. The implications which
follow from this ironic deflation should be clear to the reader, even
if Henry is not yet capable of sorting them out: if the feared unknown, the hideous dragon of war, can be successfully encountered
while one is in a trance, then Henry's former imaginings, fears,
concepts of knightly heroism, all such feverish activity of his weak
mental machinery, stand revealed as absurd. Henry, in other words,
for the first time since the novel began, is now in a position to
learn authentic self-knowledge, to perceive the reality which is
actually before his eyes to be seen, and to acquire the humility
which Wilson has already attained.

Henry's subsequent actions immensely favour this conclusion.
He accepts his own insignificance when he overhears his regiment
of 'mule drivers' ordered into an action from which few are
expected to emerge alive. And, even though he knows the danger
of the coming battle, there is no hesitation in Henry, no thought of
flight. Hence, it follows reasonably from this deliberate courage
that Henry should finally be able to experience actual combat in
full possession of all his faculties. In fact, Crane insists upon
Henry's awareness, both of the external and the inner reality,
during this charge: 'It seemed to the youth that he saw everything.
Each blade of the green grass was bold and clear . . . all were
comprehended. His mind took a mechanical but firm impression,
so that afterward everything was pictured and explained to him,
save why he himself was there' (pp. 338–9; my italics). The final
phrase simply points to Henry's remembrance of his past failures.
The frenzy of this charge, not a blind rage of battle sleep, is
described as a 'temporary but sublime absence of selfishness. And
because it was of this order was the reason, perhaps, why the youth
wondered, afterward, what reasons he could have had for being
there' (p. 339). Henry, like the other men, still shows anger, pride,
wild excitement; but such qualities are good ones for a soldier to
have because they help him stand and fight, they could hardly be
omitted from any realistic presentation of men at war, they do not

make these men less than human, and Henry never again loses his grip on his consciousness because of them. These men reveal anger and pride in this situation precisely because they are men who hold themselves responsible for their own actions and seek the good opinion of their fellow men. Henry has yet to learn that if a man satisfies his own sense of personal honesty, this is enough; the opinions of others, just one more externality, will vary with the several views which others take of one's actions. Chapter 21 prepares Henry for this stoic lesson.

The elated regiment returns from their charge, only to be taunted by veterans who observe how little ground was covered. Henry soon accepts the view that the extent of the charge was comparatively 'trivial', even though he feels 'a considerable joy in musing upon his performances during the charge' (a joy which is not unreasonable when we recall that only yesterday Henry had fled in panic from this same situation). When a general states yet another point of view—that the charge was a military failure, and the 'mule drivers' now seem to him to be 'mud diggers'—the lieutenant's defence of his own men implies that a military failure is in itself no criterion of the performance of the men doing the fighting. And the chapter ends with Wilson and Fleming being told of the praise they have received from the lieutenant and colonel of their own regiment. Wilson and Fleming have every right to feel pleased at this praise; and the fact that they 'speedily forgot many things', that for them 'the past held no pictures of error and disappointment', does not indicate that they are mere automatons at the mercy of external circumstance: it indicates that in their first flush of pleasure they have not yet assimilated and considered this praise in the total perspective which is specifically demanded by the several points of view presented in this very chapter. There is no time for assimilation of anything at this point because the novel immediately roars on into yet another battle, a final skirmish in which Henry's actions confirm the self-control he has recently acquired. During this fight all the men act like veterans by tending strictly to business and Wilson even captures an enemy flag; after the battle he holds this prize 'with vanity' as he and Henry, both still caught up in the excitement of the moment, congratulate each other. The time for reflection and assimilation comes only with the final chapter when Henry walks away from the battle-field and is again free to probe into his own mind.

The endless critical squabbles which have arisen over this final chapter hinge upon a single question: does Fleming achieve any moral growth or development of character? Yet any Crane student should be able to answer this question almost without consulting this chapter at all—without reading Crane's description of Henry's change of soul which requires at least two pages in most editions. To claim that Fleming does *not* achieve any growth or development is to ignore many quite obvious statements of his gradual moral progress that are scattered throughout the novel, the entire function of Wilson's role, and the fact that Crane must have had some reason for endowing Henry—unlike the earlier protagonists —with awareness and a conscience. It is also well to remember that Crane is trying to be psychologically realistic: this is the *first* time Henry has full opportunity to reflect upon all the experiences which have crowded the past two days of his life, he is still a young lad not yet even twenty-four hours removed from the very nadir of self-abasement, and, like Wilson whose development preceded his own, Henry is still 'capable of vanity. Even in the final chapter of the novel, Crane still writes as of a process that is going on. Fleming's mind, he says, "was under-going a subtle change"; nevertheless, the final paragraphs describe that change in detail, and the unmistakable traits of genuine maturity . . . are present.'[21]

Crane devotes the first two pages, over a fourth of the chapter, to a careful preparation for the important matters which follow. The battle is over for the day, and, as the regiment ironically marches back over the same ground they had taken at great cost, the reader is taken directly into Henry's mind. He begins by rejoicing that he has come forth, escaped, from 'a land of strange, squalling upheavals'. The deliberately ambiguous language here should suggest *all* of Private Fleming's various battles, with the

21 Westbrook, 'Revolt-Search', pp. 199–200.

enemy, the 'arrayed forces of the universe', and his own weaknesses. Then Henry attempts to consider all that has happened to him from the point of view of the new perspective he has attained by living through these past two days. And here Crane is again explicit, neither ironic nor ambiguous:

> he began to study his deeds, [both] his failures, and his achievements. Thus, fresh from scenes where many of his usual machines of reflection had been idle . . . he struggled to marshal all his acts.
>
> At last they marched before him clearly. From this present view point he was enabled to look at them in spectator fashion and to criticize them with some correctness, for his new condition had already defeated certain sympathies. (pp. 365–6)

Henry's 'procession of memory' begins with the most recent events, his public deeds which are recalled with delight because they tell him 'he was good'. This recollection seems reasonable, so far as it goes; these public deeds, after all, have been good. But the next sentence reveals Henry's error a few moments before he himself corrects it: 'He recalled with a thrill of joy the respectful comments of his fellows upon his conduct' (p. 366). Henry, in short, begins with his old error of judging himself by the opinion of others, by his external reputation. The entire remaining portion of his self-analysis consists of the assaults made upon this public image by the shameful recollections of his private deeds until, finally, an equilibrium is attained in which both public and private views of the self take permanent position in a realistic, balanced judgement. These emotionally powerful memories of his private misdeeds originally fell under three headings: his desertion from the regiment's first engagement, his 'terrible combat with the arrayed forces of the universe', and his desertion of the tattered man. In the final version, the first act of desertion merged with the more vividly personal abandonment of the tattered man, and the resolution to the theme of Henry's battle with the universe was largely omitted.[22]

[22] Although the resolution of this excised theme (*Omnibus*, pp. 367, 369) is presented ambiguously—Henry's 'deity laying about him with the bludgeon of correction' for whom 'no grain like him would be lost' can only be an illusion in Crane's amoral universe—Henry's conclusion resembles Crane's own view:

Thus, the great image which dominates these final pages as an inexorable 'spectre of reproach' is the 'dogging memory of the tattered soldier—he who, gored by bullets and faint for blood, had fretted concerning an imagined wound in another; he who had loaned his last of strength and intellect for the tall soldier; he who, blind with weariness and pain, had been deserted in the field' (p. 367). The great care with which Crane makes Henry recall all the ramifications of this incident implies the deep impression it has made upon the youth. He cringes when this spectre looms before him: 'For an instant a wretched chill of sweat was upon him at the thought that he might be detected in the thing. As he stood persistently before his vision, he gave vent to a cry of sharp irritation and agony' (p. 367). If read correctly this passage does not reveal a selfish vanity; it reveals only the continuity of Henry's thought. He is still basking in the warmth of his public deeds when this private horror suddenly pierces and deflates, for him, his public image of himself. In order to live with this awful ghost Henry has to redress his own judgement of himself: he retains a concern for his external reputation—few men of any age desire to have their shameful deeds made public—but this vision finally forces him to accept the characteristic position of the mature man that his own inner view of himself is vastly more important than the external opinions of others.

Henry never entirely banishes this ghost—an attainment which would be as impossible in Crane's world as it would be in Hawthorne's—but he is able to place it in perspective, 'to put the sin at a distance'. An excised passage which follows reveals that Henry handles this sin as any intelligent man of conscience would handle it, as a means of trampling upon his own ego to prevent his committing such a sin again. 'This plan for the utilization of a sin did not give him complete joy but it was the best sentiment he could formulate under the circumstances, and when it was com-

---

'those tempestuous moments were of the wild mistakes and ravings of a novice who did not comprehend. He had been a mere man railing at a condition. . . . The imperturbable sun shines on insult and worship' (p. 367). See Fryckstedt, 'Tupenny Fury'.

bined with his success, or public deeds, he knew that he was quite contented' (p. 369). Henry is being neither vain nor callous in this decision; he is merely being practical and realistic. No better use of a past sin is possible in Crane's world. And if this sin is a real and permanent part of his past, so are his good actions during the day's fighting: if Henry is to see himself as he really is, he must consider both 'his failures, and his achievements'.

Once he attains this balanced view of himself, he is able to foresee 'some new ways' of life for him in the future: 'He found that he could look back upon the brass and bombast of his earlier gospels and see them truly. He was gleeful when he discovered that he now despised them' (p. 369). Henry's weak mental machinery, in short, has undergone considerable readjustment. His eyes have finally opened, and he is now able to begin perceiving correctly the reality which has been before him and largely unchanged since the novel began. Henry's personal honesty can now assert itself in morally significant action, and he is ready to begin the difficult practice of manhood in an amoral universe.

With this conviction [my italics] came a store of assurance. He felt a quiet manhood, nonassertive but of sturdy and strong blood. He knew that he would no more quail before his guides wherever they should point. He had been to touch the great death, and found that, after all, it was but the great death. He was a man. (p. 369)

I am unable to find much irony in the closing paragraphs of the novel. Henry is exhausted from all his battles and gratefully marching to a rest. Only the most romantically obtuse reader at this point could believe in the actuality of 'an existence of soft and eternal peace', but the image aptly describes how inviting the coming rest must seem to a weary young soldier. Certainly Henry is not fooling himself; his quiet confidence that he will 'no more quail before his guides wherever they should point' would be meaningless if he really anticipated an existence of soft and eternal peace. And the final image seems to me merely an emblem of what has just happened to Henry. He has attained authentic self-knowledge and a sense of manhood after long and fierce battles with his own moral weaknesses; hence it seems entirely appropriate that Crane should end this tale with the image of a golden ray of sunlight appearing through hosts of leaden rain clouds. Irony has its function earlier in Crane's pattern, before the protagonist becomes aware of the reality he struggles to perceive correctly.

Two postscripts to the above reading of the novel particularly suggest themselves for brief comment: Henry's relation to the larger group formed by the regiment, and Crane's literary debt to Howells. The minor question of Henry's relationship with the group[23] seems to me to be answered by the general function of Crane's imagery in this novel. Crane emphasizes Henry's sense of personal isolation whenever the youth's imagination violently distorts the realities of war, his own capabilities and weaknesses, or the external universe; such an emphasis implies that his isolation from his fellow men is itself merely one more illusion, that so far as all the other soldiers are concerned Henry is always what his mother tried to tell him he was—'jest one little feller amongst a hull lot of others'—and that his real problem, here as elsewhere, is to free himself from distortion and grasp the reality which has been present to him since he joined the regiment. Thus Crane again seems comparatively unconcerned with the external fact; the significant struggle from 'isolation' to identification is one more of the various battles which are to be won or lost within the mind of Private Fleming. Crane's debt to Howells, however, is an important matter.

In a copy of the 1896 edition of *The Red Badge* Crane wrote the following inscription: 'To W. D. Howells this small and belated book as a token of the veneration and gratitude of Stephen Crane for many things he has learned of the common man and, above all, for a certain re-adjustment of his point of view victoriously concluded some time in 1892.'[24] A letter that Crane wrote to Lily

---

[23] See Eric Solomon, 'Structure of "The Red Badge" ', p. 231; A. W. Hart, 'Social Outlook', pp. 163–4; Friedman, 'Criticism and the Novel', p. 361.

[24] *Letters*, p. 62. Crane dated this inscription 17 August 1895, a date when the Appleton 1896 issue should not have been available. The book was not presented until 1896 (*Letters*, p. 62, n. 76), probably as a New Year's gift (see Howells's letter to Crane, *Letters*, p. 102); hence Katz argues that 'Crane's misdating must be considered intentional, a way of backdating his expression of gratitude to Howells' (Katz, ed., *Poems*. p. 192).

Brandon Munroe, apparently in the Spring of 1894, also speaks of a change in attitude, and dates this change from about the time that Crane and Lily parted in August 1892; it is more revealing than the inscription to Howells.

My career has been more of a battle than a journey. You know, when I left you, I renounced the clever school in literature. It seemed to me that there must be something more in life than to sit and cudgel one's brains for clever and witty expedients. So I developed all alone a little creed of art which I thought was a good one. Later I discovered that my creed was identical with the one of Howells and Garland and in this way I became involved in the beautiful war between those who say art is man's substitute for nature and we are most successful in art when we approach the nearest to nature and truth, and those who say —well, I don't know what they say . . .

If I had kept to my clever, Rudyard-Kipling style, the road might have been shorter but, ah, it wouldn't be the true road. The two years of fighting [i.e. from about August 1892 until the date of this letter] have been well-spent. And now I am almost at the end of it. This winter fixes me firmly. . . . It has made me better, it has widened my comprehension of people and my sympathy with whatever they endure. And to it I owe whatever I have achieved and the hope of the future. In truth, this change in my life should prove of some value to me, for, ye gods, I have paid a price for it. (*Letters*, pp. 31–3)

When Crane presented the inscribed *Red Badge* to Howells he could have used instead a copy of either the first edition of *Maggie* or *The Black Riders*, and he could not have been unaware that Howells strongly preferred *Maggie*.[25] Hence, his choice of *The Red Badge* implies that his novel best reveals the readjustment of point of view for which he thanked Howells. Certainly, if my dating of Crane's works thus far is at all correct, *The Red Badge* has to be the first work he produced after his readjustment.

Crane reported Garland's lecture, 'Howells Discussed at Avon-

---

[25] See *Letters*, p. 102. Fifteen years after Crane's death Howells still called *The Red Badge* his 'worst book' ('Editor's Easy Chair', *Harper's Monthly*, CXXX [Apr. 1915], 797). Howells's most revealing estimate of Crane is presented in 'Frank Norris', *North American Review*, CLXXV (Dec. 1902), 769–78. On Howells's steadfast preference for *Maggie*, see Cunliffe, 'American Background', p. 33; Thomas A. Gullason, 'New Light on the Crane–Howells Relationship', *New England Quarterly*, XXX (Sept. 1957), 389–92.

By-The-Sea', for the New York *Tribune* on 18 August 1891 (p. 5);
he was, therefore, acquainted with Howells's ideas almost two
years before he met him. The only scholar who has written
extensively about both authors argues that 'from April 1893
forward, relationships were close between Howells and Crane for
as long as Crane remained in New York', that Crane was indebted
to Howells for 'friendship, encouragement, and for a skillful, untiring effort both in print and behind the scenes to get the audience
and reputation Crane deserved', and that Crane in turn understood
Howells 'almost uniquely well. Crane's interview of Howells for
the New York *Times*, October 28, 1894 ["Fears Realists Must
Wait", p. 20], elucidated Howells' theory more plainly and effectively than perhaps any other single statement—including Howells'
own.' Nevertheless, 'it would be absurd to intimate that the
essential Crane was a little Howells.'[26] A literary theory or creed,
in short, is not at all the same thing as a literary practice. Howells's
theory, as Crane reported it in the *Times*, could almost outline
Crane's letter to Hilliard about a man being born with his own
pair of eyes. Fiction should have a purpose other than mere
entertainment but should avoid direct preaching, for 'it is the
business of the novel to picture daily life in the most exact terms
possible, with an absolute and clear sense of proportion', because
fiction is 'a perspective made for the benefit of people who have
no true use of their eyes'. As such, it is implicitly didactic: 'When
people are introduced to each other they will see the resemblances,
and won't want to fight so badly.' Thus, a writer should not write
'what people want', but must remain 'true to his conscience'; and
such a writer, given skill, 'cannot be defeated' if he perseveres.

In literary practice this theory led Howells to the skilful
examination of the ordinary, the day-by-day portrayal of the
normal in terms of circumstantial realism; and it led Crane to

---

[26] Edwin H. Cady, *The Realist at War: The Mature Years, 1885–1920, of
William Dean Howells* (Syracuse, 1958), pp. 212–18; cf. Jumper, pp. 149–50,
and Linson, *My Stephen Crane*, ed. Cady, pp. 30–1. Although Crane mentions
Garland, I am unable either to find much influence or to trust Garland's
recollections of a man he could not begin to understand; see Robert Mane,
'Une Rencontre Littéraire: Hamlin Garland et Stephen Crane', *Études Anglaises*,
XVII (janvier–mars 1964), 30–46.

psychological realism, the careful analysis of what goes on within a representative mind labouring under intense emotional stress. The same creed thus accommodated two subjects as mutually distinct as the prose styles of the two men, and Crane's craftsmanship can reasonably be considered his own accomplishment. Moreover, Crane's use of the word 'readjustment' does not imply the formation of a whole new attitude; the psychological plot of *The Red Badge* is present in the early sketches—which Crane himself said were written 'when I was clever' (*Letters*, p. 59)—and the irony which informs its prose first sharpened itself on the whetstone provided by Asbury Park.

Crane's readjustment occurred in his attitude towards mankind, and hence he was justified in calling it a change in his life which cost him dearly. Howells and the values he personified, according to Crane's inscription, must gradually have brought him to consider the whole of his protagonists, and thus widened his comprehension and sympathy in terms of a more humanistic *use* of his ironic vision and his 'one trump' pattern. *The Red Badge* is considerably more humanistic than the earlier work simply because Henry is more completely human, because Crane views his protagonist's struggles from within Henry's own mind instead of from the godlike position he assumed above and external to the inner selves of the little man and Maggie, and because this novel embodies an affirmative view of man not offered in the earlier work. The *Sullivan County Sketches* tend towards satire partly because of rudimentary characterization and the consequence that intensity has to depend more upon prose style than upon character, and partly because Crane never allows his campers to learn anything from their own experience. *Maggie* is an improvement, but in this book the 'sense of proportion' is hardly 'absolute and clear', and the resulting 'perspective' is acceptable only so far as the reader is able to accept the cast-iron innocence of the protagonist. The youth of the 'Experiment in Misery' occupies a position somewhere between Maggie and Henry: he attains authentic knowledge of a moral reality, and to do so he has to confront and overcome his own illusory notions with his own intelligence; but the reality he has to perceive is the death-in-life state which results when a man wilfully abandons his own humanism.

If such distinctions are acceptable, it should follow that Crane's readjustment in attitude was indeed a major change in his life. The price it demanded was more or less the mastery of a new crafts-manship which would allow him to identify his own sympathies more closely with the inner life of his protagonists as they struggle to fulfil their own human potentialities. The ironist's aesthetic detachment remained intact. But *The Red Badge* implies a 'widened comprehension of people' and 'sympathy with whatever they endure' through Crane's commitment to a more truly realistic portrait of man's moral qualities, a view in which both the good and the bad ones are honestly offered in a 'perspective made for the benefit of people who have no true use of their eyes'. The technical evidence, apart from Henry's moral completeness, is Crane's proficiency with third-person limited narration; and, again, the portrayal of the youth of the 'Experiment' serves to illustrate a transitional stage between the omniscient narration of the earlier work and the technique of *The Red Badge*.[27] The distinctive changes in this novel, in short, are all in the general direction of Howells's own approach to fiction and Howells's own compassionate view of mankind. Hence, Crane chose the right book for his inscription. Perhaps his readjustment in attitude helped him accept the irony of Howells's failure to appreciate the novel which most embodied it.

Crane's change in attitude was permanent. It is confirmed by the poems and quite explicitly set forth in his letters to Nellie Crouse.

[27] Cf. Jumper, pp. 169–70.

IV

THE IRONIST'S MORAL NORM

IN the most extensive critical study of Crane's poetry now available, Daniel G. Hoffman argues that

The poems ... are particularly useful to the critic who wishes to understand Crane's sensibility. In his verse Crane defines or implies his essential convictions about man's relations to God, to nature, to women, and to his fellow-man. These convictions are the assumptions on which his fiction is based.[1]

Scholars tend to agree, in theory at any rate. Crane himself claimed to prefer *The Black Riders* to *The Red Badge* because 'the former is the more ambitious effort. In it I aim to give my ideas of life as a whole, so far as I know it, and the latter is a mere episode, or rather an amplification' (*Letters*, p. 159). But the comparative dearth of criticism of the poems suggests either an unwillingness to grapple with them as poetry or a reluctance to risk the critic's view of the fiction in the crucible they provide. Hoffman has not shunned this risk, and his reading of the poems seems frankly coloured by at least three critical assumptions which were generally applied to Crane's fiction during the mid-1950s. Specifically, to use Hoffman's own topics, his view of Crane's convictions about

---

[1] *The Poetry of Stephen Crane*, p. 20. Criticism before Hoffman is not very useful, the most noteworthy essay being a study of influence: Carlin T. Kindilien, 'Stephen Crane and the "Savage Philosophy" of Olive Schreiner', *Boston University Studies in English*, III (Summer 1957), 97–107. Three excellent critical studies have appeared since Hoffman: Max Westbrook, 'Stephen Crane's Poetry: Perspective and Arrogance', *Bucknell Review*, XI (Dec. 1963), 24–34; Harland S. Nelson, 'Stephen Crane's Achievement as a Poet', *Texas Studies in Literature and Language*, IV (Winter 1963), 564–82; Yoshie Itabashi, 'The Modern Pilgrimage of *The Black Riders*: An Interpretation', *Tsuda Review*, no. 12 (Nov. 1967), 1–41. Ruth Miller, 'Regions of Snow: The Poetic Style of Stephen Crane', *Bulletin of the New York Public Library*, LXXII (1968), 328–49, offers common-sense observations about his technique as an ironic, dramatic poet.

man's relation to God assumes that Crane, like Arnold, was 'after all' a Christian; his view of Crane on man's relations to women is admittedly influenced by Berryman's Freudian theories; and his conclusions about Crane on man's relations to nature and to his fellow man imply the traditional pigeon-holing under naturalism. Given such assumptions, Hoffman is able to conclude that Crane

views, and makes us feel, the reality of a universe where force is law, where love is doom, where God is cold, where man's lot is fated misery, where hope is narrowed to the possibility of courage, and the reward of courage is self-sacrifice. None has surpassed him in the imaginative expression of this sensibility of isolation. (pp. 278–9)

Hence, if one approaches the poems without a commitment to any of these three critical assumptions one's reading will not agree with Hoffman's.

Crane apparently began writing poetry in February 1894,[2] immediately after finishing *The Red Badge*, and *The Black Riders* volume was complete by September. As a result of this single sustained creative burst *The Black Riders* possesses a certain coherence which is missing from *War Is Kind*, the sense of purpose characteristic of an original and important piece of work. That *The Black Riders* is such a work is implied by Crane's stubbornness with his publishers:

I should absolutely refuse to have my poems printed without many of those which you just as absolutely mark 'No.' It seems to me that you cut all the ethical sense out of the book. All the anarchy, perhaps. It is the anarchy which I particularly insist upon. From the poems which you keep you could produce what might be termed a 'nice little volume of verse by Stephen Crane,' but for me there would be no satisfaction. The ones which refer to God, I believe you condemn altogether. I am obliged to have them in when my book is printed. (*Letters*, pp. 39–40)

[2] See Olov W. Fryckstedt, 'Crane's *Black Riders*: A Discussion of Dates', *Studia Neophilologica*, XXXIV (1962), 282–93; Donald Pizer, 'The Garland–Crane Relationship', *Huntington Library Quarterly*, XXIV (Nov. 1960), 75–82. Crane's letter to Garland, 9 May 1894 (*Letters*, pp. 36–7), implies that he was writing *George's Mother* and the poems for *The Black Riders* at the same time. The volume was published in late April or May 1895; it was the first book to appear with Crane's name on it.

Crane did not entirely win this battle with Copeland and Day because at least seven poems were finally rejected;[3] if they had been included the coherence of the volume's statement, as will be seen, would have been even stronger. *War Is Kind*, on the other hand,

partakes rather of the quality of gleaning than sowing, and is dominated by the careless off-handedness that Crane assumed in closing a business affair. . . . Only the embarrassingly tedious 'Intrigue' cycle and twelve of the individual poems are first printings. Of the twelve poems, no more than nine could have been written for the volume. (*Poems*, ed. Katz, Introduction, p. xlix.)

Crane, in brief, had something of importance to say by means of *The Black Riders*, and even a casual reading reveals that the omission of the 'anarchy' and the poems about 'God' would have wrenched the over-all impression violently away from what exists. What does exist is a reasonably complete outline of Crane's mature philosophical position, the moral reality which his ironic awareness allowed him to accept. The poems in *War Is Kind* do not significantly alter this philosophical stance. Written intermittently from the fall of 1894 until they were collected for the press in 1899, these poems essentially restate, re-explore, redefine the position set forth in *The Black Riders*, and occasionally extend it in particular areas; but they do not constitute an original statement comparable to the earlier volume, and Crane thus was unable to summon a comparable interest in their publication. *All* of Crane's poetry, in other words, forms a distinct unit in itself. As such, it is the one major work he produced in which he is free of the restrictions imposed upon his fiction by his 'one trump' pattern of psychological progression to awareness. The poems present the moral norm which controls this ironic pattern in his fiction. It should follow, therefore, that any critique of Crane's fiction which ignores the poetry is likely to be inadequate; any conclusions about his fiction which run contrary to the values set forth in the poems are likely to be wrong.

[3] Katz, ed., *The Poems of Stephen Crane*, poems numbered *78, 91, 119, 120*. The other three apparently have been lost (Katz, Introduction, pp. xxvii–ix).

My concern with the poems is limited to the wish to understand Crane's acute sensibility which had to adapt itself, emotionally and spiritually, to his own awareness of a world dominated by pain, chaos, and rampant human weakness.[4] His means of adaptation, the realities which his perception of human experience and his personal honesty allowed him to accept, do indeed include 'man's relations to God, to nature, to women, and to his fellow-man'. These essential realities, like the sensibility that affirmed them, remain the same in the poetry, the fiction, and in Crane's own life; only the formal means of their expression changes.[5]

Man's relations to nature, as implied in *The Red Badge*, are easily described: nature in Crane's view is external to man and the moral life of the mind. The essential *lack* of relationship is best expressed in the poem anthologists have made famous:

> A man said to the universe:
> 'Sir, I exist!'
> 'However,' replied the universe,
> 'The fact has not created in me
> A sense of obligation.' (*WK 96*, p. 102)[6]

The universe and all its furniture—including lower animals (*BR 55*, p. 59), birds (*BR 2*, p. 4; *U 72*, p. 75; *P 116*, p. 128), trees (*U 71*, p. 75), even angels (*BR 54*, p. 58) and one's own creations once they have been created (*BR 31*, p. 33)—merely constitute the given setting in which man's life has to be lived. This externality is occasionally beautiful and therefore aesthetically gratifying, as in *WK 101*, p. 107, but it is always amoral, mechanical, 'flatly indifferent' to human life; it has neither the obligation to sustain nor the urge to destroy man. Hence, man's human 'agony' takes place in 'grey-green woods impassive' (*WK 94*, p. 100); 'the sky

---

[4] Cf. Earle Labor, 'Crane and Hemingway: Anatomy of Trauma', *Renascence*, XI (Summer 1959), 189.

[5] Cf. Westbrook, 'Perspective and Arrogance', p. 31.

[6] Here and subsequently *BR* stands for *The Black Riders*, *WK* for *War Is Kind*, *U* for uncollected poems, and *P* for posthumously published poems. The text is always from *The Poems of Stephen Crane*, ed. Joseph Katz, and the number in italics refers to Katz's numbering.

and the opulent sea, / The plains and the hills' are 'aloof' from man (*WK 79*, p. 85).

Self-loving man, however, is reluctant to accept his separation from external nature because he implicitly interprets the lack of relationship as an assault upon his ego. Mrs. Johnson's attempts to revenge herself upon the universe, George Kelcey's tilting with the nervous and abashed horizon, Henry Fleming's sentimental notion that mother nature has an aversion to tragedy are all comforting illusions; and whenever man endows externals with moral qualities existing within his own mind he merely reveals himself to the aware observer. The stupidity of Mrs. Johnson, of the little man who believes a cave gapes at him, their pointless rage and readiness to take offence, are caught and commented upon by the poem of the man who inadvertently compares himself to a 'stupid ass' (*BR 55*, p. 59):

> A man toiled on a burning road,
> Never resting.
> Once he saw a fat, stupid ass
> Grinning at him from a green place.
> The man cried out in rage:
> 'Ah! do not deride me, fool!
> I know you—
> All day stuffing your belly,
> Burying your heart
> In grass and tender sprouts:
> It will not suffice you.'
> But the ass only grinned at him from the green place.

A more subtle illustration of the same human failing results when two illusory views of a morally neutral externality are contrasted with each other:

> To the maiden
> The sea was blue meadow
> Alive with little froth-people
> Singing.
>
> To the sailor, wrecked,
> The sea was dead grey walls

> Superlative in vacancy
> Upon which nevertheless at fateful time
> Was written
> The grim hatred of nature. (*WK 78*, p. 84)

The maiden's obvious happiness is inferred only from the attributes with which she endows the sea. The wrecked sailor, like Melville's Pip, is unhappily alone in an immensity superlative in vacancy, but in this superlative vacancy there can be no grim hatred towards him. The sailor either accepts the *post hoc* argument which the Book of Job rejected or, more probably, he wishes to invest his coming death with a dignity it does not possess: hatred is better than nothing, and death at the will of a superior antagonist is more comforting to the ego than impersonal annihilation in (not *by*) an element where there are 'no temples' and 'no bricks' to throw at them. The sailor's illusion matches the maiden's; each is the opposite of the other. A failure to understand this poem probably accounts for its rejection from *The Black Riders* even though an accepted poem provides the essential commentary. This other poem contains the maiden, now weeping, the wrecked sailor, now drowned, and the sea, now personified; but again the sea is unable either to sustain or to destroy human life intentionally:

> ' . . . the king of the seas
> Weeps too, old, helpless man.
> The bustling fates
> Heap his hands with corpses
> Until he stands like a child
> With surplus of toys.' (*BR 38*, p. 40)

Those who seek a moral dimension in externality delude themselves with all the futility of the arrogant fool who pursues the horizon (*BR 24*, p. 26); they are the 'quick stream of men' who direct their feet towards an illusion—and in Crane's world, as will be seen, an institutionalized, codified conception of God is as morally empty as any other external. The man who stands 'musing in a black world' learns by experience that he will have to look within himself to find any sort of moral guide (*BR 49*, pp. 52–3).

Such a view of amoral nature divorced from man is obviously

naturalistic, and Crane might be mistaken for a naturalist if this were the end of his concern with the subject. But the separation itself is merely the given or fixed part of the relation between man and nature; it is absolute, and all that the aware and honest man can do about it, as Fleming learns, is accept it. That part of the relation which is not fixed, which is always capable of development or degeneration, is man's inner or moral reality of the mind as it copes with externality. And Crane's persistent emphasis upon the essential superiority of man's inner reality over all externals aligns him firmly with the humanistic tradition which reaches from Plato to Wallace Stevens: the recurring pattern in his fiction implicitly presents this emphasis, it receives its most thorough exploration in 'The Open Boat', it forms a large part of Fleming's journey to manhood, without it 'The Men in the Storm' would be mere newspaper realism, George Kelcey and the assassin fall alike because their inner world has degenerated beyond the capability of coping with externals, an awareness of the primacy of man's moral reality is gained by Maggie at the cost of her own happiness, and the theme is powerfully set forth in the poems.

The image of external reality is usually harsh, forbidding, in some way threatening—the sea, a desert, 'angry' mountains—in order to imply that external nature even at best confronts man with a challenge which he must acknowledge: the challenge of an omnipresent, fixed condition of being ultimately beyond the control of the individual who necessarily depends upon it for his physical survival. In one of the poems featuring desert imagery the spirit of a dead man (according to the final line) returns from the 'land of the farther suns':

> And I was in a reptile-swarming place,
> Peopled, otherwise, with grimaces,
> Shrouded above in black impenetrableness.
> I shrank, loathing,
> Sick with it.

Yet when this spirit asks 'him' what place this is, the answer is that this is a world: 'This was your home' (*BR 29*, p. 31). The implication is clear that this man when alive had not considered his home

to be any such place; with death and his experience of the ideal
which it is impossible to possess in the physical world has come
perspective. His attainment of the land of the farther suns reinforces the point of his question and the answer he receives: he was
one of Crane's good men on earth who lived the good life and
found happiness in the reptile-swarming place. The same point is
made in another desert poem, but the approach is from the opposite
direction:

> I walked in a desert.
> And I cried:
> 'Ah, God, take me from this place!'
> A voice said: 'It is no desert.'
> I cried: 'Well, but—
> The sand, the heat, the vacant horizon.'
> A voice said: 'It is no desert.' (*BR 42*, p. 45)

The 'I' of this poem has yet to learn what the spirit of the previous
one had realized as a man, the necessity of accepting the desert and
making the best of it. The speaker, like George Kelcey, wants to
leave a less than ideal reality for somewhere else, and 'for Crane
there is no someplace else' (Jumper, pp. 192–3). The instruction of
the voice has to be accepted; it 'is given the last word, there is no
irony to justify discrediting what it says, and a quiet assertion,
throughout Crane's poetry, is associated with genuine wisdom'
(Westbrook, 'Revolt-Search', p. 78). The voice's advice implies
that with acceptance the speaker's mind will impose its own moral
force upon the external. The result will be a continuous tension,
Crane's view of the human situation, something more than desert
but inevitably less than ideal; and within these boundaries both
happiness and significant achievement are available to the aware
man who maintains his personal honesty in the continuous struggle
required to sustain the tension.

This remarkably stoic cast of Crane's humanism is stressed in
two other desert poems. In the first the speaker is aware of the
bleak external reality, but he toys with the notion of actually
possessing an ideal:

> There was, before me,
> Mile upon mile
> Of snow, ice, burning sand.
> And yet I could look beyond all this,
> To a place of infinite beauty;
> And I could see the loveliness of her
> Who walked in the shade of the trees.
> When I gazed,
> All was lost
> But this place of beauty and her.
> When I gazed,
> And in my gazing, desired,
> Then came again
> Mile upon mile,
> Of snow, ice, burning sand. (*BR 21*, p. 23)

The speaker looks beyond the external to 'see' within his own mind the ideal of beauty in the 'place' and the woman, and this inner reality effectively overcomes the forbidding desert landscape; but the moment he desires to possess the ideal, the stern physical reality reasserts itself. Man pursues the ideal for the sake of the pursuit, the purpose and direction which make his pilgrimage across the desert meaningful and distinguish him from other animals. To deny the pursuit, as does the spirit in the final poem of *The Black Riders* (*68*, p. 72), is to deny one's own humanity, and what was once a man then becomes, at best, a mere scavenger of the desert like the assassin. But, Crane says, let an honest man have no illusions that the ideal can ever be attained in this desert world of externality beyond the individual's control.[7]

The remaining desert poem, perhaps the best of the four, gathers the themes of the previous ones:

> In the desert
> I saw a creature, naked, bestial,
> Who, squatting upon the ground,
> Held his heart in his hands,

---

[7] This is Crane's attitude towards his own ideal of personal honesty (*Letters*, p. 110), toward Tolstoy's aim 'to make himself good' (*Letters*, p. 116), and it is written into his note congratulating Mark Barr upon the birth of a son (*Letters*, p. 232). See also *BR 35*, p. 37; *64*, p. 68.

And ate of it.
I said: 'Is it good, friend?'
'It is bitter—bitter,' he answered;
'But I like it
Because it is bitter,
And because it is my heart.' (*BR 3*, p. 5)[8]

If one reads 'life' for 'heart' this poems portrays heroic man as
Crane conceives him. Nothing in the portrait is gilded; external
nature is desert, man is bestial, life is honestly assessed as bitter
without any hint of a better reality than the present, which for
Crane—as for Marcus Aurelius and Epictetus—is apparently all
man has. This man, having accepted the desert and the bitterness
—like Fleming once he accepts the reality of combat and his own
weaknesses—is able to be content with life under the given conditions. His fiercely stoic existence thus implies a dignity powerful
enough to impose itself upon the grim externality—'The dignity
of the accursed; / The glory of slavery, despair, death' (*WK 86*, p.
92)—and the speaker rightly honours this human dignity in calling
this creature 'friend'.

Another hero such as the heart-eater is the little man who faces
threatening mountains.[9] In one poem (*BR 37*, p. 39) the speaker
sees the peaks assemble on the horizon and begin marching
towards him, but the poem immediately ends and the point remains
implicit: faced with this challenge the speaker will have to act,
and his response will reveal both his manhood and the extent of his
understanding. Another poem presents the same situation except
that the assembled mountains are angry and the little man has
chosen his course of action:

Once I saw mountains angry,
And ranged in battle-front.
Against them stood a little man;
Aye, he was no bigger than my finger.
I laughed, and spoke to one near me:

[8] Cf. *BR 9*, p. 11; *23*, p. 25; *WK 81*, p. 87.
[9] For the relevance of this image to Crane's work in general, see James B.
Colvert, 'Stephen Crane's Magic Mountain', *Stephen Crane: A Collection of
Critical Essays*, ed. Maurice Bassan (Englewood Cliffs, 1967), pp. 95–105.

'Will he prevail?'
'Surely,' replied this other;
'His grandfathers beat them many times.'
Then did I see much virtue in grandfathers,—
At least, for the little man
Who stood against the mountains. (*BR 22*, p. 24)

This little man, thanks to the humanistic tradition inherited from
his grandfathers, is aware that mountains are after all only mountains, no matter how formidable they may appear, and of course he
will prevail. Externalities may kill him, as they kill the oiler in 'The
Open Boat', but they cannot in any way injure the moral reality
within him, within his own power of control. This little man—like
the heart-eater, Wilson and Fleming after their acceptance of
experience, Dr. Trescott, the men in the open boat, Manolo Prat,
the nameless men of 'War Memories'—is well equipped to live the
good life in Crane's world. All are

men who have the honesty to perceive their own unimportance in an
indifferent universe and the courage to believe in a code of humanistic
values in spite of a fate that mocks these values. They do not quail . . .
nor do they rage. . . . No day dreams are needed to sublimate an
objective reality that is almost always harsh. They accept their lot . . .
and struggle forward as best they can. (Westbrook, 'Revolt-Search',
p. 166.)

Crane's convictions about man's relations to God, to women, and
to his fellow man arise more or less as corollaries to his view of
man's relation to nature.

Nature as an amoral material externality is the logical consequence of such an act of creation as Crane describes. God may
have 'fashioned the ship of the world carefully', but just as he was
about to attach the rudder his attention wavered and the world got
away from him:

So that, forever rudderless, it went upon the seas
Going ridiculous voyages,
Making quaint progress,
Turning as with serious purpose
Before stupid winds.

> And there were many in the sky
> Who laughed at this thing. (*BR 6*, p. 8)

God as creator exists, the poem implies, but so far as the world is concerned he might just as well not exist; God, in short, is as remote from external nature as external nature is from man. His creation has escaped his jurisdiction and now moves of its own momentum without purpose or direction—a view which would have been acceptable to Hardy's Tess, London's Wolf Larsen, Mark Twain's mysterious stranger, and which can be found in the *Meditations* of Marcus Aurelius.

The analogous poem describing how the relations between this God and man were created was rejected from *The Black Riders* and did not achieve publication until after Crane's death. God reveals to man a 'glorious apple', a magnificent apple from the 'inner thoughts of heaven's greatest'. God places it within man's reach and then orders man to 'sit for sixty years / But—leave be the apple':

> The man answered in this wise:
> 'Oh, most interesting God
> What folly is this?
> Behold, thou hast moulded my desires
> Even as thou hast moulded the apple.'

What appears to God to be merely a test of obedience, in other words, is in reality an insult to the humanity he has himself created; and the fact that man is able to point out to God the lapse of logic in this bit of business in itself proclaims man's independence. Nevertheless, man proceeds to externalize this moral reality in a literal fact of action so that even God will understand what has already happened: he eats the apple.

> 'Look you, foolish god
> If I thrust behind me
> Sixty white years
> I am a greater god than God
> And, then, complacent splendor,
> Thou wilt see that the golden angels
> That sing pink hymns

Around thy throne-top
Will be lower than my feet.' (*P 120*, pp. 132–3)

Once again the created has escaped the jurisdiction of the creator, but the difference between the escape of physical nature and that of man is important: the ship of the world escaped by chance, and thus it became the amoral externality; man escaped by way of his wilful and purposive rejection of factual appearance to affirm an existing moral reality, and thus he attained the human situation as Crane perceives it—full moral responsibility in an amoral universe. And God is left as remote from both man and nature as the gods are for Lucretius. To believe otherwise, Crane implies, is to succumb to the usual illusion of endowing externality with moral qualities; but here the illusion is the more absurd—essentially a human act of creation—because, while external nature at least has the power of an effective force upon man's physical life, God relative to both man and nature is absolutely inert both morally and physically.

The powerless position of this deposed God is lyrically set forth in one of the finest poems—which even Hoffman (p. 96) admits 'is Crane's most complete denial of God'. Four regular stanzas with an all-important refrain portray the bitter reality of solitary death at sea and enclose a nine-line passage of illusion implicitly evoked in the victim's mind by his hopeless predicament.

> A man adrift on a slim spar
> A horizon smaller than the rim of a bottle
> Tented waves rearing lashy dark points
> The near whine of froth in circles.
>> God is cold.

> The incessant raise and swing of the sea
> And growl after growl of crest
> The sinkings, green, seething, endless
> The upheaval half-completed.
>> God is cold.

> The seas are in the hollow of The Hand;
> Oceans may be turned to a spray
> Raining down through the stars

Because of a gesture of pity toward a babe.
Oceans may become grey ashes,
Die with a long moan and a roar
Amid the tumult of the fishes
And the cries of the ships,
Because The Hand beckons the mice.

A horizon smaller than a doomed assassin's cap,
Inky, surging tumults
A reeling, drunken sky and no sky
A pale hand sliding from a polished spar.
                    God is cold.

The puff of a coat imprisoning air:
A face kissing the water-death
A weary slow sway of a lost hand
And the sea, the moving sea, the sea.
                    Gold is cold. (*P 113*, p. 125)

A normal identification with the suffering man will, at first reading,
make the coldness of God seem a mere turning away or refusal of
help, an interpretation which gives God a power of choice he does
not possess. This poem, a meditation on man's *physical* plight—
alone, by accident or chance, in an amoral universe—is a third-
person limited narration, like *The Red Badge*, in which there are
only two active 'characters': the man and the sea, humanity and
externality. God is entirely passive; his position is fixed in the
first refrain, and it never changes. This refrain, in other words, is
always the narrator's comment, and from the first it implies the
'superlative vacancy' presented in the final stanza. The first two
stanzas, except for the initial line which gives the situation, do not
mention the man at all, but the images of the sea are most often
visual and implicitly seen from the viewpoint of the dying man on
the spar. What is all too easily overlooked is that God is considered
from the same viewpoint, and that—as the final stanza should
suggest—this viewpoint, except for the extremities of isolation and
immediate death, is the normal one for man in Crane's world (a
more satisfactory image of it being the four men adrift in the open
boat). The nine-line passage at the centre of the poem results from

the narrator entering the mind of his protagonist at the moment of crisis, the usual technique in Crane's fiction; and so far as the drowning man himself is concerned, his thoughts reveal that he has abandoned all rational hope of rescue—that is, he would have no such thoughts as these if he were watching a ship's boat pulling toward him—and his futile, last-gasp wish is for a miracle. Moreover, nothing in the poem suggests that either protagonist or narrator really believes such a miracle could happen; when it fails to happen there is no reaction from either except the narrator's flat statement that God is cold; and the connotations of 'Because The Hand beckons the mice', which have deteriorated from those of 'gesture of pity toward a babe' in the parallel line, imply the collapse of the dying man's frantic wish even as it is formulated. This entire passage is an indirect statement only so far as it implies the protagonist's final clutch at life. It is also a direct statement—the seas *are* in the hollow of The Hand—of the manner in which the creator should be able to control his own creation according to the Christian myth. As such it is the opposite of the only other direct statement in the poem: God is cold. The conditional mood of the second and fifth lines of this passage follows from the direct statement in the first line, the required condition being a God warm with the power of creative or regulative force. Hence, God's coldness applies to his relation with external nature as much as it does to his relation with man. This is the coldness of the 'high cold star on a winter's night' which is the only answer 'The Open Boat' offers men who 'desire to confront a personification and indulge in pleas': a remoteness beyond all power, beyond even awareness of either the force of the sea or the plight of the mice. The superb final stanza presents what remains after human life is extinguished: the cold clay, now as cold both morally and physically as the vacancy which has always surrounded it, merges with the pointless and incessant motion of 'the sea, the moving sea, the sea'; and God is indeed cold.[10]

[10] This poem, unpublished until 1929, was written before June 1898 (Hoffman, p. 94). For an excellent interpretation at variance with mine, see Hoffman, pp. 94–9.

This icy remoteness of a dispossessed creator, however, like the fact of man's separation from nature, is merely the fixed part of the relationship between man and God. Again it is absolute, and man can only accept it; again man's ego militates against such acceptance—far more violently than it rejects the reality of an amoral nature—and again Crane's main interest centres upon that part of the relation which is not fixed: man's mind as it copes with this defunct God. This relation between man and God, as might be expected from Crane's Methodist upbringing, is easily the most important of the four noted above. It looms constantly as the main authority behind Crane's three principal integrating devices in the poems: two opposed concepts of 'God'—by no means two 'Gods', as is usually claimed—two opposed concepts of truth, and two opposed voices—in Westbrook's excellent terms, the voice of arrogance and the voice of perspective.[11] The two concepts of 'God', and incidentally the two voices, are presented in *BR 51* (p. 55):

> A man went before a strange god,—
> The god of many men, sadly wise.
> And the deity thundered loudly,
> Fat with rage, and puffing:
> 'Kneel, mortal, and cringe
> And grovel and do homage
> To my particularly sublime majesty.'
>
> The man fled.
>
> Then the man went to another god,—
> The god of his inner thoughts.
> And this one looked at him
> With soft eyes
> Lit with infinite comprehension,
> And said: 'My poor child!'[12]

[11] The general form of these devices should recall Crane's preoccupation with the parallel scene in his fiction and his tendency to use running patterns of opposed imagery: saloon and tenement in *Maggie*, saloon and church in *George's Mother*, Fleming's illusory notions of a moralized externality and his own isolation in *The Red Badge*.

[12] See also *BR 53*, p. 57, the other poem which best presents both concepts

Also, the opposition between a particularized majesty and an infinite comprehension implies the two opposed concepts of truth which are best set forth in *BR 28* (p. 30):

> 'Truth,' said a traveller,
> 'Is a rock, a mighty fortress;
> Often have I been to it,
> Even to its highest tower,
> From whence the world looks black.'
>
> 'Truth,' said a traveller,
> 'Is a breath, a wind,
> A shadow, a phantom;
> Long have I pursued it,
> But never have I touched
> The hem of its garment.'[13]

As these two poems suggest, Crane's three opposed pairs unite into one: one term from each pair is associated consistently with its cognate from each of the other two, and none of the three terms on either side of the resulting opposition is ever associated with the other triumvirate.

---

of 'God'. Hereafter, the capitalized form 'God' will refer only to the Christian God. Crane's attack, as Westbrook argues in 'Perspective and Arrogance', is aimed not at God but at human concepts which Crane considered absurd. Although the attacked notions clearly imply the fundamentalist Christian God of Crane's mother's family, I henceforth use the form 'god' to indicate a particularized human concept whether this concept is attacked or affirmed.

[13] A third stanza states that the narrator 'believed the second traveller'. The two concepts of god are merged with the two concepts of truth in *BR 39*, p. 41:

> The livid lightnings flashed in the clouds;
> The leaden thunders crashed.
> A worshipper raised his arm.
> 'Hearken! Hearken! The voice of God!'
>
> 'Not so,' said a man.
> 'The voice of God whispers in the heart
> So softly
> That the soul pauses,
> Making no noise,
> And strives for these melodies,
> Distant, sighing, like faintest breath,
> And all the being is still to hear.'

The voice of perspective draws Crane's deepest sympathy; [representative of the sort of mind that affirms the concept of a god of the inner thoughts,] it is characterized by humility, kindness, a quiet determination, and by a consistent belief in a truth which is symbolic, elusive, but always real. The voice of arrogance—representing the values Crane attacked in his prose and fiction as well as in his poetry—is characterized by pride, dogmatism, often by an aggressive manner, and by a stubborn insistence on a literal truth [and such is the type of mind that affirms the concept of an external god complete with church and professional advocates].[14]

For Crane, the external 'god of many men' has no objective existence, so far as I can determine, except the inert remoteness described in 'A man adrift on a slim spar'. It is instead a concept, an illusion created by the huddled procession of men either incapable of awareness or too cowardly or too selfish to accept what their awareness reveals to them—precisely those most apt to insist violently upon a literal, institutionalized, fixed truth; in so far as their insistence succeeds it both releases them from the labour of further thought and preserves their pet illusion from attack by other men. Crane's analysis of the several attributes men have contributed to this concept reveals its absurdity. One of his favourite approaches is to assume that this god does exist as an all-powerful, all-knowing, and all-just authority, and then portray him in action woefully beneath such godlike qualities. This god, who rages at man to 'grovel and do homage', thus punishes children for sins they did not commit (*BR 12*, p. 14), menaces fools (*BR 13*, p. 15), blusters, swaggers, and threatens (*BR 53*, p. 57), terrorizes man with natural violence (*BR 39*, p. 41), summarily condemns man in spite of woman's love (*BR 25*, p. 27), and proclaims that might is right (*WK 102*, pp. 108–9). Such are the very qualities with which Crane had endowed Pete, Jimmie, and Mrs. Johnson; the concept exposed in these poems merely amounts to another Bowery lout writ large. Other poems align with 'A man adrift on a slim spar' in stressing the lack of power of this presumed

---

[14] Westbrook, 'Perspective and Arrogance', p. 25: 'The voice of perspective, with reasonable consistency, is affirmed; the voice of arrogance, without exception, is mocked.'

omnipotent god. All he can offer man is a hope (*BR 30*, p. 32); and as Crane's man actively possesses only the present he replies

> If I should cast off this tattered coat,
> And go free into the mighty sky;
> If I should find nothing there
> But a vast blue,
> Echoless, ignorant,—
> What then? (*BR 66*, p. 70)

In another poem everything in the universe, like the drowning man, looks to this powerless concept for salvation (*WK 89*, p. 95). And in an apocalyptic vision the fact that 'God lay dead in Heaven' arouses no emotion: this fact is trivial beside the moral reality of woman's love—the very love which the 'stern spirit' of *BR 25* spurns:

> But of all sadness this was sad,—
> A woman's arms tried to shield
> The head of a sleeping man
> From the jaws of the final beast. (*BR 67*, p. 71)

So much for the concept of the Peck family god. There is no 'war in heaven' so far as Crane is concerned; the war takes place exactly where it always does in his work, within the mind of his human protagonists.

Crane's examination of the people who affirm this illusory god justifies the absurdity of the concept they have created and pointedly recalls his ironic observations of Founder Bradley and the Ocean Grove ministers. These are the people who would organize mankind into rows for no apparent reason except the fact of organization itself (*BR 5*, p. 7), who demand that everyone think as they think (*BR 47*, p. 50). Crane again assumes the existence of the external god, and then argues that the church, an institution man has created, can have no connection with him (*BR 32*, p. 34; *59*, p. 63). Also, if such a god did exist he would not be over-eager to acknowledge the church as Crane sees it. The professionals are either hypocrites (*BR 50*, p. 54; *57*, p. 61; *63*, p. 67) or simply 'surpliced numbskulls' (*WK 79*, p. 85; *97*, p. 103), asses who deal in printed lists and burning candles (*WK 85*, p. 91) as well as black valises; and, of course, if people seeking a god in such externals disagree, the result is as many gods as there are individuals (*BR 34*, p. 36), while those who do agree unite to become the quick stream of men in pursuit of an illusion. The professionals and the huddled processions they lead affirm a sterile tradition containing 'no meat for men' (*BR 45*, p. 48), not because of the worth or worthlessness of the tradition, but because of their own lack of manhood; for example, they watch passively while 'a god in wrath' beats a man:

> The people cried:
> 'Ah, what a wicked man!'
> And—
> 'Ah, what a redoubtable god!' (*BR 19*, p. 21)[15]

In so far as these people resemble Founder Bradley, the rest of the analogy has to apply: their concept of god is merely an illusory value which, like Bradley's absurd bathtubs and fire engines on the boardwalk, retains its place only because such people accept it without question.[16]

[15] Crane's attitude towards tradition never varies; he consistently rejects the empty form (best shown in *BR 27*, p. 29), and affirms the value—the tradition of grandfathers who beat the mountains, the military tradition of the United States regulars. In *P 119*, p. 131, ousted from *The Black Riders*, he rejects the formal tradition of marriage when the reality of love is absent.

[16] A few poems remain. The external god is mentioned, but not as the subject of the poem, in *BR 18*, p. 20; *68*, p. 72; *WK 80*, p. 86; *93*, p. 99. Hoffman (p. 88) argues that *WK 101*, p. 107, offers 'a synaesthetic evocation of natural beauty, regarded as praise of God and proof of His existence'; but as Crane elsewhere inevitably insists upon the futility of ascribing moral qualities to nature, the ironic reading implied by the last three lines is justified: if God's existence is affirmed only in moments of natural beauty, he is frequently off duty as, for example, in 'Nebraskans' Bitter Fight for Life' (Philadelphia *Press*, 24 Feb. 1895, p. 25). Hoffman (pp. 158–74) understandably emphasizes 'The Battle Hymn' (*P 129*, pp. 142–3), which he published for the first time, and 'The Blue Battalions' (*U 74*, pp. 76–7), which Crane withheld from *War Is Kind*. Westbrook dismisses both poems in a footnote ('Perspective and Arrogance', p. 30, n. 11); Nelson ignores 'The Battle Hymn', but argues at length for rejecting 'The Blue Battalions' on formal grounds ('Achievement as Poet', pp. 575–7). There are other reasons for rejecting it. 'When a people reach the top of a hill' is suspect because this image in the poems always implies the literal truth which Crane rejects; the image of 'the eyeless,/The God-led, turning only to beckon./Swinging a creed like a censer' presents the quick stream of undis-

No one wishes to claim that Crane had any leanings towards this concept of god; the problems arise in assessing the concept that Crane does affirm. What Crane says is plain enough: the voice of this god 'whispers in the heart' (*BR 39*, p. 41); he is the god of a man's 'inner thoughts' who looks upon the individual with 'soft eyes/Lit with infinite comprehension' (*BR 51*, p. 55; *33*, p. 35); he is described as 'those eyes of my soul', and the only fear he ever inspires is the 'fear to see grief upon that face' (*BR 53*, p. 57). Two poems insist that each individual possesses his own god of this kind, that this is morally right (*BR 34*, p. 36), and that one individual can in no way injure the god of another:

> Perchance, friend, he is not your god;
> If so, spit upon him.
> By it you will do no profanity. (*BR 53*, p. 57)

And this is about all that Crane reveals; but it should be enough to show that this god is not the God of Crane's father (see Hoffman, chapter 3), not 'the God of Elijah—the God who is . . . in the still small voice (I Kings 19:11–12)—and the New Testament God of love' (Nelson, p. 570).

Crane's emphasis veers away from Christianity in the direction of a common-sense stoic humanism. His describing this god as the eye of the soul obviously implies not the Christian God of love, but the conscience, the individual's private awareness of his responsibility towards his personal honesty. And hence the attributes of pity and infinite comprehension—not love—reasonably follow from this eye of the soul 'seeing' man's moral burden in an amoral universe and the strength and endurance required to bear it. This god of the inner thoughts, like the conscience but unlike the New Testament God, offers no hint of any reward for righteousness; the upheld personal honesty, conduct which does

---

criminating lemmings in huddled procession; and Crane elsewhere never calls human beings 'the tools of nature's impulse'. Most important, however, the tone of both poems, like that of *P 124*, p. 137, is evidence that Crane attempted in poetry what he had already succeeded in doing in prose: a deliberate abandoning of irony to produce commercially acceptable goods for a sentimental market. See also Joseph Katz, ' "The Blue Battalions" and the Uses of Experience', *Studia Neophilologica*, XXXVIII (1966), 107–16.

not bring 'grief upon that face', is always its own reward even when it leads to death. Most revealing of all, this inner god, exactly like one's own pair of eyes, is confined strictly to the individual; another individual as personally honest may spit upon this god without profanity, and such a stance is hardly Christian.[17] Crane's inner god, his concept of the conscience, embodies the personal aspect of the individual's 'quality of personal honesty'; but in order to understand Crane's thought at this point one has to leave the poetry and return briefly to the prose.

When Crane says a man is born with his own pair of eyes he recognizes that awareness is a power which varies with the individual; when he notes man's quality of personal honesty he endows man with moral responsibility which, in itself, apart from the way in which it is fulfilled, does not vary with the individual because the acceptable standard of conduct is always defined by the society to which he belongs. Honesty in conduct, as judged by one's peers, has to mean action in accordance with some recognized norm; and hence an individual's honesty, so far as society at large is concerned, also depends in part upon the individual's awareness: he must perceive the acceptable norm correctly in order either to act honestly in accordance with it or to act *honestly* at variance with it if, to the best of his judgement, he finds it inadequate. Maggie, though personally honest, still falls socially because of her lack of awareness, and Crane holds her responsible for giving in to Pete in so far as her fate results from her choosing an untenable position; but he reserves his ironic attack for those who choose to act *dishonestly* in terms of the reality that their own limited awareness can reasonably be expected to make available to them—Pete, Jimmie, Mrs. Johnson, the Bowery tramps, George Kelcey, Fleming when he deserts the tattered man—and external society's

[17] Crane inevitably scorns all dogma. He never hints that the Christian church will offer any real help or comfort to anyone, here or hereafter. He ignores the entire Christian eschatology. If Crane had intended his concept of god to mean the Christian God within man there should appear, somewhere in the canon, at least some sympathetic mention of Christianity. I find no such reference apart from the laconic statement that his mother was 'more of a Christian than a Methodist' (*Letters*, p. 242). Father Donovan of *The O'Ruddy* appears only in that part of the novel which, at the least, has to be ascribed to Robert Barr.

judgement of their actions is irrelevant to Crane's condemnation just as society's judgement of Maggie is irrelevant to Crane's refusal to condemn her as a person. Externality affects the individual's power of assent only to the extent that awareness is experiential, that the range of alternative choice in a particular situation can depend upon the scope of the individual's awareness, and that the physical circumstance limits the possible choice; but within these limitations the power of assent to a given action remains with the individual, no matter what social or physical pressures are brought to bear on him; and in this sense of the moral *act* of choice one's honesty is private, one's conscience is personal, unaffected by externality either physical or social. The sea may kill the man on the spar, but he himself has chosen to cling to the spar and live as long as possible. The social force aligned against Dr. Trescott in 'The Monster' is overwhelming, but he chooses to resist it. The external reality in most of Crane's work eventually reveals to the protagonist his own misapprehensions and stupidities, but the peculiar impact of Crane's best stories could not be felt—by either protagonist or reader—without the implication that the protagonist has *chosen*, if through no more than a failure to maintain self-control, to let some weakness such as fear or vanity subvert his common sense; the ironic deflation, the shame Crane's protagonist suffers at the end of his progression to awareness, presupposes that his past actions were in his own power. Thus, in Crane's world, although a man is not held responsible for the extent of his awareness, he is held absolutely responsible for whatever actions he chooses on the basis of whatever awareness he commands, and he, privately, personally, holds himself fully responsible for his own failings no matter how society may judge or fail to judge them; those personally dishonest characters who shirk the latter responsibility are, without exception, condemned with the full lash of Crane's irony.

Crane's concept of the conscience makes life in such a world both bearable and meaningful, and his image of a god of the inner thoughts seems singularly appropriate. This eye of the soul is to the individual's inner or moral reality what his own eyes are to the external reality, the personal awareness of the moral reality of the self. As such, its judgements claim precedence of all external forces including, if necessary, the socially recognized values affirmed by other men; and it compensates for the weakness of a person's mental machinery because it allows every individual to be personally honest no matter what the extent of his awareness of the external reality. Life is thus bearable because the self is a private reality apart from what others may think of it, apart from whatever external forces are aligned against it. Life is meaningful, morally significant, because every individual has the power to choose what is morally right for himself within whatever scope of awareness he possesses, and thus he can maintain his moral world intact as his awareness increases. Crane's god of the inner thoughts can be deposed only by the wilful dishonesty of the individual himself. Maggie listens to the voice of her conscience whispering in her heart, honestly makes a wrong choice, and therefore—in spite of society's judgement and the external forces that drive her to prostitution for survival—goes to her death without seeing 'grief on that face'; her moral reality, which endures in the face of social scorn and her own misery, implies the pity and infinite comprehension of the personal world within, the very qualities society withholds from her. Dr. Trescott honestly chooses a course of action which brings misery upon himself and his wife, and he also endures in the infinite comprehension of an ungrieved conscience. Manolo Prat, in 'The Clan of No-Name', knowingly chooses to die rather than bring grief upon that face. Henry Fleming sees a full measure of grief in the eye of his soul, suffers because of it, and, once he realizes that a grieving conscience outranks the judgements of his peers, sets his moral world in order with the aim of avoiding such grief wherever his guides may point thereafter. George Kelcey sees the same grief and spends his energy trying to look the other way. That he will eventually succeed is implied by the moral exhaustion of the assassin, a man who—like the 'successful man' (*WK 92*, p. 98), his social and economic opposite but moral twin—has been wilfully dishonest for so long that the eye of his soul has closed for ever. 'Not one Crane hero is judged by external values, by practical success or failure. Circumstance neither rewards nor punishes. Crane's emphasis, rather, is on the hero's unassuming devotion to duty and to humanistic values.'[18] Society, the external world, sees and judges facts, the literal truth; the conscience, the eye of the soul, sees and judges the moral reality beyond the fact of a person's overt action, the moral truth— 'a breath, a wind,/A shadow, a phantom'. And a quiet acceptance of whatever this god of his inner thoughts affirms as moral truth characterizes the good man leading the good life in Crane's desert world.

Elijah enjoyed no monopoly of the still small voice. Plato makes Socrates in the *Apology* speak of his little god within which always forbids but never commands, and Marcus Aurelius often refers to 'the deity which is planted in thee'. Crane's inner god embodies these classic concepts of the conscience in that every irrelevant emotional excess has been purged away; what remains is too simply and severely functional to be the Christian God of love. Also, although 'Crane's biographers have continued to insist that his mother held religious views much more narrow and more condemnatory than those of her husband', Dr. Crane's Methodism must have been generally acceptable in view of the important positions he held in the church. Hence, as might be expected, 'There is no reason to believe that serious doctrinal or temperamental differences existed between Jonathan Crane and his wife. ... The distinction between the justified and the unregenerate remained sharp in his theology, and he had by no means given up the fiery pit.'[19] Yet the available evidence strongly suggests that Dr. Crane's practice, his application of this doctrine, was considerably more humane than that of his wife. Crane himself, at any rate, implies such a judgement: 'He was a great, fine, simple mind' (*Letters*, p. 94). 'He was so simple and good that I often think he didn't know much of anything about humanity' (p. 243). Just when Crane came to terms with what his father represented is

[18] Westbrook, 'Perspective and Arrogance', p. 31.
[19] Stanley Wertheim, 'Stephen Crane and the Wrath of Jehova', *Literary Review*, VII (Spring 1964), 500.

impossible to say—probably by 1892 when he renounced the 'clever school' of writing, certainly before he wrote chapter 21 of *The Red Badge* which implies his own stoic-humanist position— but his sharp distinction between the values he accepted and his father's monumental innocence should recall his earlier assessment of his mother. Jonathan Crane assuredly emerged from the fire of his son's irony more intact than his wife had before him because the virtues of what Berryman calls his 'saintlike life' were immense: hard and incessant labour in behalf of his fellow men, patience, compassion, humility, gentleness, endurance, selfless devotion to his duty as his own eye of the soul defined it for him. These enormously *practical* values, salvaged from the father's humanism by a son too discerning to accept the father's innocence and too personally honest to support what he could not accept, emerge as Crane's ideal of man's relation to his fellow man. But in so far as affirmation of the God of Crane's father depended upon the father's innocence, this God could not have been acceptable to the son.

Crane's ideal of man's relation to his fellow man follows not in spite of his ironic view of mankind, but because of it. The poems show again and again that in this reptile-swarming place, where only man can be believed in because nothing external to man is worthy of one's faith, even man's weak mental machinery is all too often dominated by his own moral flaws. Chief among these sins against the individual's god of the inner thoughts is vanity (*BR 52*, p. 56), man's persistent refusal to acknowledge his own fallibility:

> I stood upon a high place,
> And saw, below, many devils
> Running, leaping,
> And carousing in sin.
> One looked up, grinning,
> And said: 'Comrade! Brother!' (*BR 9*, p. 11)

The true 'sage' accepts his brotherhood among the imperfect (*BR 58*, p. 62), and so does the poet who writes with 'this red muck/Of things from my heart' (*BR 46*, p. 49); but men generally hold out until the last moment before admitting their own limitations (*BR 33*, p. 35). The 'high place' which affords the illusion of superiority to those who attain it always implies some sort of literal truth which for Crane is only provisional (*BR 26*, p. 28), but which for the vain man is final, a position 'from whence the world looks black' (*BR 28*, p. 30). This literal truth may be the fact of one's public good deeds, and Crane implies that all public good deeds are tinged with an alloy of vanity (*BR 16*, p. 18; *18*, p. 20; *60*, p. 64), it can be the fact of material wealth (*WK 95*, p. 101), and it can even be an accomplishment of one's own creation achieved in honest sweat of the face:

> Many workmen
> Built a huge ball of masonry
> Upon a mountain-top.
> Then they went to the valley below,
> And turned to behold their work.
> 'It is grand,' they said;
> They loved the thing.
>
> Of a sudden, it moved:
> It came upon them swiftly;
> It crushed them all to blood.
> But some had opportunity to squeal. (*BR 31*, p. 33)

A public good deed has to be judged by the moral reality of its motivation, a vain fool surrounded by wealth and 'a crash of flunkeys' is still a vain fool precisely as a just man defeated is still just (*WK 80*, p. 86), and Crane provides his own commentary on the 'huge ball of masonry':

> A man saw a ball of gold in the sky;
> He climbed for it,
> And eventually he achieved it—
> It was clay.
>
> Now this is the strange part:
> When the man went to the earth
> And looked again,
> Lo, there was the ball of gold.

Now this is the strange part:
It was a ball of gold.
Aye, by the heavens, it was a ball of gold. (*BR 35*, p. 37)

The moral reality of any human achievement—such as writing *The Red Badge*—is the combination of those inner forces of intelligence, endurance, effort, the virtues evoked by man's pursuit of the ideal and which made the achievement possible. But the literal fact of an attained accomplishment is merely the clay which can be set upon a high place for the external world to see, the sort of thing that can be reported in a newspaper (see *BR 11*, p. 13; *WK 87*, p. 93). The ideal, truth, reality, is always moral, an inner reality like the birds in the basket (*BR 65*, p. 69), and the illusion of confusing any literal externality with the ideal or moral truth is analogous to opening the basket and allowing the birds to fly away. Similarly, the poet advises the old man who waits to see ideal justice upon earth to pass on to 'more tender lands' (*BR 64*, p. 68).[20] And in the desert world where a continuous present poses a continuous challenge, where nothing but death is final, a man's complacent admiration for the literal result of even his own past achievement is a delusion of his vanity and laziness. Man has to descend immediately from the attained fact and begin again the pursuit of what will then be again the ball of gold. But such a doctrine is too strenuous for many men—such as George Kelcey— to accept; even when they realize its truth they do their best to ignore it:

I was in the darkness;
I could not see my words
Nor the wishes of my heart.
Then suddenly there was a great light—

'Let me into the darkness again.' (*BR 44*, p. 47)

The good man's relation to his fellow men, Crane argues, will be to help them stand firm against the tempting darkness, to teach them to accept what the great light of awareness reveals of their own

---

[20] Two poems imply that the reality of war is moral and personal, not the literal fact of action (*BR 14, 15*, pp. 16, 17).

inner reality and their place among other men in an amoral universe.

Those poems which discuss not primarily the nature of truth in general, but the individual's quest for his own truth can almost be called by-products of the intense writing Crane poured into the scenes of Fleming's wanderings in the forest, a portion of *The Red Badge* that seems to be the full rendition of a motif which, for Crane himself, apparently assumed the authority of an archetype. There is no 'high place' anywhere in this enchanted forest; the quest for one's own moral truth is always a plunge into 'direful thickets' after leaving the huddled procession (*BR 17*, p. 19), a lonely attempt to pick out a path through thick 'weeds' each of which becomes 'a singular knife' (*WK 88*, p. 94). A fragment from 'The Battle Hymn', written late in Crane's life, repeats the metaphor:

> And if the path, the new path, lead awry
> Then in the forest of the lost standards
> Suffer us to grope and bleed apace; (*P 129*, p. 142)

and two poems, at first glance unrelated to any personal quest, complete the metaphor by spelling out—with all the persistently indefinite horror of a nightmare—the threat of death that lurks in this enchanted forest:

> There is a grey thing that lives in the tree-tops
> None know the horror of its sight
> Save those who meet death in the wilderness
> But one is enabled to see
> To see branches move at its passing
> To hear at times the wail of black laughter
> And to come often upon mystic places
> Places where the thing has just been. (*P 121*, p. 134)[21]

---

[21] The fugitive nature of this 'thing' is also that of Crane's view of truth; hence, the kind of death implied is not the literal death of the body. Fleming encounters death in the forest but is not destroyed, Manolo Prat accepts literal death in order to avoid moral death in the forest, and the 'death-demon' that chatters unseen in the 'tree-top' kills the 'lone hunter' in *WK 94*, p. 100, so as to preclude his future happiness implicit in the image of the woman seeking him. *BR 27*, p. 29, relates to the metaphor because the 'youth in apparel that

Crane's entire metaphor is an extremely condensed statement of his view of mankind.

All the good men in Crane's world—a comparatively small group—have to make a successful journey through the enchanted forest. Those of the huddled procession are exempt from the plunge into the thicket: cowardly men will not make the attempt because the lone journey requires courage; vain fools cannot undertake the journey until they first acknowledge their own fallibility (*BR 36*, p. 38); and lazy men lack the moral force of commitment that the journey demands. All such people are ironically safe from the threat of 'death' in this forest because they lack the manhood, the moral 'life' which can be killed; the lazy, the vain, and the cowardly are merely the drones of the world, not—at least at the beginning of their moral life—primarily vicious, not necessarily hypocrites or personally dishonest, although they usually become so if they continue to indulge their own weaknesses. Each good man has to plunge alone into the direful thicket of his inner self because no one else, not even the most learned (*BR 20*, p. 22), can accompany him or make this journey for him. The enchanted forest is appropriately a limbo of 'lost standards' because the personal search for moral truth is undertaken only when a man is psychologically on the run like Fleming fleeing from the regiment, when a man can no longer accept the traditional truths which have been institutionalized by the civilization he has inherited. The process of institutionalizing a moral truth, for Crane, implicitly makes it a literal truth, i.e. institutionalization removes it from the individual's personal realm of values affirmed by his god of the inner thoughts and makes it public property, another example of the ball of gold being turned into clay by men who then are effectively crushed by it because they do not realize that an ideal, a moral truth, cannot be thus possessed in this world.[22] The path which the good man gropes and bleeds

---

glittered' meets death at the hand of an assassin, in 'a grim forest'; but the assassin clearly implies formal tradition, and thus this fatuous youth never gets beyond the edge of the forest.

[22] See Westbrook, 'Revolt-Search', *passim*.

to discern in the forest leads to awareness of the moral reality of the self and its real place among other men in an indifferent universe, a truth which may well be 'bitter as eaten fire' (*BR* 7, p. 9) as it is for Fleming when he deserts the tattered man, for Manolo Prat when he walks knowingly to his physical death, for Dr. Trescott when he stands firm against all Whilomville, for George Kelcey the morning after Bleecker's drunken party, for the correspondent in 'The Open Boat' when he realizes that the inescapable human lot is to be adrift by chance in a frail vessel on an amoral sea. Once the end of the path is attained, the lone hunter is faced with a decision. He can accept the moral reality of his self and its place in the world—as Fleming, Manolo Prat, Dr. Trescott, and the correspondent do—and then conduct himself as a man with the approval of his personal god of the inner thoughts. Or he can refuse to act in accordance with his own awareness, a refusal which overrules the conscience and thus brings moral death; the grey thing then springs from the tree-tops, and the wail of black laughter follows the hypocrite, the personally dishonest man—Pete, Jimmie, Mrs. Johnson, George Kelcey, the assassin, the 'successful man'—as he emerges, morally dead, from the forest.[23]

The final stage of the journey is best set forth in *The Red Badge* and 'The Open Boat': a return to the regiment, a commitment to one's fellow men which arises from the awareness acquired in the depths of the forest. Both Fleming and the correspondent learn of their own human weakness and fallibility, both learn that nature is amoral and apart from man's life of aspiration and suffering, both learn the value of brotherhood, and both end their dark journey with a quiet commitment to the group, mankind in general who, aware or unaware, are caught in the same human predicament that the Crane hero has just discerned and accepted at the end of his terrible path through the forest. The specific virtues of this commitment are set forth in only one poem:

[23] The relation between Crane's metaphor and Conrad's *Heart of Darkness* should be noted. Kurtz, whom Marlow distinguishes morally from the worthless pilgrims, also meets death in the forest and acknowledges the horror of his defeat. Marlow even states that 'a fool is always safe'.

'What says the sea, little shell?
What says the sea?
Long has our brother been silent to us,
Kept his message for the ships,
Awkward ships, stupid ships.'

The pines on the shore who ask the question are the image of vain
and unaware men—vain because of their attitude towards the
ships, unaware because they have to ask the question—and the
sea, as usual in Crane's work, is the emblem of external nature.
Hence, the first advice that the sea offers is compassion for the
plight of man in the desert world:

'The sea bids you mourn, oh, pines,
Sing low in the moonlight.
He sends tale of the land of doom,
Of place where endless falls
A rain of women's tears,
And men in grey robes—
Men in grey robes—
Chant the unknown pain.'

And when the pines ask again, the sea names the virtues valued
by the weeping women and the men aware of pain:

'The sea bids you teach, oh, pines,
Sing low in the moonlight,
Teach the gold of patience,
Cry gospel of gentle hands,
Cry a brotherhood of hearts.
The sea bids you teach, oh, pines.'

But then the pines reveal their shallowness, implied in the first
stanza, by asking 'Where is the reward, little shell?' And, as un-
selfishness is the prerequisite of moral life in Crane's world, the
shell returns the only answer possible to those whose vanity
disqualifies them from understanding themselves and their
responsibilities in this land of doom:

'No word says the sea, oh, pines,
No word says the sea.
Long will your brother be silent to you,

Keep his message for the ships,
Oh, puny pines, silly pines.'[24]

However, the immense worth of compassion, teaching, patience, gentleness, brotherhood—the practical virtues affirmed by Crane's father—remains unaffected by the failures of those too undiscerning to realize that in such a world as this the practice of man's ideal relation to his fellow man is always its own reward.

At this point the meaning and function of the title poems of the two collections should be apparent. 'The Black Riders' presents a single powerful metaphor:

> Black riders came from the sea.
> There was clang and clang of spear and shield,
> And clash and clash of hoof and heel,
> Wild shouts and the wave of hair
> In the rush upon the wind:
> Thus the ride of Sin. (*BR 1*, p. 3)

Crane's use of 'Sin' follows reasonably from his defining the conscience as the 'god' of the inner thoughts—both terms having been salvaged from the tradition he rejected—but the two words have to be quite strictly associated because Crane seldom concerns himself with sin in any Biblical or theological sense of disobedience to divine command. Crane's awesome black figures burst forth from the sea into a wild tumult of action which can no more be stopped than the rush of the wind, and the implication is that these wild riders gallop eternally out of control across the plane of Crane's universe. Their association with 'Sin' implies that the metaphor identifies the real source of misery and suffering in the world: the universal human weaknesses which eternally ride man himself and lead him to sin against his own conscience, the moral flaws which emerge into the universe simultaneously with man, and which the poems in the collection examine. 'War Is Kind' more explicitly offers the same general meaning. War, the greatest mischief that limited man is capable of, is plainly ascribed to man's own weakness by the second and fourth stanzas.

[24] *WK* 77, pp. 82–3. As 'a fair copy dated 28 December 1895' exists, this poem was written shortly after those of *The Black Riders* (see Katz, p. 193).

These 'little souls who thirst for fight', born only to 'drill and die', are men who blindly follow an 'unexplained glory' and believe those who 'point for them the virtue of slaughter,/Make plain to them the excellence of killing' (*WK 76*, p. 81); and the first, third, and fifth stanzas show the misery which results from this man-created folly. Thus, both title pieces serve to set forth the essential subject of the poems which follow.

Crane's thought concerning man's relation to women has evoked some strange speculation, but the view of love set forth in some seven poems in the two collections suggests neither a juvenile nor a monster; it implies a discerning intelligence which is not to be gulled by externals or by any sentimental notions of permanence in romantic love.[25] Love, like beauty, truth, brotherhood, exists only within the mind and, while it can and must be pursued in practical action, it cannot be ideally realized in actual life which necessarily includes the external, the beloved. *BR 8*, p. 10, states that ideal beauty, even that of a woman loved, exists in the heart of the lover, not in the external woman herself; and *BR 21*, p. 23, presents the futility of desiring to possess ideal beauty—again associated with a loved woman—in the external world. What seems to me Crane's finest love poem equates his treatment of love with his treatment of ideal beauty:

> Should the wide world roll away,
> Leaving black terror,
> Limitless night,
> Nor God, nor man, nor place to stand
> Would be to me essential,
> If thou and thy white arms were there,
> And the fall to doom a long way. (*BR 10*, p. 12)

Love between man and woman, an extension of the ideal of

[25] I omit the 'Intrigue' poems from consideration. They are incredibly bad pieces, and no artist deserves judgement on the basis of his poorest work. Moreover, judgement about them probably should remain tentative until considerably more is known of how they came into being. At present we know only that Crane sent them to his agent from Havana in October 1898, during probably the darkest and most troubled period of his life, and that he dismissed them with one curt sentence: 'The "Intrigue" lot goes to Heinemann' (*Letters*, p. 189).

brotherhood between man and man, can endure as long as man endures. In the imaginative universe of this poem the world, God, other men, everything else—even a place to stand—are collapsing into black terror and infinite night; and given love, the poem says let the rest go. Everything except love in this poem is external to the lover, and the fall to doom is the inevitable death which in Crane's world awaits the lover and the fool alike. But love exists within the mind, and the fact of inescapable oblivion in the future is itself just one more authority for the worth of love in the present. Finally, the mood is conditional—nothing else *would be* essential *if* the speaker's love were accepted and returned by the woman—, but because the fulfilment of the condition is not within the power of the individual lover the poem affirms the value of love in its own right, apart from whatever fate it may meet in the response of the beloved.

This view of love reappears in other poems. In *BR 67*, p. 71, God is dead and again the universe is dying, but the climactic image is that of the woman trying to shield the head of her sleeping lover and thus prolong their fall to doom as long as possible. The lover in *BR 23*, p. 25, rejects realms of distant beauty for the desert world:

> Since she is here
> In a place of blackness,
> Here I stay and wait.

The speaker in *WK 100*, p. 106, asking the 'workman' to make a dream for his love, details the externals of sunlight, breezes, flowers, meadows, and in the final line reminds him that there must be a man in this dream; without man, obviously, love cannot exist, no matter how beautiful the external settings. Externality is also rejected by the beloved whose lover merely professes his love and pleads that he is held back by

> Man's opinions, a thousand thickets,
> My interwoven existence,
> My life,
> Caught in the stubble of the world.

The beloved knows better:

> If love loves,
> There is no world
> Nor word.
> All is lost
> Save thought of love
> And place to dream. (*BR 40*, pp. 42–3)

In *BR 25*, p. 27, a weeping woman and a 'stern spirit' meet at the
grave of 'a wicked man'; and the poem's implicit affirmation of the
woman's love over the spirit's justice, as index of the man's
character while living, implies that the spirit has judged by the
literal fact while the woman has known and loved the real man in
spite of the fact:

> If the spirit was just,
> Why did the maid weep?

And in *WK 81*, p. 87 (first published in October 1896), a ship on
the sea at night is again the metaphor of man in the midst of the
amoral universe; love in this poem stands for man's whole moral
life as he voyages from darkness to darkness. Life without love,
the poem implies, is merely a bleak journey amidst

> . . . a far waste of waters
> And the soft lashing of black waves
> For long and in loneliness.

Thus, again, love remains an affirmed ideal no matter what sort of
response one's commitment meets in the external world; the pursuit
of any ideal depends upon the moral strength of the pursuer. Love
between man and woman requires the same moral commitment as
brotherhood between man and man; either relation is subject to
the same pitfalls in the way to any reciprocal fulfilment, and is
deserving of the same gentleness, patience, and loyalty.

So long as Crane treats love as an ideal he is sure of himself and
of what he wants to say; the diction of these poems is characteristically hard and taut, and their burden of thought occasionally
seems too great to be borne by so few words. Moreover, when he

considers young women ironically—as in his treatment of Maggie's innocence, the situation of Nell in 'A Desertion' (*New York City Sketches*, pp. 189–92), the portrayal of Margharita in 'The Clan of No-Name'—there is nothing noticeably wrong with either his perception or his writing. He clearly was interested in prostitutes and prostitution, as much as (but, so far as I can determine, no more than) he was interested in other forms of human weakness. And the letters imply that his relations with Lily Brandon Munroe and Nellie Crouse, both exceptionally lovely women, were healthy and normal. Yet in Crane's attempts to consider the external woman herself—not ideal love, not man's relation to woman—there is an inept sense of tension and fumbling. The sentimentalism of his day was always waiting to engulf him whenever he abandoned the security of his ironic perception, and thus we have such curious puppets as Grace Fanhall and Marjory Wainwright. It seems reasonable to insist that Crane was singularly ill equipped to write about women in the 1890s; neither his affirmation of love as an ideal nor his view of man's relation to women could teach him how to write without irony about woman herself, and he wrote at a time when pretty young women were not supposed to be considered ironically. His seven letters to Nellie Crouse, written early in 1896, less than a year after the appearance of *The Black Riders*, seem to be his last futile attempt to bridge the gap between the personal god of his inner thoughts and the conventional mind of a young woman. As such, these letters are the other important revelation of his own thoughts about life and how it should be lived, virtually a résumé of the poems; and thus they provide both a postscript in confirmation of the above reading and a convenient summary of the development of Crane's mind to early 1896 when the world at large first heard of him.

In the first letter Crane only once peeps out from behind the mask of light raillery he has assumed: 'The lives of some people are one long apology. Mine was, once, but not now. I go through the world unexplained, I suppose' (*Letters*, p. 86). And in the second letter he adds, 'You have no idea how it simplifies matters' (p. 97). The apologetic lives are those of the huddled procession because they are dominated by illusory values—Maggie trying to live according to her hopeless innocence, Pete, Jimmie, and Mrs. Johnson wasting life in pointless rage at the universe to hide their own hypocrisy, George Kelcey, Bleecker, the Bowery tramps implicitly apologizing for their moral failures by drinking and telling themselves they live like kings, Fleming rationalizing his own weaknesses as he gropes for his path through the forest, all the arrogant fools of the poems who chase their own pet horizons. Crane's awareness and honesty have forced him to leave this quick stream of men and formulate his own philosophy; he will simply act in accordance with the god of his inner thoughts and accept the fact that most people will not understand his actions, a decision which simplifies matters because, so far as Crane himself is concerned, it discriminates between reality and illusion and frees him from worrying about external judgements based upon the literal fact of his actions. But, having deftly implied that her life is not one of apology, he will try to explain himself to Miss Crouse, he says; he will confess, even if it ruins his egotism for a fortnight. After all, writes the stoic, 'it is a very comfortable and manful occupation to trample upon one's own egotism' (p. 98).[26]

His direct attempt to explain himself begins in the third letter. Crane writes that he is 'minded to die in my thirty-fifth year' because life 'doesn't strike me as particularly worth the trouble'.

The final wall of the wise man's thought however is Human Kindness of course. If the road of disappointment, grief, pessimism, is followed far enough, it will arrive there. Pessimism itself is only a little, little way, and moreover it is ridiculously cheap. The cynical mind is an uneducated thing. Therefore do I strive to be as kind and as just as may be to those about me and in my meagre success at it, I find the solitary pleasure of life. (*Letters*, p. 99)

Although Crane's willingness to die young may seem to smack of

---

[26] This occupation served Crane as moral callisthenics: 'Men usually refuse to recognize their school-boy dreams. They blush. I don't. . . . I was such an ass, such a pure complete ass—it does me good to recollect it' (*Letters*, p. 119). 'I have managed my success like a fool and a child but then it is difficult to succeed gracefully at 23. However I am learning every day. I am slowly becoming a man' (p. 147). See also Crane's excellent letter to Miss Daisy D. Hill, *Stephen Crane Newsletter*, IV (Winter 1969), 1–2.

fin de siècle languor, the stoic's life of duty is an arduous burden which is never eased until death comes as the release, and the ultimate pleasure involved—fulfilment of the commands of conscience under all circumstances—is indeed solitary. As there is no other reward here or hereafter, human kindness, not faith in the God of Crane's father, is the final position of the wise man. Pessimism and cynicism, offered as two more versions of the apologetic life, had been portrayed earlier in the poems:

> Once there was a man,—
> Oh, so wise!
> In all drink
> He detected the bitter,
> And in all touch
> He found the sting.
> At last he cried thus:
> 'There is nothing,—
> No life,
> No joy,
> No pain,—
> There is nothing save opinion,
> And opinion be damned.' (*BR 48*, p. 51)

This 'wise' man has merely found out that the world is a desert, but he has not yet either accepted the desert for what it is or discovered his own humanity. His cynical pessimism is thus merely one more arrogant apology, a philosophy bought cheaply because he has yet to become aware that—precisely because there is much truth in his bitter view of life—brotherhood, love, kindness, justice, the other values of Crane's creed, are necessary if human life is to be meaningful under such conditions, an awareness that the heart-eater has attained. Man's success in the practice of such virtues will be meagre at best, partly because of his own weak mental machinery, partly because others are prone to misunderstand his best efforts: 'There is only one person in the world who knows less than the average reader. He is the average reviewer' (*Letters*, p. 99). Thus, a man has to accept his own vision of his duty and do it in spite of criticism or applause. Human kindness in such a world, however, is the value affirmed by 'an intensely practical and experienced person' (p. 101).

Crane's development of this philosophical position in his next letter requires the distinction between moral values, within the mind and thus within the power of the individual, and externals. He begins by belittling his own success because he has 'lost all appetite for victory, as victory is defined by the mob' (p. 105). Such a claim follows directly from *BR 31*, p. 33, without either snobbery or false modesty. Crane probably caught himself basking in the sudden popularity achieved by *The Red Badge* and realized that this huge ball of masonry he had placed upon a mountain-top would crush him if he did not put it out of his mind and get back to work; as long as he hesitated he was guilty of Fleming's sin of judging himself by the opinions of other men regarding the literal result of his past achievement. Besides, as Fleming also learns, a man's external reputation varies with the different views different individuals take of his public deeds, and is thus something not entirely within the power of the man himself. The poems bluntly reject it:

> Why do you strive for greatness, fool?
> Go pluck a bough and wear it.
> It is as sufficing. (*BR 52*, p. 56)

Hence, while it is true that even the literal fact of success which the mob can appreciate has to be pursued and achieved over and over again in a continuous present which extends to the grave, Crane is concerned with the moral victory or defeat that remains strictly personal:

I will be glad if I can feel on my death-bed that my life has been just and kind according to my ability and that every particle of my little ridiculous stock of eloquence and wisdom has been applied for the benefit of my kind. From this moment to that deathbed may be a short time or a long one but at any rate it means a life of labor and sorrow. I do not confront it blithely. I confront it with desperate resolution. There is not even much hope in my attitude. I do not even expect to do good. But I expect to make a sincere, desperate, lonely battle to remain true to my conception of my life and the way it should be lived, and if this plan can accomplish anything, it shall be accomplished. (*Letters*, p. 105)

For Crane, real victory or defeat equates with his view of truth as 'a breath, a wind, / A shadow, a phantom', the moral outcome of a lifelong struggle to uphold the code of conduct which emerges from the poems. The commitment to justice, kindness, brotherhood, teaching for the benefit of mankind is made without hint of laying up treasure in heaven, without even the illusion of significant accomplishment (in any literal sense) upon earth: precisely as the little shell implies in bringing the sea's message to the pines, the man who is aware will pursue this ideal merely because it is his duty to do so given the conditions of life in which he finds himself. In the next paragraph Crane tries to make his meaning clear to Miss Crouse by speaking directly of his inner self, without humour or irony:

When I speak of a battle I do not mean want, and those similar spectres. I mean myself and the inherent indolence and cowardice which is the lot of all men. I mean, also, applause. . . . [With the arrival of fame] for the first time in my life I began to be afraid, afraid that I would grow content with myself . . . would be satisfied with the little, little things I have done. For the first time I saw the majestic forces which are arrayed against man's true success—not the world—the world is silly, changeable, any of it's [*sic*] decisions can be reversed—but man's own colossal impulses more strong than chains, and I perceived that the fight was not going to be with the world but with myself. I had fought the world and had not bended nor moved an inch but this other battle—it is to last on up through the years to my grave. (*Letters*, p. 105)

Because the real scene of struggle—in Crane himself, in the poems, and in the fiction—lies within the mind of the protagonist, victory or defeat is also significant only in a personal or moral sense. Man's *true* success occurs when he is able to control his own majestic inner forces by means of his own will so that his mind stays healthy and strong in the continuous performance of his duty; defeat occurs when the will relaxes its grip and the colossal impulses seize control—a view of man which is at least as old as

Plato's *Republic*. These impulses, examined in the poems and fiction and specified here as inherent indolence, cowardice, and the vanity which gluts itself upon external applause, are the universal black horsemen which ride all men and spur them to sin against their own conscience. Externals, favourable or unfavourable, are trivial in themselves and are quickly dismissed as silly, but the 'singular knives' which line a man's pathway to moral truth are eternally in position to slash him the moment he falters. And, as Crane also confessed to Howells, the greatest temptation to turn from the path stems not from hardship or abuse but from applause: 'I am, mostly, afraid . . . that some small degree of talk will turn me ever so slightly from what I believe to be the pursuit of truth, and that my block-head will lose something of the resolution which carried me very comfortably through the ridicule' (*Letters*, p. 106). Ridicule and hardship present an obvious challenge, and one's normal response is to fight; but the will tends at first to relax in the warmth of a favourable opinion of oneself, and if this temptation is not overcome indolence will reinforce vanity to make one content with resting upon past success. The resulting inertia will then become increasingly difficult to overcome because cowardice, finally, will also block the path; after a great public success a failure would hurt one's vanity unbearably, and thus one's inherent cowardice whispers that if one merely remains indolent and does not try a new venture there will be no danger of such a failure. And once this final stage has been reached, the wail of black laughter again sounds through the forest to signify the moral death of yet another man.

This immensely important letter won Crane Miss Crouse's picture, and he answered with a note of thanks. But the sixth letter resumes the argument with a discussion of the gentleman, or 'real aristocrat', in an attempt to place before Miss Crouse the distinction between illusion and reality. The obvious problem is that correct form, which can be learned and practised by anyone, does not make a man an aristocrat; and in order to discern the inner reality beneath the façade one must be able to penetrate to the moral nature of the man before passing judgement. The danger in too great a commitment to manners and social forms—essentially the same as that of allowing vanity, indolence, and cowardice to lead one to think solely in terms of literal success or failure—is that in devoting oneself to an externality one is apt to slight the inner reality; and without the inner worth behind the form, the form itself becomes a lie, as in Crane's caricature of the millionaire's wife in 'An Experiment in Luxury'. Given the moral reality within, Crane implies, the form—'merely a collection of the most rational and just of laws which any properly-born person understands from his cradle'—will take care of itself. Crane does not care for 'the man with the high aims and things', particularly 'if he was at all in the habit of talking about them'. Talking about them implies high aims bent towards literal accomplishment, and these are not the sort of aspirations that Crane accepts as real; the man who would make himself great because of the reputation with which the mob would flatter him Crane inevitably considers ridiculous. But there is also the man who, like Tolstoy, would make himself good; and for such a man Crane quietly foresees the failure as clearly as he admires the moral strength that even the pursuit of such an ideal implies.

Miss Crouse dismissed Crane with her next letter, and his reply closes with a view of death which is no more Christian than the rest of his philosophy is. Death is merely the release from pain and moral responsibility: 'the calm unfretting unhopeing [*sic*] end of things—serene absence of passion—oblivious to sin—ignorant of the accursed golden hopes that flame at night and make a man run his legs off and then in the daylight of experience turn out to be ingenious traps for the imagination' (*Letters*, p. 120). Crane, left alone in the amoral universe without the fulfilment of love which makes the desert bloom, has to confront again the continuous present which looms before him more bleakly now than before: 'The future? The future is blue with obligations—new trials—conflicts.' But the struggle continued for four more years. To struggle and labour with the moral strength of the real aristocrat was the first principle of Crane's stoic code of conduct.

With *The Red Badge*, *The Black Riders*, and the Crouse letters one attains a kind of plateau in the study of Crane: his development, both in his personal philosophy and in the technical resources of his talent, was substantially complete by early 1896. The ironic vision with which he began was now firmly controlled and directed by the code of values which apparently defined itself by about 1893; and the combination of this vision and this philosophical stance will be found henceforth in his unmistakable prose. His technical development—away from the starkness and deliberate verbal intensity of the *Sullivan County Sketches*, towards flexibility, comparative simplicity, and a psychological realism in which the intensity is less a matter of language and more a matter of character—was carefully cultivated in his news articles and sketches, and it received its greatest single impetus from his discovery of the resources available in the third-person limited point of view. By 1896 he had attained the fluent level of craftsmanship which made possible the machine-like production of story after story, many of which were not at all unmistakable Crane, during the remaining four years as debt and death closed in upon him.

V

'ANY SORT OF STUFF THAT WOULD SELL'

FROM 1896 until his death Crane's life was lived on the run. In September, against the advice of everyone, he testified on behalf of Dora Clark who had been accused of soliciting while in his company; and the New York journalists, who did not understand *The Black Riders* as well as they did the police and the public's inability to discern reality from sensationalism, were amazed to be 'confronted with a man who said that his honor dictated a most unpractical course of action and who really meant what he said'.[1] By November an aroused police department had made New York entirely too hot for him, and Crane left for Florida and a fling at gun-running into Cuba. He met Cora Taylor, proprietress of the Hotel de Dream in Jacksonville; but he did not get to Cuba because the *Commodore* sank beneath him on New Year's Day. In March he sailed from New York to report the Graeco-Turkish War for the New York *Journal* and the Westminster *Gazette*, and was in Greece until June. Then he and Cora, who had followed him abroad from Florida, returned to England and lived as man and wife at Ravensbrook, Oxted, Surrey. By April 1898, having had enough of debts, social parasites, and—one suspects—of Cora, he left for New York and the Spanish-American War, and did not return until January 1899. Crane and Cora moved to Brede Place, Sussex, in February; and 'at the end of a heartbreaking struggle of eighteen months to reduce his thousand-dollar debt by writing too much, he expired, owing five thousand dollars'.[2] Crane was twenty-eight when he died from

---

[1] Fryckstedt, 'Crane in the Tenderloin', p. 147.

[2] A. J. Liebling, 'The Dollars Damned Him', *New Yorker*, XXXVII (5 Aug. 1961), 50. 'Two audits were required to establish that he had been in debt for over £905 and that Cora would be without further support' (Joseph Katz, 'Cora

tuberculosis at Badenweiler in Germany on 5 June 1900.

The conditions under which Crane laboured during these last four years are of some importance because he produced a lot of second-rate work; a man doubly trapped as he was has to have money, and pieces such as the Whilomville tales, even *Great Battles of the World*, 'sold readily and earned twice the rate of his best, most painstaking fiction'.[3] One trap was his health; Crane knew what was wrong with him, probably before he left New York for Greece.[4] The other trap, this one of his own making, closed when he accepted Cora. Her letters reveal a good woman who gave herself whole-heartedly to Crane, suffered with him faithfully to the end, and assumed the crushing burden of making funeral arrangements on begged or borrowed money—burial was at Hillside, New Jersey—and ordering an impossible estate; but they also imply a sentimental woman whose taste and approach to life differed violently from Crane's, and who seems to have been almost as careless with money as Crane himself was. The Spanish-American War offered the possibility of escape from both traps, and Crane's conduct in Cuba—both in the violence of his exertion and his blatant courting of enemy fire—suggests a deliberate attempt to free himself. When he found himself still alive at the war's end he disappeared in Havana; and, although he soon surfaced, it was nearly four months before he could bring himself to return to Cora and the mess—social and financial—awaiting him in England. His hesitation, like his last letters, clearly implies the immense cost of this particular act of personal honesty. Hence, 'if there is an authentic mystery in the legend of the later Crane,

---

Crane and the Poetry of Stephen Crane', *Papers of the Bibliographical Society of America*, LVIII [1964], 470). A brief chronology of Crane's life is provided by T. A. Gullason, ed., *The Complete Novels of Stephen Crane* (Garden City, 1967), pp. 793–6.

[3] James B. Stronks, 'Stephen Crane's English Years: The Legend Corrected', *Papers of the Bibliographical Society of America*, LVII (1963), 347. Stronks finds that *Harper's* paid 5¼ cents per word for the *Whilomville Stories* while 'The Bride Comes to Yellow Sky', 'The Open Boat', 'The Blue Hotel', and 'The Monster' earned an 'average of only 2.7 cents per word'—at a time when Kipling occasionally received 23 cents per word.

[4] See Helen R. Crane, 'My Uncle, Stephen Crane', p. 28; *Letters*, p. 184.

it is that, in his sweating desperation to stave off bankruptcy . . . he occasionally managed to write incomparably well'.[5] However, a brief look at his second-rate work, both for what it contains and what is missing from it, will dispel part of even this mystery.

Crane's most conspicuous failure seems to be his first try at the conventional novel which he assessed correctly as 'pretty rotten work' (*Letters*, p. 87). Although his sketches prove that by 1896 he could handle the sentimental mode in short pieces, *The Third Violet* (1897) shows that he could not sustain it even to the length of a short novel. Several worthwhile themes lurk hidden beneath the banality: there is the autobiographical interest best described by Follett (*Work*, III, xvii–xxi); Hawker and Hollanden embody respectively the typical points of view introduced with the little man and the quiet man of the Sullivan County tales (except that Hollanden is never quiet); Crane probably voices his own fear in Hollanden's decline from a 'prophet' to a 'trained bear of the magazines' (Howells's phrase) through economic necessity; and he satirizes the urge to run all over the world in search of fit subjects for one's art. Perhaps the most important of these thematic possibilities is the social clash between Hawker (penniless, rural, an artist) and Miss Fanhall (wealthy, urban, a socialite) who are both opposed to the middle-aged female voices of arrogance who rule the porch at Hemlock Inn, a motif which at once recalls Crane's sixth letter to Nellie Crouse and edges toward his usual concern with the distinctions between illusion and reality. But none of these ideas survives the tedium of the main characters— Hawker, who is mildly a snob and wholly an oaf, and Miss Fanhall, who would be at home in one of Steele's sentimental comedies. Also, the tone of Crane's prose telegraphs the failure before one has read a dozen pages. Irony has been abandoned along with

---

[5] Stronks, p. 349. For Crane's exertion in Cuba, see Beer, *Crane*, pp. 195–206, and Richard Harding Davis, 'Our War Correspondents in Cuba and Puerto Rico', *Harper's*, XCVIII (May 1899), 941, 947; for his suicidal exposure to fire, see Davis, p. 942; concerning his disappearance in Havana, see Edwin H. Cady, *Stephen Crane* (New York, 1962), pp. 62–7. A good account of the whole Cuban episode is given by Stallman, *Crane*, pp. 350–421.

Crane's austere detachment from his characters, and the tight control evident in the best sentimental sketches such as 'Mr. Binks' Day Off' is not present to compensate. Crane's temporary artistic exhaustion is implied by his dumping wholesale into the novel at chapter 19 portions of an earlier sketch, 'Stories Told by an Artist', and by the striking resemblance of the 'awf'ly clever' dialogue to that of *The Light that Failed*: Hawker and Hollanden mimic Dick Heldar and Torpenhow, and Grief's harangue about foreign art subjects is close kin to Heldar's harangue about 'His Last Shot'.[6] Crane, in short, revived his 'clever Rudyard-Kipling style' to float *The Third Violet* on the backwash of the creative surge that had produced *The Red Badge*, *George's Mother*, and *The Black Riders*.

Active Service (1899), Crane's second attempt, is a much longer novel which in spite of its faults is still readable. The plot is conventional romanticism; Professor Wainwright is the gruff father complete with soft heart, his wife is absurd; Carl Van Doren found Nora undismayed by 'snubs which would batter an ordinary woman into a pulp'; and Marjory is incomprehensible to everyone including the author. Yet Crane the craftsman is once more in fair control of pace and tone: once past Marjory's initial encounters with her father and Coleman the canter through an unfailing series of external adventures falters only when Marjory and Coleman are forced to play an occasional scene alone; and the tone, because Coleman is *presented* as partly a blockhead instead of merely being one, like Hawker, is light and relaxed. Coleman continually conceives romantic notions of himself and what he will accomplish—much like Fleming during the farewell scene with his mother—and these illusions are continually deflated either by circumstance or by Coleman's own blunders. Such a presentation of the protagonist occasionally allows Crane to sketch the outline of the psychological pattern found in his better work. Coleman, for example, has a paralysing fear of Nora's urge and ability to defeat his campaign for Marjory; yet when he finally tells Nora in public that she has no claim upon him, after worrying

[6] See *Work*, III, 220–1; *The Light that Failed*, ch. 4.

himself to desperation, Nora simply collapses. The hero's reaction should sound familiar:

Coleman found himself wondering why he had not gone flatly at the great question at a much earlier period, indeed at the first moment when the great question began to make life exciting for him. He thought that if he had charged Nora's guns in the beginning they would have turned out to be the same incapable artillery. Instead of that he had run away and continued to run away until he was actually cornered and made to fight, and his easy victory had defined him as a person who had, earlier, indulged in much stupidity and cowardice. (*Work*, IV, 242)

Thus, Crane's irony and the stylistic energy which it generates are not entirely banished from this novel. As the above passage suggests, however, this energy is not concentrated into the intense metaphor and implication of his best work, but deliberately spun out to more or less overt statement; the result is that Crane's irony, as in several of the New York sketches, relaxes to a wry humour. *Active Service* is by no means vintage Crane, but it is a long step in the right direction away from *The Third Violet*.[7]

Crane's final attempt, *The O'Ruddy* (1903, completed by Robert Barr), is to *Active Service* roughly as *Active Service* is to *The Third Violet*: the prose moves well beyond explicit statement to achieve garrulity, and the tone further lightens from humour to burlesque. As a result, *The O'Ruddy* gallops along with all the admitted absurdity of a costume-piece in which almost no attention is paid to costume, and the most puzzling thing about it is Crane's ability to turn out such gay and apparently effortless froth while dying amidst the howls of his creditors. O'Ruddy is Crane's real aristocrat in the role of a *picaro*, whose adventures begin with an abrupt lurch—his past history is given and he is on the road by the second page—and thereafter bounce merrily from episode to episode as he blunders his way to marriage with Lady Mary,

---

[7] For further comment, see Carl Van Doren, 'Introduction,' *Work*, IV, x, xii–xiv; T. A. Gullason, 'Stephen Crane's Private War Against Yellow Journalism,' *Huntington Library Quarterly*, XXII (May 1959), 203–4; Gullason, 'The Jamesian Motif in Stephen Crane's last Novels', *Personalist*, LXII (January 1961), 80–2.

another such aristocrat in her own right. Crane's typical pre-occupations are revealed by the kind of encounters his hero faces: O'Ruddy regularly has to penetrate beneath various façades—the fierceness of Jem Bottles as highwayman, the terrible fencing skill of Forister, the respectability of Dr. Chord, the wit of Fullbil, servants dressed as their masters and exhibiting better manners, the nobility of the Earl of Westport and his monstrous wife—and perceive such moral realities as vanity, pretence, cowardice, hypocrisy, selfishness, innocence. There is also some social criticism which, like O'Ruddy's comments upon the absurdities of romantic stories, is usually given in the hero's comic asides and not taken very seriously. Above all there is a great deal of fun as the novel careens hilariously into a parody of the very clichés its hero has just sense enough to reject. The Crane who wrote *The O'Ruddy* is the man who years earlier had written 'At Clancy's Wake' for *Truth*; in both pieces the pressure of irony is diffused to the point of harmlessness, and the author seems genuinely free to laugh with his characters as he creates them.[8]

An awareness of the psychological pattern recurring in the important work implies the principal artistic reason behind the writing of these three novels: it reflects Crane's need to achieve a longer form not structurally dependent upon this pattern which is better suited to the short story. Although *The Third Violet* seems to represent a false start, it should be noted that, once Coleman decides to leave New York, *Active Service* becomes Crane's first novel of the road and its hero also casts the shadow of the literary rogue: he is the most sophisticated character and is able and willing to manipulate those around him, he uses his power and position to aid his progress towards a personal goal, he seizes whatever opportunity circumstance offers and allows chance events to be interpreted to his credit, he keeps an eye out for his own physical comforts, and he even has the ability to influence others

---

[8] See also Gullason, 'Jamesian Motif', pp. 82–4. Crane's work probably stops with chapter 25; see Beer, *Work*, VII, Introduction, p. xi; *Letters*, p. 266; Bernard O'Donnell, 'An Analysis of Prose Style to Determine Authorship: *The O'Ruddy*, a Novel by Stephen Crane and Robert Barr', unpublished Ed.D. thesis (Harvard, 1963).

with an assumed appearance of innocence. Hence, the last two novels suggest that a successful long form new to Crane could have been the picaresque with a likeable, blundering *picaro*, an absolute minimum of sentimental love scenes to slow the pace, a firm ballast of colour and suspense in external incident, and powered by two dependable Crane strengths—his humour and his craftsmanship. Either *Active Service* or *The O'Ruddy* could have become this novel—not memorable literature, but thoroughly enjoyable light comedy, finished, good of its kind—if Crane could have taken time to edit and polish it carefully; but what time he had was spent writing in the form he handled better.

At least three of the six stories in *The Little Regiment* (1896) provide a kind of subject index to much of Crane's less distinguished work thereafter. He was in a comic predicament when he published this collection: he had become famous for a 'war' story and the publishers were clamouring for more, yet he knew no more about war in 1896 than he had when he created Henry Fleming. Crane obliged, of course, with six stories which are no more about war than *The Red Badge* is. 'A Mystery of Heroism', in which the significant action occurs within the mind of the 'hero', is first-rate Crane. 'The Veteran', an unnecessary epilogue asserting that Fleming grew from a scared youth to manhood during the battle of Chancellorsville, would be a mere series of events without little Jim, who is 'visibly horror-stricken' when his 'most magnificent grandfather' admits he ran from battle; little Jim's hero reveals his selfless courage when he dies in a futile attempt to save his colts from a burning barn, but this story does not even use war as a setting. Nor does 'An Indiana Campaign', which deserves to be called an excellent Sullivan County sketch. Old Tom Boldin (and to a lesser extent Peter Witheby) is Crane's little protagonist faced with the unknown—supposedly a rebel hiding in the woods—and he has to confront it because, with the able-bodied men away at war, he is the head of the townspeople. His fear is implied by his illusions: 'The field of corn . . . was a darkly mystic place whose recesses could contain all manner of dangers. . . . Above the tops of the corn loomed the distant foliage of Smith's woods, curtaining the silent action of a tragedy whose horrors they imagined' (*Work*, II, 116). And Boldin's mind compensates by conceiving an illusory 'dream of triumph' to keep his feet advancing. When the unknown is experienced—'ol' Milt' Jacoby', the town drunkard—the situation collapses and the story ends. Unlike 'A Ghoul's Accountant', however, this story never cheats the reader; the reality is never represented as more than it actually is, and both terror and day-dream are entirely products of Boldin's weak mental machinery. By making the frightened townspeople wait together at the edge of the cornfield, Crane for the first time forced a whole town into the position of the protagonist, a feat he was soon to repeat more significantly in 'The Monster'. And his means of resolution, a simple collapse in which nothing happens, recalls 'Horses—One Dash' (late 1895) and anticipates 'The Five White Mice' (1898).[9] The remaining three stories, however, are more relevant to his later work.

'A Grey Sleeve' is a suspense story masquerading as a romantic meeting between Union officer and Confederate belle, and Crane studiously avoids their confrontation as lovers until the end— even then brief and hurried because the officer has to ride after his departed company. The suspense is well managed as the reader gradually learns what is in the house, what the girl holds behind her back, who is upstairs, whether the corporal really saw the sleeve, how the captain will resolve the situation. Crane's one trump is lightly drawn upon when the troopers approaching the house hesitate: 'There was some subtle suggestion—some tale of an unknown thing—which watched them from they knew not which part of it. . . . At last the captain swore and said: "We are certainly a pack of fools" ' (*Work*, II, 131). Also, this officer is an authentic Crane hero: when the girl's brother calls him a liar he

---

[9] Both stories concern merely the appearance of a moral reality, courage, a pretence which saves the protagonists from death. Both are structurally broken in the middle: 'Horses' ends in an artistically inconsequential chase, and the sluggish first part of 'Mice' entails an awkward shift in tone to the tense confrontation in the second part. Rage as the protagonist's reaction was explored in 'The Cry of a Huckleberry Pudding'. The kind of resolution these tales feature is best used in 'The Bride Comes to Yellow Sky'.

quietly continues attending to business. 'Three Miraculous Soldiers' is a still better story of the same type, an excellent tale of hare and hounds told from the third-person limited point of view within the mind of the heroine. She is one of Crane's more believable female characters because, until the final page, she functions only as an intelligence facing an unknown situation. The pattern of fear, illusion, and deflating experience occurs superficially when she believes someone is hiding in her kitchen (*Work*, II, 61–2); like Fleming she endows the external world with her own emotions; and she day-dreams of acting like a romantic heroine, although all she can do at the crisis is watch the action through a knot-hole. But Crane here uses his pattern only to create suspense in an unflagging tale of external event which is expertly spun out to its maximum length. Hence, these two stories seem to be the first examples of the conventional adventure-suspense yarn that Crane was often to spin, usually with ironic humour, usually with finished craftsmanship: 'Flanagan and His Short Filibustering Adventure' (1897), 'God Rest Ye, Merry Gentlemen' (1899), 'The Lone Charge of William B. Perkins' (1899), 'The Sergeant's Private Madhouse' (1899), 'The Revenge of the *Adolphus*' (1899), 'His Majestic Lie' (1900).[10] Crane does not have enough to say in these stories to make them important, yet all are well written and provide good reading.

'The Little Regiment' introduces a theme which informs an important group of stories that miss greatness because Crane has too much to say in them; he becomes so emotionally aroused by their subject that he loses his artistic detachment, and the prose becomes implicit propaganda seasoned with explicit preaching. This theme is the brotherhood existing among men who are thrown into the cauldron of war; and 'The Little Regiment' is the least of these stories partly because of a slick tone that wavers toward sentimentality, partly because the protagonists actually are brothers and the literal relationship obscures the more important one, but primarily because the remaining stories in this group— 'The Price of the Harness' (1898), 'Virtue in War' (1899), 'The

---

[10] All except 'Flanagan' were included in *Wounds in the Rain* (1900).

Second Generation' (1899), and 'The Clan of No-Name' (1900)[11]
—were all written after Crane had experienced war for himself.
The Dempster brothers are veterans who accept their insignificance and expertly do their work without fear or illusions of glory,
and their deep feeling for each other is masked by profanity, a
bantering contempt, and indifference in their outward behaviour.
All these attributes reappear more significantly in the later stories
because, while the men of the little regiment have to fight only the
opposing army, after Crane's own experience of war his heroes
have to cope with two enemies and put up with an aggravating
nuisance while they are doing it: the nuisance is the innocent, the
untrained and unaware volunteer whose military uselessness
aggravates because he continually gets in the way when work has
to be done; the two enemies are the literal foe in the field and the
more unconquerable moral foe of infamy in those personally
dishonest people on their own side who, both at the front and safe
at home, have wormed themselves into responsible positions.
These poltroons, as Crane calls them,[12] who create 'the miserable mismanagement and corruption of the army command, the
inadequate supplies and inedible food sent to the front, the political
interference with soldierly conduct of the war',[13] remain
poltroons even when, like Caspar Cadogan of 'The Second
Generation', they are commissioned officers; and hence they simply
'are no damn good'. The brotherhood theme develops logically
as the moral answer to this moral foe; it becomes increasingly
identified as the hallmark of a class of men, the Regulars—a title
which Crane invests with moral value, and which immediately
distinguishes the real soldiers from the innocent fools in the
volunteer regiments—who oppose both the poltroons' infamy and
the innocents' uselessness with the professional soldier's code of
competence and duty.

    In 'The Price of the Harness' Crane, observing from a point
outside the story, offers propaganda in favour of his Regulars, but

---

[11] All four included in *Wounds in the Rain*.
[12] *Poems*, P 127, p. 140.
[13] Hoffman, *Poetry*, p. 157.

there is little overt preaching, possibly because the moral foe is mentioned only once: a young lieutenant is called the heir to 'those traditions of fidelity and courage which have been handed to him from generation to generation, and which he has tenaciously preserved despite the persecution of legislators and the indifference of his country' (*Work*, IX, 25). The Regular's code of conduct, set forth in the actions and attitudes of Nolan, Grierson, Watkins, and Martin—men who accept their position in the regiment and do their jobs—arises as a consequence of their situation in the midst of a shooting war. This code includes a competent professionalism, the practical ability to do efficiently whatever the situation requires; a stoic endurance of whatever suffering the situation may bring; an unquestioning obedience as duty to those whose duty it is to command; and selfless identification with one's brothers so that the regiment can function in combat as a unit. The resulting brotherhood, an essential element of the Regular's code and never self-conscious or acknowledged overtly, is the mutual recognition and respect that exist among real professionals working together against a common antagonist. No one can force a man to assume this code of conduct. Each Regular practises it for the sake of himself and his fellow men faced with the same danger. Hence, this story contains probably Crane's most explicit statement about the source of moral values in his world: the young lieutenant 'raises his illumined face toward his purpose . . . his sky of the ideal of duty; and the wonderful part of it is, that he is guided by an ideal which he has himself created, and has alone protected from attack' (*Work*, IX, 25–6). This code is the real harness the Regular wears, an implicit moral uniform; in a world full of poltroons, and innocents unable to discern a poltroon from a Regular, it is an honour to wear it. Crane was extremely angry when an editor changed the title (*Letters*, p. 193).

The poltroons have a greater role in 'The Clan of No-Name' and, although this story is the best of the lot, Crane's disgust is proportionally more obvious. Mister Smith, the Spanish officers and men, and Margharita's 'fat and commercially excited' mother are made contemptible; Margharita is implicitly scorned, in the

final section, for giving herself to Mister Smith after Manolo
Prat's death; but Manolo, Rodriguez, Bas, and the Cuban *practicos*
are heroic. The heroes belong to the nameless clan identified only
by the soldier's code of conduct; the others do not belong, nor are
they capable of understanding the 'mystic tie' which binds the
clan together. Manolo is as young and untried as Fleming, but
when he assumes his officer's uniform he also assumes the moral
harness it implies. He runs to join men in a trap—militarily a useless action—not because he wants to, but simply because 'there
was a standard, and he must follow it, obey it'. This moral code
is thus shown to be at once greater than the individual who creates
it:

He knew that he was thrusting himself into a trap whose door, once
closed, opened only when the black hand knocked; and every part of
him seemed to be in panic-stricken revolt. But . . . the men of his
kind . . . *were governed by their gods*, and each man knew the law and
yet could not give tongue to it, but it was the law; and if the spirits of
the men of his kind were all sitting in critical judgment upon him even
then in the sky, he could not have bettered his conduct. (*Work*, II,
167; italics mine.)

Hence, Manolo dies with 'the approval and the benediction of his
brethren'; and neither the military futility of his death, the innocence or poltroonery of the others, the irony of Mister Smith's
'winning' Margharita to the implicit satisfaction of her mother, nor
the 'victory' of the Spanish troops in any way affects either his
moral princeliness or the code of conduct he dies to uphold.

'Virtue in War' and 'The Second Generation' are lesser stories,
artistically, because Crane lashes the poltroons and the innocents
with open contempt. His most effective means of assault lies in
defining and exploiting the great moral gulf which separates the
Regulars, such as Major Gates, from both the innocent, Lige
Wigram, and the poltroon, Caspar Cadogan. The innocent may or
may not prove teachable, but the poltroon is hopeless. Both
stories hammer away at the same point—that 'virtue' in war *is* the
thorough knowledge, acceptance, and expert practice of the
Regular's moral harness; those who fail to uphold this code are not

virtuous in combat because they add unnecessarily to the suffering and death the Regulars have to endure. The brotherhood theme in both stories is implicit in the Regular's instant recognition of his own kind and his refusal to have anything to do with those who will never be of his own kind. Even the poltroons sense this moral separation: as Caspar Cadogan tells his father, 'the other men, you know. I couldn't get along with them, you know. They're peculiar, somehow; odd; I didn't understand them ... didn't hitch, somehow. They're a queer lot. They've got funny ideas.' Their brotherhood is thus part of the code itself, inseparable from it in the same way as the power of awareness in a Crane character is inseparable from an ungrieved conscience. Hence, the Regular is another authentic Crane hero who stands against mountains both physical and moral: 'the best man standing on two feet on God's green earth'.[14]

Crane's handling of the Regular's code in these stories duplicates important aspects of his presentation of the moral code set forth in the poems. The outstanding clue to this analogy was noticed by Hoffman when he pointed out that the fourth line of the poetic riddle prefixed to 'The Clan of No-Name' does not correspond physically to anything in the tale itself: 'There is no sea in the story: "The hard waves" that "see an arm flung high" are those around the open boat, the waves closing over the man adrift on a slim spar' (*Poetry*, pp. 153–4). The sea is always Crane's favourite emblem of the amoral universe; and man's situation in the midst of this godless externality is the philosophical basis for the moral code of the poems just as man's situation in the midst of a shooting war is the basis for the Regular's code of conduct. In both poems and stories there are three general classes of characters: the personally dishonest men who have met their death in the enchanted forest become the poltroons; the drones of the huddled procession who never enter the forest become the innocent volunteers; and the good men who successfully negotiate the forest become the Regulars. The poltroons, like their dishonest counterparts of the poems, are primarily self-seeking; the innocents and

[14] 'Regulars Get No Glory', New York *World*, 20 July 1898, p. 6.

the drones of the procession are primarily unaware; and the good man in the amoral universe, like the Regular at war, *because* of his awareness of the reality surrounding him, is committed to brotherhood, to a life of action in a continuous present, and to a stoic endurance of whatever hardship may befall him in fulfilling his duty as he understands it.[15] The Regular, like his brother of the poems, gets no glory; and like Major Gates, he may be killed where the innocent and the poltroon escape without a scratch; nevertheless, he is of the kind who are 'governed by their gods' of their inner thoughts, and who therefore share that brotherhood which 'The Open Boat' defines as 'the best experience' of life, the silent recognition, respect, and—if need be—benediction of their kind. None of these five stories is artistically important, but together they are important to those who would understand Crane.

Another subject index like *The Little Regiment* is provided by a letter Crane wrote to his agent early in 1899: 'My short stories are developing in three series. I. The Whilomville stories. (always to Harpers.)/II. The war tales./III. Tales of western American life similar to "Twelve O'Clock." '[16] This listing concerns the stories produced during the last frantic year and a half after Crane's return from the Spanish-American War.

The fourteen Whilomville tales are best considered 'obviously

[15] The good man, poltroon, and innocent reappear in a piece published on 24 February 1895. Another authentic Crane hero, L. P. Ludden, was 'the secretary and general manager of the commission' administering relief to the drought area of Nebraska in the winter of 1894–5: 'he is the most unpopular man in the State of Nebraska. He is honest, conscientious and loyal; he is hardworking and has great executive ability. He struggles heroically with the thugs who wish to filch supplies, and with the virtuous but misguided philanthropists who write to learn of the folks that received their fifty cents and who expect a full record of this event' ('Waiting for the Spring', *Prairie Schooner*, XXXVIII [Spring 1964], 21).

[16] *Letters*, p. 214. The first Whilomville tale, 'His New Mittens', went to *McClure's Magazine*; the other thirteen went to *Harper's*. The war tales are those collected in *Wounds in the Rain* after magazine publication. All eleven in the original collection have been mentioned except 'Marines Signalling Under Fire at Guantanamo', a reprinted article, and 'War Memories', examined below. For comment on the collection, see Gullason, 'The Significance of "Wounds in the Rain" ', *Modern Fiction Studies*, V (Autumn 1959), 235–42. Crane's only remaining second-rate war tales are the brief 'Rudyard-Kipling style' first three episodes of 'The Kicking Twelfth'.

minor, but uncontestably honest and clear-sighted' (Jumper, p. 249). Written at top speed under the mounting pressure of debt, they are remarkable for their consistently high level of craftsmanship, for excellent dialogue and humour, and for Crane's absolutely unsentimentalized view of children as amoral, selfish, mean, vain, loud-mouthed, cowardly, fickle, infinitely romantic, and given to brutal mob action—an immensely appealing pack of miniature wolves. The fact that such qualities are precisely the ones Crane always damns in adults implies the principal contribution these stories offer to an understanding of his mind. He obviously holds adults morally responsible for 'seeing', by the time they reach adulthood, that their indulgence of such weaknesses is personally dishonest; but Crane's children are never held responsible to their own personal honesty. They are still at the age when awareness is free. Moral responsibility does not come at birth, with one's own pair of eyes; a child is given a certain amount of time to develop his awareness. Eventually, however, no matter what the extent of his awareness, he is held fully responsible for whatever action he undertakes. Maggie, Fleming, George Kelcey are all caught at roughly that period in life when this moral axe falls; none is entirely ready for the moral responsibility thrust upon him, yet Maggie unknowingly assumes it when she chooses Pete, Henry also assumes it unknowingly when he decides to enlist, and George—having chosen to work and support his mother and himself—is saddled with it when his story begins. Each progresses through painful experience to an awareness of the real significance of the moral responsibility he has innocently accepted.

Crane's children, however, in Whilomville as in the Bowery, are not held responsible for seeing the reality which confronts them. Thus, the child's word is one of illusion, and its only boundaries are *physical* limitations such as fatigue, hunger, chance—as when Jimmie Trescott throws a stone at Peter Washington and breaks the carriage lamps—, parental authority, and superior force. Structurally, Crane usually starts a story moving towards the fulfilment of any desire at all, and the movement continues until it runs into one of the physical limits of the child's illusory world.

The result is warm humour because the adult reader soon senses
that illusion and reality have been aligned into a collision course,
and he happily anticipates the result (as in 'The Angel Child', 'The
Lover and the Telltale', 'The Stove'), or he is amused at the *non
sequitur* with which the childish mind seeks to cope with the
result ('Lynx-Hunting', 'The Knife', 'The Fight', 'The City
Urchin and the Chaste Villagers'). The reader rarely gets a direct
flick of the lash. In 'A Little Pilgrimage' Crane is unable to resist
calling a disgusting character 'an ideal Sunday-school superinten-
dent—one who had never felt hunger or thirst or the wound of the
challenge of dishonour; a man, indeed, with beautiful fat hands
who waved them in greasy victorious beneficence over a crowd of
children' (*Work*, V, 186); and 'Making an Orator' flails at the
futility of forcing children to recite memorized pieces. The
artistic touch which consistently distinguishes these tales is
Crane's refusal to make light of the child's values and desires when
they are considered from the child's own point of view; in 'Shame',
for example, when Jimmie is ostracized for bringing his lunch to
the picnic in a tin pail no character in all Crane's fiction is more
desolate than he is. But Whilomville and its adult population
brought Crane to the intensity of his best work only once (as will
be seen)—in 'The Monster'.

Two of Crane's eight 'tales of western American life' are major
stories, three others—'Horses—One Dash', 'The Wise Men', and
'The Five White Mice'—have been mentioned above, and the
best of the three remaining is 'A Man and—Some Others' (1897).
Bill, the sheep-herder protagonist, morally battered by a long life
of extremely questionable motivation, dies in a brave stand against
eight Mexicans who want him off the range. Bill ends as a man
because he does not act during his last fight as he had acted, for
example, during his fight with the three sailors in a Bowery
saloon. In the saloon Bill is Crane's typical swaggering bully who
this time gets what he deserves, but the gun-battle is forced upon
him—he must either fight or yield his right to the common range,
and thus he is confronted with the 'wound of the challenge of dishonour'. His manner of response implies Crane's admiration: he

'gloomily' sees 'nothin'' else to do' except fight an unjust attack, and he quietly tells the stranger what is about to happen and advises him to ride on and stay out of it. The fact that Bill dies because his own foolish pride leads him to mismanage the fight does not diminish the manhood of the stand he makes; and the stranger recognizes that 'the dignity of last defeat, the superiority of him who stands in his grave, was in the pose of the lost sheepherder' (*Work*, XII, 83). This story has one serious violation of tone—a comic purple passage describing what the Mexicans load into their shotguns. An early passage, however, makes an essential point about all Crane's Western tales:

'Well, why in the name of wonder don't you go get the sheriff?' cried the stranger.
'Oh, hell!' said Bill. (p. 75)

Even if a sheriff were available in the superlative vacancy of the plains the challenge would still be ultimately to the honour of the individual, and Bill is aware of it. The West in Crane's work, like war, like the sea, merely provides the setting in which men have to be aware or unaware, personally honest or dishonest, just as in New York.

Critics agree that 'Twelve O'Clock' (1899) and 'Moonlight on the Snow' (1900), the last and least of the lot, seem to be parodies of Bret Harte. If 'Twelve O'Clock' has a point beyond the grotesquerie of its ending it has to be the familiar one that violence, suffering, and death are stupidly gratuitous when they result merely from human weakness. The cowboys are drunk; Jake is naïve and quick to anger; Placer is surly; Big Watson is drunk and quarrelsome; and after the first killing the citizens who wish to stop violence in the town shoot an innocent cowboy as he rides away. The cuckoo declaiming over the corpses provides comment —grotesque, contrived, but still appropriate—upon this whole array of multiple human failure leading to needless death. 'Moonlight on the Snow' is rather more interesting because Crane lays greater stress upon motivation. The town of Warpost suddenly resolves to reform, not for the sake of being good, but to attract money from real-estate speculators. When the gambler kills a man under justifiable circumstances the town wants to hang him, not for the sake of justice, but to 'sell real estate'; and the gambler mocks this hypocrisy until the whole town is glad to see him arrested for mere grand larceny. The story also provides a gloss on 'The Bride Comes to Yellow Sky' by showing Potter and Wilson working together for the law as sheriff and deputy.

This hasty survey of some thirty-five short stories[17] and three novels should show that there was no deterioration of Crane's talent—a defence which is largely unnecessary because 'The Upturned Face' was written only about six months before his death. Most of these tales were written frankly for immediate cash, and editors generally got their money's worth in the craftsmanship of simply good story-telling. More important, however, the work examined here is distinguished by the absence of Crane's psychological pattern. When it is present, as in 'An Indiana Campaign' and to a lesser extent in 'Three Miraculous Soldiers' and *Active Service*, Crane uses it as a conventional plot device to evoke suspense in a series of adventurous events, not as an instrument for probing the mind suffering under stress. Without his pattern, these stories lack the intensity of his better work; the prose is more conventionally relaxed, the irony tends toward humour (unless Crane is angry, as in 'Virtue in War'), and the metaphorical language gives way in the direction of explicit statement; these stories, in short, generally do not imply a hidden freight of truth lurking beneath the surface of what is said. Crane still exploits the distinctions between illusion and reality, and usually his characters in these stories—Tom Larpent, Caspar Cadogan, Lige Wigram,

---

[17] Four other tales deserve brief mention. The three Wyoming Valley stories, 'The Battle of Forty Fort', 'The Surrender of Forty Fort', and 'Ol' Bennet and the Indians', written in the Fall of 1899 (*Letters*, p. 232), resulted from Crane's plans for a novel of the revolutionary war which he did not live to write. They are excellent adventure stories which leave no doubt of their precise historical setting. See D. G. Hoffman, 'Stephen Crane's Last Novel', *Bulletin of the New York Public Library*, LXIV (June 1960), 337–43. 'An Illusion in Red and White' (published May 1900) concerns a murderer's planting indelible illusions in the minds of his children by associating these illusions with the murder of the mother which the children witnessed.

Manolo Part, Little Nell, Coleman, O'Ruddy, Tom Boldin, the Regulars—succeed in proportion to their capacity to make such distinctions; but, again, the result is essentially a well-told tale of action and external event. The conspicuous absence of Crane's established pattern from this second-rate work implies that, as he confessed to Willa Cather, he still needed his one trump as the conceptual basis for his greatest stories.

VI

'THE MATTER THAT PLEASED HIMSELF'

D**URING** the latter half of his writing life Crane produced eight major stories and one excellent sketch. These, in the probable order of their composition, are 'A Mystery of Heroism', 'The Open Boat', 'The Monster', 'The Bride Comes to Yellow Sky', 'Death and the Child', 'The Blue Hotel', 'War Memories', 'An Episode of War', and 'The Upturned Face'. Upon these works Crane lavished artistic care, and wrote, incomparably well, the matter that pleased himself.

'A Mystery of Heroism' (published August 1895) shows young Fred Collins, in the midst of one of Crane's excellent imaginary battle scenes, making an unnecessary journey across a shell-torn meadow for water. This incredible dash is sheer stupidity: his colonel—who significantly calls him a 'lad'—asks him, 'Don't you think that's taking pretty big risks for a little drink of water?', and the men of his regiment comment, 'We ain't dyin' of thirst, are we? That's foolishness' (*Work*, II, 100–1). Collins goes for exactly the same reason that the little man climbs the 'holler tree', that little Horace Glenn in 'Showin' Off' rides his velocipede over a six-foot bank: he makes an idle boast, his comrades jeer at him, and stung by their taunts his boy's pride rules his intelligence. Crane says as much when, the moment Collins leaves the regiment, his physical situation is used to dramatize his moral isolation—through vanity—from his fellows with more common sense:

When Collins faced the meadow and walked away from the regiment, he was vaguely conscious that a chasm, the deep valley of all prides, was suddenly between him and his comrades. It was provisional, but the provision was that he return as a victor. He had blindly been led by quaint emotions, and laid himself under an obligation to walk squarely up to the face of death. (p. 102)

Hence, there is nothing really heroic about this stupid action.

What has occurred within Collins's mind implies a variation of Crane's psychological pattern: Collins, idly gazing at the well from across the meadow, conceives romantic notions of heroism, and these illusory clichés not only precede, but also bring about, the unknown experience which—because of his boast and his pride—he now has to undergo. Also, in this tale terror does not strike the protagonist until his progress through the unknown is halfway completed: Collins crosses to the well in a bemused trance, like Fleming's battle sleep, as his dazed mind gropes for 'the form and colour of this incident' which he believes can be considered 'dramatically great'. He wonders why he feels no fear in a situation which his clichés tell him should evoke fear, concludes that he is therefore a hero, and that 'after all, heroes were not much'. But then, after recalling shameful acts in his past and deciding he is not a hero because—again according to romantic tradition—'heroes had no shames in their lives', he ends by believing 'he was an intruder in the land of fine deeds', a conclusion which is correct even though his reasons for it are wrong. Collins is no hero, not because of past mistakes, not because he succumbs to romantic clichés, but because his action is without worthy motivation.

As often happens in Crane's stories, the protagonist (now at the well) is 'suddenly smitten with the terror' as he lies 'with his face turned away' from the source of danger. His face 'staring white with anticipation' of death, Collins starts comically back across the meadow: because 'in running with a filled bucket, a man can adopt but one kind of gait . . . Collins ran in the manner of a farmer chased out of a dairy by a bull' (p. 105). Crane's use of the comic at this point implies that he does not 'accept the simple Old Testament idea that the performance of a hazardous action in itself constitutes heroism. . . . Indeed, Crane consistently presents Collins as absurd in the main actions of his exploit.'[1]

In the meadow, however, Collins passes a dying officer who

---

[1] James W. Gargano, 'Crane's "A Mystery of Heroism": A Possible Source', *Modern Language Notes*, LXXIV (Jan. 1959), 23.

asks for a drink, and though at first he runs on, he stops and comes back to grant the dying man's request. This willed and selfless act of charity performed in extremely hazardous circumstances is genuinely heroic, and by contrast it implies the absurdity of the rest of Collins's action. This contrast is emphasized in the two welcomes Collins receives: the dying man contemplates him with 'the faintest shadow of a smile on his lips', but the regiment gives him 'a welcoming roar. The grimed faces were wrinkled in laughter' (p. 106). When two lieutenants start to drink from the bucket the usual deflation after the fact of experience is presented by implication: 'The bucket lay on the ground, empty.'

This ending is sufficiently ambiguous to have caused the belief that the 'skylarking lieutenants' spill the water (e.g. Jumper, p. 246), a reading which the text by no means requires; in view of both the story's structure and title this has to be an error. Collins having risked his life to no purpose to begin with, the emptiness of the bucket implies the emptiness of both his romantic notions of heroism and his whole exploit so far as the regiment is concerned and, more important, so far as Collins himself is concerned: Collins spilled the water *en route*, and thus he risked his life to bring back an empty bucket. Crane's pattern is now complete: Collins's illusions of heroism have been deflated by experience, his fear has been proved an unnecessary encumbrance because nothing happened to him; and the moral emptiness of his whole experience implies that Collins, if he is intelligent, will have learned from this incident to refrain henceforth from idle boasting, from allowing himself to become obliged through pride to walk squarely up to the face of death. But the significance of his heroic deed within this empty experience escapes both the regiment and Collins himself: the watching regiment considers it just one more exciting part of Collins's mad dash across the meadow; and Collins, because giving a man a drink of water will not fit his romantic images of heroism, because he is not motivated by the desire to be heroic but simply wishes to give the man a drink and leave as soon as possible, and because he is wholly intent upon reaching safety, attaches no significance to this incident. Hence the mystery promised in the title. This story implies a definition of heroism much the same as the definition of a good deed implied by the poems: neither the heroic act nor the good deed rings true when it is at all deliberately done so that one's vanity can in any way feed upon praise for the literal fact; both are authentic when done only for the sake of the action itself, when vanity is entirely absent. The mysterious authenticity of such selfless action is that phantom moral truth of goodness or heroism which will not yield even the hem of its garment to one's deliberate pursuit.

Crane students generally agree that 'The Open Boat' (published June 1897) is 'the crown of all his work', the one story which 'would, even if he had written nothing else, have placed him where he now undoubtedly stands', an 'impressionist masterpiece'.[2] Crane originally subtitled it a 'tale intended to be after the fact', and Ralph D. Paine claimed that soon after the sinking of the *Commodore* he heard Crane read parts of the first draft to Captain Ed Murphy in Jacksonville 'to get it right'.[3] The important parts of the story are indeed after the fact, not the fact itself, which Crane immediately dashed off for the newspapers in prose 'as lifeless as the "copy" of a police court reporter';[4] and nothing more clearly illustrates the essential insignificance of external fact in a Crane story than a comparison of 'The Open Boat' with his own news report of the disaster. Yet a sentence near the end of his report—'The history of life in an open boat for thirty hours would no doubt be instructive for the young, but none is to be told here and now'—indicates that Crane had already seized upon that part of his adventure which 'suited the purposes of his art, for "The Open Boat" begins precisely where the newspaper account ends. It is clear . . . that the writer made his selection almost immediately' (Colvert, 'Development', p. 243). The report conveys the

---

[2] See, respectively, Wells, 'English Standpoint', p. 237; Harold Frederic, 'Stephen Crane's New Book', New York *Times*, 1 May 1898, p. 19; Lang, p. 145. Mrs. Lang (p. 34) considers the four men in the open boat to be the ideal image of Crane's 'philosophy of life'.

[3] *Roads of Adventure* (Boston, 1922), p. 168.

[4] Cather, 'When I Knew Stephen Crane', p. 235. See 'Stephen Crane's Own Story', New York *Press*, 7 Jan. 1897, p. 1.

literal truth of the fact; Crane's structure imposed upon the fact in the work of art conveys the moral truth of the human experience; and the moral truth, in this story, becomes his 'most powerful statement of the "Crane world," and thus the most effective presentation of the stoic humanist theme' (Jumper, pp. 194–5).

The four men riding the waves in their ten-foot dinghy are obviously worried about capsizing and drowning at any moment because 'each froth-top was a problem in small-boat navigation'; and, as several readers have noted, Crane exploits this constant threat by alternating, for purposes of contrast, the point of view from within the boat with that of a detached—and unthreatened—observer: 'Viewed from a balcony, the whole thing would doubtless have been weirdly picturesque. But the men in the boat had no time to see it, and even if they had had leisure, there were other things to occupy their minds.' Even a careless reading will reveal that, beginning with the ninth brief paragraph of the second section, one of the principal thoughts occupying their minds centres on an unknown experience (unknown at least to the correspondent through whose mind the story is transmitted) which they all realize will soon have to be undergone: the extremely dangerous business of passing through the surf to reach land. Crane leaves no doubt that this coming experience is a main concern: the surf and its hazards are mentioned at least fifteen times before the boat swamps and the men enter into their unavoidable action. Given this focus for the thoughts of the men, the story acquires a strong sense of movement and progression even at the surface level of physical action: the men relax when they first near the shore, and they even light cigars in expectation of being rescued soon; but when no boat comes, their sense of security changes to renewed fear of the impossible surf, and they return to sea to spend a dismal night in comparative safety; then, in the morning, when they finally resolve to attempt the surf unaided, the tension mounts steadily—for the reader but not, as will be seen, for the men themselves—as they wait for their boat to sink beneath them. Earlier, however, they fear this coming experience, and they formulate certain thoughts which reassure them and thus brace them to undergo it. To emphasize both the thoughts themselves and their psychological function, Crane presents them in the form of an incantation:

If I am going to be drowned—if I am going to be drowned—if I am going to be drowned, why, in the name of the seven mad gods who rule the sea, was I allowed to come thus far and contemplate sand and trees? [This much of the incantation is given three times.] Was I brought here merely to have my nose dragged away as I was about to nibble the sacred cheese of life? It is preposterous. If this old ninny-woman, Fate, cannot do better than this, she should be deprived of the management of men's fortunes. . . . But no; she cannot mean to drown me. She dare not drown me. She cannot drown me. Not after all this work. (*Work*, XII, 41)

Then Crane immediately underscores the illusory nature of these thoughts by ending the paragraph with cutting irony: 'Afterward the man might have had an impulse to shake his fist at the clouds. "Just you drown me, now, and then hear what I call you!" ' Nevertheless, the incantation recurs to the men as they await the inevitable, and the same illusion is stated in another fashion: 'It was certainly an abominable injustice to drown a man who had worked so hard, so hard. The man felt it would be a crime most unnatural' (p. 51). Normally such notions are pierced and deflated by the climactic experience of the unknown.

In this story, however, Crane varies his pattern by making it set forth gradually the moral truth he wishes to communicate. The terrible night spent in the open boat prolongs their ordeal so long that awareness comes to the men *before* their encounter with the surf; this is the only Crane story in which both the protagonist's fears and illusions are dissipated, in which he attains the full awareness typical of the intelligent man after the fact of experience, before the feared unknown is undergone. The illusory notions cease about one-third of the way through section six when the protagonist 'knows the pathos of his situation', and he immediately recalls the soldier of the Legion dying in Algiers. He is fully aware of nature's indifference before the boat swamps, knows that his extremity is at 'the grave-edge', and 'it merely occurred to him that if he should drown it would be a shame'. When he is trapped in the current he thinks only 'I am going to drown? Can it be possible? Can it be possible?' And before the boat swamps, Crane explicitly states that the men have conquered their fear: 'The correspondent, observing the others, knew that they were not afraid. . . . There were no hurried words, no pallor, no plain agitation'; and the correspondent himself is so weary that he 'did not care'. When the men are finally dumped into the surf the injured captain clings to the overturned dinghy and is swept in to shore; the cook in his life preserver paddles himself in with one of the oars; the correspondent, also with part of a life preserver, has a comparatively easy task of swimming to shore after being trapped temporarily in a particular current; but the oiler, physically the best man of them all, is drowned at the last moment. The only response his death evokes in the others is implicitly a mature, calm acceptance: there are no 'shrill, seething sentences', no bursts of 'tupenny fury' at fate or external nature, nothing but the quiet acknowledgement that for the body of the oiler the land's welcome can only be the grave. Their comrade's death brings no great revelation to the others because they have already come to an awareness, before abandoning the boat, that a man can drown a few feet off shore as readily as any number of miles out at sea, that both his comparative fitness to survive and the amount of work he has done are irrelevant to this simple truth, and that man's moral realities of justice or injustice have no application whatsoever to external nature. The story ends with the famous line, 'they felt that they could then [i.e. after undergoing their whole experience, including their brother's death] be interpreters'.[5] However, because the subject of their interpretation is 'the great sea's voice' which the little shell tried to interpret to the pines, because they can now interpret to man his real role in the midst of amoral nature, Crane's variation of his psychological pattern causes this story to open outwards, as it were, to set forth the moral norm

[5] For the impact of this concluding sentence, see Morgan Blum, 'Berryman as Biographer, Stephen Crane as Poet', *Poetry*, LXXVIII (Aug. 1951), 303.

implied by the poems. Crane's world view and the stoic humanism it demands of man gradually emerge as the protagonist's fear and illusion give way to his deepening awareness of reality. And this protagonist is no untried youth to begin with. 'He is represented as an experienced, cynical, somewhat dogmatic individual. His initiation is not into manhood, as is Fleming's, but into a new attitude towards nature and his fellow-men.'[6]

Scholars disagree over the role of nature: Greenfield claims that nature 'is *the* antagonist' in this story; Mrs. Lang (by way of Emerson) and R. P. Adams (by way of Whitman) argue that man's unity with nature is the lesson learned by the interpreters; and, of course, others offer the naturalistic doctrine that nature as an overwhelming, mechanical, and indifferent force 'raises a question, not only about the ultimate value of heroic behavior, but even about the possibility of its existence'.[7] Yet Crane at least tries to be precise in his statement. External nature in 'The Open Boat', as in all Crane's work, is neither cruel, 'nor beneficent, nor treacherous, nor wise. But she was indifferent, flatly indifferent' (p. 56).[8] Hence, if chance or human error brings a man into so precarious a situation that he desires 'to confront a personification and indulge in pleas, bowed to one knee, and with hands supplicant, saying "Yes, but I love myself" ', his answer will not be reassuring: 'A high cold star on a winter's night is the word he feels that she says to him. Thereafter he knows the pathos of his situation' (p. 51). Logically, the last depth of this pathos—man's utter moral loneliness in the universe—is probably his realization that nature's absolute indifference precludes even antagonism. Although man's weak mental machinery may perceive external nature differently

[6] Peter Buitenhuis, 'The Essentials of Life: "The Open Boat" as Existentialist Fiction', *Modern Fiction Studies*, V (Autumn 1959), 244.

[7] Greenfield, 'Unmistakable Crane', p. 564; Lang, pp. 62–5; Adams, 'Naturalistic Fiction: "The Open Boat" ', *Tulane Studies in English*, IV (1954), 139–44; Greenfield, p. 564; John W. Shroeder, 'Stephen Crane Embattled', *University of Kansas City Review*, XVII (Winter 1950), 128; W. B. Stein, 'Stephen Crane's *Homo Absurdus*', *Bucknell Review*, VIII (May 1959), 170.

[8] Beer's quotation, 'Philosophy should always know that indifference is a militant thing' (*Crane*, p. 158), will not apply to Crane's view of nature. Crane wrote it in reference to Englishmen's top hats (*Work*, XI, 139), and it thus comments upon indifference in morally responsible human beings.

under different circumstances, as *WK 78* illustrates—as indeed Crane's manipulation of point of view in this very story illustrates —this externality is inevitably a moral blank, a fixed condition of being. And in Crane's world any transcendental unity achieved by moral man with amoral nature is the illusion of an innocent:

> The belief that the individual can reach at least a partial understanding of the human condition in relation to external nature—that he can 'interpret' nature—is not necessarily a romantic notion; it is eminently classical. The romantic 'solution' to the problem is a mystical union with . . . natural forces, so that the questions are not answered; they merely dissolve in intuitive understanding. . . . The classical view is that nature is truly 'external', at least to those attributes which differentiate man as man; knowledge, and a conscious choice of action based upon that knowledge, is man's only guide through the labyrinth of nature, even though the knowledge is always partial. Whatever unity exists is predicated upon the common humanity which the individual shares with humankind. (Jumper, p. 198)

The fact that man's moral identification with his fellow man is independent of external nature has to mean that externality, no matter how unsuitable to human life it may occasionally become, raises no questions about either the possibility of heroic behaviour or its ultimate value in the moral world of man: 'The belief that courage is a reality is not proved when a wave rescues the correspondent or disproved when another wave drowns the oiler. Man's values are defined *in* actuality, but they are not defined *by* actuality.'[9] Hence, one of the best readings that this story has received claims 'a slowly changing three-fold view of nature which is revealed in the characters' thoughts: they see nature first as malevolently hostile, then as thoughtlessly hostile, and finally as wholly indifferent. This progress of ideas also accompanies the men's deepening concept of brotherhood.'[10] Because the protagonist of Crane's pattern always works his way to awareness of a

---

[9] Westbrook, 'Personal Universal', p. 359.

[10] Mordecai Marcus, 'The Three-Fold View of Nature in "The Open Boat" ', *Philological Quarterly*, XLI (Apr. 1962), 512. Marcus is aware that the first two views are illusory, that Crane himself constantly sees nature as indifferent.

reality that was available to him before his psychological journey began, and because Crane altered his pattern in 'The Open Boat' to bring this awareness to his protagonist gradually, the *moral* reality of brotherhood in this story emerges roughly in three stages to correspond with the gradual disintegration of the protagonist's illusions as he becomes increasingly aware of the *physical* reality of indifferent nature.

The first commitment is made by each to the others within the boat; and the story implies that this sense of brotherhood arose almost immediately because, by the time it is mentioned (at the beginning of the third section), the correspondent's awareness of it is well after the fact. When a man suddenly finds himself adrift in an open boat his first impression of the surrounding sea will emphasize the danger which confronts him. The mutual commitment within the group, like the brotherhood of the Regulars, is each man's moral answer of selfless co-operation in the boat to counteract the threatening physical forces outside it as effectively as possible with their united effort. Thus, most of the attributes of this particular commitment—the awareness of danger as its immediate cause, its expression only in action, its lack of explicit acknowledgement, its respect for authoritative command, its significance beyond the demands of mere duty—were soon to reappear in Crane's analysis of the Regulars' code:

It would be difficult to describe the subtle brotherhood of men that was here established on the seas. No one said that it was so. No one mentioned it. But it dwelt in the boat, and each man felt it warm him . . . and they were friends—friends in a more curiously iron-bound degree than may be common. The hurt captain . . . could never command a more ready and swiftly obedient crew. . . . It was more than a mere recognition of what was best for the common safety. There was surely in it a quality that was personal and heart-felt. And after this devotion to the commander of the boat, there was this comradeship, that the correspondent, for instance, who had been taught to be cynical of men, knew even at the time was the best experience of his life. But no one said that it was so. No one mentioned it. (p. 36)

This group feeling within the boat is emphasized by the appearance of the shark when the correspondent believes himself to be the only man awake. Although companionship will not preserve a man from a shark, 'he did not wish to be alone with the thing. He wished one of his companions to awake by chance and keep him company with it.'

After the men have been so long in the same danger that the threat has lost its edge for them—after 'their backbones had become thoroughly used to balancing in the boat'—they begin to think beyond their immediate predicament: the oiler observes that 'None of those other boats could have got ashore to give word of the wreck.' When night comes, the symbolic universality of their situation is forcefully presented by the image of enveloping darkness in which two lights, the creations of man, 'were the furniture of the world'. Shortly afterwards, the thoughts which herald the collapse of the men's illusions are presented: 'When it occurs to a man that nature does not regard him as important, and that she feels she would not maim the universe by disposing of him, he at first wishes to throw bricks at the temple, and he hates deeply the fact that there are no bricks and no temples' (p. 51). Such a passage marks a transitional state: such verbs as 'regard', 'feels', and 'dispose', like the personal pronoun, imply the personification of the old ninny-woman; but the recognition that there are neither bricks nor temples leads straight to the depersonalized, remote indifference of the 'high cold star on a winter's night'. And with this image comes awareness of the pathos of the human situation. As implied by the poems, once a good man becomes aware of the universal human condition he will also perceive the moral demands his situation implicitly makes of him. Hence, as if 'to chime the notes of his emotion', the correspondent identifies himself with, and feels compassion for, the dying soldier of the Legion toward whom previously he had been 'perfectly *indifferent*' (italics mine). This earlier indifference resulted from the correspondent's innocence. His new sense of universal brotherhood derives from his 'profound and perfectly impersonal comprehension' of man's plight. Thus, his former innocence and indifference should not only recall the people on the shore who saw the boat and did nothing, but also imply the crying need for aware interpreters of the great sea's voice.

This need is emphasized with the final stage of awareness which comes when the wind-tower, 'a giant, standing with its back to the plight of the ants', represents, 'to the correspondent, the serenity of nature amid the struggles of the individual—nature in the wind, and nature in the vision of men' (pp. 55–6). The unalterable indifference of nature is thus compared with the indefensible indifference of moral man; and the correspondent then realizes 'the innumerable flaws of his life' and vows that, given another chance, he will 'mend his conduct and his words, and be better and brighter during an introduction or at a tea'. He vows that he will no longer be indifferent toward his fellow man even in the most banal situations, that he will wholeheartedly affirm even the social clichés by means of which human brotherhood can be expressed. The vast difference between the natural world and the moral world of man, implied through the image of the wind-tower, is stressed in the final scenes of the story. When the men approach the land with its cottages there is not a sign of life—not even a dog—to be seen; hence, they 'contemplate the lonely and indifferent shore' which, without man, is as indifferent as the sea. This amorality is shattered when a man comes running down the beach flinging off his clothes to plunge into the sea 'naked as a tree in winter' and help the men. To the correspondent 'a halo was about his head, and he shone like a saint', but no Christian reference is implied by the context: this naked man is the first person to act towards the castaways as an aware moral being should, and his sainthood is earned in terms of his enthusiastic practice of simple humanity towards a suffering brother, specifically by 'a strong pull, and a long drag, and a bully heave at the correspondent's hand'. Then the indifferent shore is transformed: 'instantly the beach was populated with men with blankets, clothes, and flasks, and women with coffee-pots and all the remedies sacred to their minds. The welcome of the land to the men from the sea [i.e. of aware humankind to the living men from the sea] was warm and generous.' But the oiler is dead, and his death poignantly underlines the distinction:

what remains—as in the final stanza of 'A man adrift on a slim spar'—is no longer a part of the moral world of living man; thus, the land's welcome to the 'still and dripping shape' can 'only be' a lonely and indifferent grave. The human commitment to brotherhood in this story enlarges from the immediate group to universal mankind to the social forms man has created for communicating his humanity to other living men; and the whole progression, as in the poems, is offered as the logical corollary of man's alien position in an indifferent universe.

Three apparent misreadings deserve brief comment. The progress of the men in the boat is no romantic death and rebirth (see Adams, pp. 144-5); they progressively acquire awareness—in the classic sense of gradual accomplishment through painful effort—of an already existing reality which is both physical (the indifference of nature) and moral (the necessary brotherhood of man). Similarly, nothing in the story suggests that the oiler is a Christ figure, or that his death is in any way sacrificial.[11] The oiler does no more than the others to get the boat ashore: each man does his best, and if Billie is more capable than the others this mere physical distinction has to be ascribed to the chance grouping of these four men in the boat, not to his moral credit. Moreover, he has his full reward and enjoys it while still living, his active participation in the brotherhood, which is the best experience of life. When his death occurs the time of the common struggle of each for the good of all within the boat has passed, and each man in the surf has to fend for himself. The oiler is killed by mere chance, a death which could have come to any of the others with exactly the same significance in context. This death signifies the immense value of brotherhood among living men because, while contingency remains in externals, as Jumper puts it, the moral realities which make human life meaningful to the living are not in themselves contingent upon external effect:

blind chance is of the essence of the material world. Only in the world of humanity is there the possibility of purposeful action. The sole

---

[11] See Hoffman, *Poetry*, p. 172; Cady, *Crane*, p. 154.

remnant of theology that survives in Crane's world is the stoic human will. . . . A world view which cannot take such a contingency into account will ill prepare its holder for the realities of life.[12]

Billie's death, in short, suggests that Crane's humanism is realistic, neither romantic nor sentimental. Finally, Crane's protagonist, the correspondent, is also his spokesman in this story.[13] The correspondent's consciousness is the vehicle which transmits the story to the reader, his mental machinery copes with the external reality and develops the philosophical conclusions which derive from his chastening experience. There is no irony aimed at his position to undermine his authority for the reader—the rescuer dashing down the sand should legitimately appear 'like a saint' to the exhausted correspondent—and Crane himself, in several stories and poems, obviously affirms both the view of external nature and the moral commitment that his spokesman here brings to the reader.

To be an 'interpreter' of the great sea's voice to man is to 'teach', with the 'gold of patience', the 'gospel of gentle hands'. Crane's tale after the fact documents the human position in an unfeeling universe where man's presence is an accident; and thus it 'cries a brotherhood of hearts' as a necessity for man's very existence in this eternally open boat.[14]

'The Monster' (written by 9 September 1897) has evoked critical comment ranging from dogmatic rejection to the claim that it is 'the greatest short story written by an American'.[15] The

---

[12] Jumper, p. 197; see also Westbrook, 'Revolt-Search', p. 74.

[13] Questioned by Hoffman, *Poetry*, p. 278; James B. Colvert, 'Style and Meaning in Stephen Crane: *The Open Boat*', *Texas Studies in English*, XXXVII (1958), 44–5; Cady, *Crane*, pp. 153–4.

[14] For the facts of Crane's experience, see Stallman, *Crane*, pp. 244–54; William Randel, 'From Slate to Emerald Green: More Light on Crane's Jacksonville Visit', *Nineteenth-Century Fiction*, XIX (Mar. 1965), 357–68. For Crane's mature flexibility of style compared with that of his earlier work, and analysis of specific devices used in this story, see Colvert, 'Development', p. 249; Adams, pp. 138–41; Hoffman, *Poetry*, pp. 276–7; Jumper, pp. 185–6; particularly Buitenhuis, pp. 245–7, and Brennan, 'Limits of Irony', pp. 190–200.

[15] See Stallman, *Omnibus*, p. 11; Winifred Lynskey, 'Crane's *Red Badge of Courage*', *Explicator*, VIII (Dec. 1949), item 18; Stein, '*Homo Absurdus*', p. 169; the quoted praise attributed to Howells by M. Solomon, 'Stephen Crane: A Critical Study', *Masses and Mainstream*, IX (Mar. 1956), 39.

assumption that Whilomville is based on the Port Jervis that Crane knew is confirmed in a letter from Brede Place, 2 March 1899, to his brother William: 'I suppose that Port Jervis entered my head while I was writing it but I particularly dont [*sic*] wish them to think so because people get very sensitive and I would not scold away freely if I thought the eye of your glorious public was upon me'[16]—a sentence which also suggests the importance of 'The Monster' in which Crane scolds away freely at the lack of humanity in the innocent society of a small American town.

This story carefully presents a dilemma, and it is therefore a unified structural whole. The protagonist is not Dr. Trescott, of course, who is one of Crane's greatest heroes: he is firmly guided by his stoic acceptance of his duty at whatever cost, he never wavers, he undergoes no struggle toward awareness and feels no shame for his actions; although he suffers as much as the protagonist in any Crane story, he is the monster's antagonist, the fixed rock which shatters the lances of the protagonist. Henry Johnson will not qualify either, but he identifies the protagonist because of the peculiar sense of horror Crane is able to centre on a man whose appearance is set forth only in the flat statement that 'he now had no face'. ' "The Monster" is a "problem" story . . . one of the best of its kind in American fiction. . . . Crane was not interested in depicting Henry Johnson as the monster; the monster is society.'[17] The people of Whilomville assume the normal position of the protagonist in Crane's psychological pattern.

Given the protagonist and the pattern, both the structure and the distinctive effectiveness of 'The Monster' are readily understood. Crane's usual pattern is broken off in this story at the point where his protagonist normally undergoes the unknown experience.

[16] William White, 'A Stephen Crane Letter', *The Times Literary Supplement*, No. 3108 (22 Sept. 1961), 636; see also Edna Crane Sidbury, 'My Uncle, Stephen Crane, as I Knew Him', *Literary Digest and International Book Review*, IV (Mar. 1926), 248. Sy Kahn argues that Crane scolds against personal wrongs: 'Stephen Crane and the Giant Voice in the Night: An Explication of "The Monster" ', *Essays in Modern American Literature*, ed. R. E. Langford, Guy Owen, W. E. Taylor (Deland, Florida, 1963), pp. 35–45.

[17] Thomas A. Gullason, 'The Symbolic Unity of "The Monster" ', *Modern Language Notes*, LXXV (Dec. 1960), 663; see also Kahn, p. 37.

Hence, this experience never occurs, no awareness comes, nothing is resolved, and the dilemma results. The protagonist, Whilomville society, is confronted with an unknown, Henry Johnson as a monster, which cannot be avoided because Dr. Trescott refuses to shirk his duty to the man who saved his son's life. Because the monster is an unknown quality, the people fear him; and because of this fear their imaginations create all sorts of illusions about how terrifying he is: the real source of horror associated with Henry lies not in Henry himself, but—as usual in Crane's work since 'Uncle Jake and the Bell-Handle' (1885)—in the ballooning illusions within the mind of the protagonist. Although 'The Monster' ends at this point, all the necessary elements of the usual pattern are present, and Crane could easily have continued the story to a typical one-trump resolution if such had been his desire. The reader, like Dr. Trescott, knows that Henry is completely harmless, that his terrifying power is, like his face, really only an absence of all capability. If the pattern had been completed, the townspeople, raised to a pitch of fear and illusion over some incident, would suddenly have realized (or experienced) Henry's total harmlessness, and thus they would have progressed to an awareness of the reality which had been available to them before their progression began. Then would have followed the usual ironic deflation of illusion, dissipation of fear, and the lingering sense of shame as they recalled their earlier conduct. But Crane's use of the truncated form of his pattern ends the story with a perfect psychological impasse.

The road to this impasse has been constructed with considerable care. The twenty-four sections of 'The Monster' divide readily into two equal portions which might well be subtitled 'appearance' and 'reality'. The first four sections are given to a deceptively warm portrait of small-town life which innocently introduces the Trescotts, Reifsnyder's barber shop, the Farraguts of Watermelon Alley, and the good people of Whilomville. Sections five to nine present the fire which will burn away the façade of this town's respectability to reveal the meanness hidden beneath; and the climactic episode of Henry's heroic action and disfigurement

—certainly one of the most intense and brilliantly impression-istic scenes Crane ever wrote—occurs midway, in section seven.[18] These sections offer several examples of Whilomville's penchant for irrational action: the mob's obvious enjoyment of the excite-ment which breaks the monotony of their lives, the rivalry of the hose companies and their partisans, the man who tears the shutters from the burning house, the rumours, the theatrical removal of the three 'bodies' through a crowd of gaping onlookers (who should recall the mob around the fallen Italian and in the police court of Crane's Bowery sketches). Section ten gives both the actual result of the fire—the destruction of the house, the condition of Dr. Trescott, Jimmie, and Henry—and the more important emotional result: the assumption of Henry's heroic death, the sentimental newspaper editorial 'built from all the best words in the vocabulary of the staff', and Bella Farragut's announcement of her engagement to the dead hero. Sections eleven and twelve are the climax of the first part. In an excellent scene between Dr. Trescott and Judge Hagenthorpe, who never had a son to be saved from burning to death, the judge pronounces the sentence upon the doctor that becomes the hidden fulcrum of the irrational mob-persecution in the second part: 'He is purely your creation. Nature has very evidently given him up. He is dead. You are restoring him to life. You are making him, and he will be a monster, and with no mind.' Section twelve presents Henry's first appearance; Dr. Trescott takes him after dark to the home of Alek Williams and thereby reduces the whole Williams family to wailing terror.

The latter half of the story is given entirely to the composite monster as Crane examines it piece by piece. Critics who have grappled sincerely with the tale are bothered by this part because 'there is little sense of progression' (Jumper, pp. 244–5). However, there can be none of the usual progression of a Crane story because the author is deliberately constructing a stasis. The latter

---

[18] 'The smoke, flames, and the malignant, brilliantly burning chemicals are anticipatory symbols for the mean and stupid hate which the community later showers upon Henry and Dr. Trescott. . . . The heated acid which destroys Henry's face is equated with the acid malice that destroys Dr. Trescott's social standing' (Colvert, 'Development', p. 253).

half is a progressive revelation of the monster as Crane moves about
Whilomville to involve the whole town in the portrait: the mindless fear of Alek Williams and his asking for more money, the
male gossip at the barber's, the hysterical children at the party, the
collapse of Bella Farragut and her mother, the veiled warning of
the chief of police who tells Dr. Trescott that Jake Winter wants
him arrested, the female gossip in the back kitchens, the unthink-
ing cruelty of the small boys (section twenty is an excellent
'Whilomville story' in itself), the ostracism of Dr. Trescott by his
patients. Also, as Gullason argues ('Symbolic Unity', p. 665), this
piecemeal revelation of the monster implies a progressive 'indictment of society' which deepens with a gradual 'transference of the
sense of ostracism from Henry to the Trescotts'. Section twenty-
two recalls section ten: in the earlier section stupidity could have
been avoided if the newspaper and Bella had merely restrained
themselves until Henry's fate was decided; in the later section
Martha Goodwin has the ability to overcome the stupidity through
her common sense and her willingness to oppose what 'everybody'
does and says, but she becomes diverted to a banal discussion of
'where the Hannigans are going to move to'. The final two sections, as in the earlier part, provide the climax. In section twenty-
three, set in autumn, a 'friendly' delegation of Whilomville's
leading citizens, including Judge Hagenthorpe, pay a futile call on
Dr. Trescott to persuade him to be morally less than a man for the
sake of his material good. Section twenty-four, set in winter,
shows the Trescotts' isolation finally completed as the women of
the town, including Judge Hagenthorpe's sister, ostracize the
doctor's wife. An early critic noted that Crane as a man 'was
wildly impatient with hypocrisy, cant, pretence, falsehood, brutality, sentimentalism, injustice, and cruelty; as an artist, he was
unendingly patient in dealing with these very things'.[19] All of
these black riders load the collective back of Whilomville's
monster.

Dr. Trescott is securely caught between opposing principles of
what is good: his duty to Henry, his obligation to his own family,

[19] William Lyon Phelps, *Work*, V, Introduction, xii–xiii.

and his professional duty to mankind as a dedicated doctor. No matter which choice he makes, he has to suffer profoundly. Nevertheless, he does choose. Like a Regular, he fulfils his duty and accepts his suffering without complaint—when Jake Winter attacks him 'yelping . . . like a little dog' he merely walks away. This hero allowed Crane to direct his ironic vision at the idealized American small town and set forth the moral truth of what he saw:

We have no more spirited portrait of the mob-meanness of our democracy—the peculiarly American disgrace that shames us among nations. . . . The completely miserable performance of these people; their laudation of poor Henry Johnson . . . when it is supposed he is dead; . . . their insistence that he be taken out of the town to spare their sensibilities; and their desertion and ruin of the career of Dr. Trescott, his one friend—all this is of the best stuff of tragedy, a living likeness of the wilds of a cowardly tyranny, splendidly and thoroughly understood and told.[20]

'The Bride Comes to Yellow Sky' (written during the fall of 1897) seems to me one of Crane's most subtle stories. It is obviously comic; yet Crane just as obviously is sympathetic towards Potter and his new wife, two plain people who have quietly married; and he is quite without rancour in his presentation of Scratchy Wilson who, if compared with the people the newly-weds encounter on the train, is clearly one of Potter's own kind. The story implies that Wilson never really hurts anyone—not even the bar-keeper's dog—during his drunken rampages. This whole business is presented more or less as a ritual which recurs periodically, and which everyone understands and accepts: Wilson turns up drunk and shooting, all sensible citizens and dogs get down behind barricades, and Potter as town marshal goes out and takes care of him—apparently without hurting him either, although the performance once slipped far enough to leave Wilson nicked in the leg. Wilson would be another drunken lout such as Pete if the author took him seriously, but Crane's attitude is much the same towards

[20] Edith Wyatt, 'Stephen Crane', *New Republic*, IV (11 Sept. 1915), 149. For further comment, see Van Doren, *Twenty Stories*, pp. xii–xiii; Lang, p. 120; Jumper, pp. 244–5; A. W. Hart, pp. 145–8 (on society's failure to assimilate the grotesque); Westbrook, 'Social Ethic', pp. 595–6.

him as it is towards Jimmie Trescott: 'In part III Scratchy is presented consistently and sardonically by the omniscient narrator as a wild, misbehaving child.'[21] Crane's attention in this story rests less upon his characters than upon this ritualistic 'wild-West' way of life, and it is primarily because of this emphasis that the story is comic,

a hilariously funny parody of neo-romantic lamentations over 'The Passing of the West.' The last marshall [*sic*] is tamed by a prosaic marriage and exempted from playing The Game so absurdly romanticized by Street and Smith, *The Police Gazette*, and finally Owen Wister. His occupation gone, the last Bad Man, a part-time worker anyhow, shuffles off into the sunset leaving boot-tracks like the tracks of the last dinosaur.[22]

Nevertheless, behind the comic front serious business is being transacted, and an overemphasis upon what Cady calls 'The Game' can obscure the real beast that Crane is stalking. This story, after all, was written immediately after 'The Monster' which examines the manners and forms that enable 'everybody' to conform in persecuting Dr. Trescott. At least one scholar has argued that these unspoken social forms are the real subject of 'The Bride Comes to Yellow Sky', that if this tale cannot be called a small comedy of manners 'we have no traditional name for such a story. . . . In fact, it would not be saying too much to suggest that where the usual institutions of society were so few, manners (or something like manners) had often to bear the full weight of preserving public order. Crane calls it humorously man's "duty to his friends, or of their idea of his duty." '[23] Artistically, the manners or social forms are the equivalent of the wild-West ritual, alike unspoken, unwritten, universally understood and accepted. Moreover, they are implicitly presented as the subject of the story before there is any mention of the gunfight ritual: they furnish the only available excuse for the protagonist's fears and illusions.

[21] S. C. Ferguson, 'Crane's "The Bride Comes to Yellow Sky" ', *Explicator*, XXI (Mar. 1963), item 59.

[22] Cady, 'Strenuous Life', p. 382. See also Solomon, *Parody to Realism*, pp. 252–6.

[23] West, 'Author in Transition', p. 221.

Potter, the principal protagonist, fears and cannot avoid an
unknown experience that is about to happen to him, his return to
Yellow Sky with a bride; and his fears derive from his conception
of his position as town marshal. He knows that 'of course people in
Yellow Sky married as it pleased them, in accordance with a general
custom', but because he is an employee of the town he absurdly
believes he should have asked the town for permission to marry,
and he feels guilt at having gone to San Antonio and married
'without consulting Yellow Sky for any part of the transaction':

> such was Potter's thought of his duty to his friends, or of their idea of
> his duty, or of an unspoken form which does not control men in these
> matters, that he felt he was heinous. He had committed an extraordinary
> crime. Face to face with this girl in San Antonio, and spurred by his
> sharp impulse, he had gone headlong over all the social hedges. At San
> Antonio he was like a man hidden in the dark. A knife to sever any
> friendly duty, any form, was easy to his hand in that remote city.
> (*Work*, XII, 90–1)

Potter's fears and illusions steadily increase as the train nears
Yellow Sky and reach their apex in his belief that he, the town
marshal, has to sneak home from the station with his bride. On the
way, however, they suddenly confront his greatest professional
problem, drunk and rampaging. But when Wilson learns of
Potter's 'new estate' he merely says 'I s'pose it's all off now',
holsters his guns, and peacefully walks away. This is the end of
Scratchy Wilson as bad man, and the end of the recurring ritual.
But the concealed force of the story's impact derives from the
implication that Potter's absurd conception of the social requirements of his position in the town also collapses with the wild-West
ritual: Potter's illusions could have arisen only from a code of
manners which made provision for the ritual gunfight. With
marriage Potter has unknowingly assumed adult social responsibility; and 'the town itself, like Scratchy, must put away its toys,
its masquerades in the manner of Wild Bill Hickok and his ilk, for
the Bride, "dutiful, . . . plain, . . . placid" has come home to stay'
(Ferguson). Also, the reality of Potter's welcome makes his fears
ridiculous. Presumably he should receive a rise in pay because,

professionally, he is now greater than ever: while not even carrying a gun he has solved the Wilson problem for ever with only a wife. There is no 'overshadowing cultural conflict . . . of the East vs. the West' in this story. Several references to Eastern civilization are present—Wilson's shirt made in a New York sweat-shop, his boots like those of little boys in New England, the Pullman car, the plains of Texas apparently 'pouring eastward', Wilson being called 'a simple child of the earlier plains' as he reacts to Potter's marriage[24]—but they create no *conflict*. The image of the Western landscape 'pouring eastward' when seen from the moving train, for example, implies becoming, and so do all Crane's implications that Wilson as innocent bad man is 'merely a grown-up child' (Jumper, p. 242). The images of the East suggest a more mature social reality than ritual gunfighting, and Yellow Sky in the course of the story becomes socially more mature. Wilson's shock of recognition brings him awareness of a social relationship which is necessary when men have to live with one another as adults, and which was not so necessary on 'the earlier plains' where a man had room and opportunity to act like an overgrown child without hurting others. Yellow Sky is still Western at the end of the story, but the barricades—both the physical ones set up against the ritual gunfight and the illusory ones Potter sets between his conception and the reality of his position—have fallen for ever.

The attempt to view the Eastern references as a source of conflict endows Potter with attributes he does not really possess—both he and his bride are socially innocent on the train, either bullied or patronized by everyone—and it also tends to allow Wilson to usurp Potter's role as the principal protagonist. Both men acquire awareness during the story, but Wilson's progression is comparatively simple and explicit: 'by preserving a comic tone and the exaggeration of comedy, [Crane] emphasizes the significance of social definition; for if we are to say what the story is about, we must say that it is the tale of a childlike man confronting a new, and more complex, situation than his simple code

[24] See Robert Barnes, 'Crane's "The Bride Comes to Yellow Sky' "', *Explicator*, XVI (Apr. 1958), item 39.

allows for' (West, p. 222). This statement *about Wilson* is certainly correct, but Potter is ignored; and the subtlety of the story is suggested by the fact that this conclusion, word for word, applies to Potter just as much as it does to Wilson. Potter gains precisely the same sort of awareness, but his progression to it remains implicit.

When Potter goes to San Antonio and marries he places himself in Maggie's position when she accepts Pete, in Fleming's position when he first enlists: Potter assumes a code of values which he himself does not entirely perceive until his 'new estate' confronts the old ritual back in Yellow Sky. Since his marriage Potter has been living ahead of his own view of himself—again like Maggie and Fleming before they achieve awareness—and the jarring confrontation forces his understanding of his own position to catch up again with his new reality. Potter is well aware that marriage is a commitment to a new life: the elegant and unfamiliar Pullman interior 'reflected the glory of their marriage that morning in San Antonio; this was the environment of their new estate'. But, as usual, the physical or literal environment merely implies the moral reality, and it is this reality that Potter has yet to understand. When Potter and Wilson meet, Crane flashes the whole Pullman image of Potter's new estate 'somewhere at the back of his mind' to imply what this confrontation signifies to him. In short, this brief story has a parallel structure in which two protagonists progress through Crane's psychological pattern to achieve a common awareness; the obvious difference between the two is that Wilson is so innocent that he knows no fear as he acts out his own illusion, a ritual which has been defunct ever since the train left San Antonio that morning. Wilson as bad man, the gunfight ritual, Potter's fears and illusions about his position in Yellow Sky all collapse at once before the mature social reality of his new estate. ' "The Bride Comes to Yellow Sky" is a daisy,' Crane told his agent, 'and don't let them talk funny about it' (*Letters*, p. 145).

'Death and the Child' (written by December 1897) has evoked less comment than it deserves, and what comment it has received implies a much misunderstood story.[25] For several reasons it is probably the least satisfying of Crane's major works: Crane seems to pursue too many purposes at once with Peza; the reality Peza has to perceive is comparatively abstract; possibly because this is the first 'war' story written after Crane's own experience it features the panoramic scene which is not his forte; the ending seems contrived; and the child's somewhat unnatural question seems overemphasized. Nevertheless, 'Death and the Child' belongs with the matter that pleased Crane himself, because, as Jumper argues, 'it is essentially a treatment of the theme' of the later Spanish-American War stories 'stated in its converse form'. Crane's fiction of the Spanish-American War presents the Regular,

the soldier who knows his job and does it, without heroics, 'the pageantry of the accomplishment of naked duty.' In the Graeco-Turkish War story he presents a romantic amateur, egotistical and 'heroic,' attempting to dramatize his dreams of war and patriotism. . . . The technique of 'standing behind' the mind of his main character . . . functions perfectly here, for Peza is an educated and articulate man; Crane can discuss psychological and ethical issues with a sophistication which Fleming denied him. (Jumper, pp. 79–80)

The issues that interested Crane in his first experience of war are examined by means of his psychological pattern which, in this story, brings together five important elements: Peza himself, external nature, the child, the common man both as soldier and as peasant, and the officers. All are placed under the pressure of war in order to reveal their reality to the reader; but in order to understand the story the reader has to distinguish between what Crane says and what Peza says.

External nature, for example, is as flatly indifferent to Peza's ordeal as it is to the death of the oiler or to Jim Conklin's suffering. Peza, not Crane, sees it as a 'theatre for slaughter, built by the inscrutable needs of the earth' (*Work*, XII, 248). Crane's view is given at the beginning, before Peza is even introduced:

[25] See Maxwell Geismar, *Rebels and Ancestors: The American Novel 1890–1915* (Boston, 1953), pp. 106–7; Shroeder, 'Crane Embattled', p. 120; Hoffman, *Poetry*, pp. 270–1; Lang, pp. 57–9; Eric Solomon, 'Stephen Crane's War Stories', *Texas Studies in Literature and Language*, III (Spring 1961), 70.

There was upon this vista a peace that a bird knows when, high in air, it surveys the world, a great, calm thing rolling noiselessly toward the end of the mystery. Here on the height one felt the existence of the universe scornfully defining the pain in ten thousand minds. The sky was an arch of stolid sapphire. . . . The sea, the sky, and the hills combined in their grandeur to term this misery inconsequent. Then, too, it sometimes happened that a face seen as it passed on the flood [of refugees] reflected curiously the spirit of them [i.e. sea, sky, and hills] all, and still more. . . . In the dismal melody of this flight there were often sounding chords of apathy. Into these preoccupied countenances one felt that needles could be thrust without purchasing a scream. (p. 242)

Nature is thus mindless and apart from man; and its *adult* human equivalent is apathy, the absence of that moral animation which man alone possesses. But Peza, like Fleming, is 'amazed that the trees, the flowers, the grass, all tender and peaceful nature, had not taken to its heels at once upon the outbreak of battle'; and when a shell hits a tree, he believes the 'convulsive tremor' of this block of wood 'was an exhibition of pain and, furthermore, deep amazement'. One has to accept Crane's view of externality, not the illusions evoked by Peza's overheated and sentimental imagination.

The child is explicitly identified with this mindless indifference of nature. Crane calls him 'the primitive courage, the sovereign child, the brother of the mountains, the sky, and the sea'; and his eyes, 'large and inscrutably wise and sad', are compared with the eyes of a cow (p. 268). This child is equated with nature because of his complete ignorance of the moral reality in which he has been abandoned. His is the 'disinterested contemplation' which springs only from the 'empty-as-a-beerpail look that a babe turns on you and shrivels you to grass with'.[26] Because of his lack of awareness (the child's equivalent of adult apathy), his 'tranquillity in regard to the death on the plain was as invincible as that of the mountain on which he stood' (p. 250). Hence, he is the opposite of the Wordsworthian sybil, the clear-eyed well of intuitive awareness unpolluted by civilization. There are no romantic children of this sort anywhere in Crane's work.

[26] Crane quoted by Beer, *Crane*, p. 147.

This child, a 'powerful symbol' (p. 267), serves Crane as a means of giving a voice and a rudimentary mind to that which has neither mind nor voice, external nature. Thus, when the child weeps high above the battle he symbolizes the attitude of the universe (granted mind and voice) towards men who stupidly struggle to kill instead of help one another. The external universe, symbolically made sentient, looks down upon man's situation in the amoral desert and weeps at man's incredible folly in deliberately making his perilous situation worse instead of better. Similarly, when the child asks Peza, 'Are you a man?' he merely voices the implicit question that Crane's universe puts to all men. Peza therefore confronts the fundamental reality of human existence as Crane perceives it: born into an amoral world where chance may maim or kill, where the good are often unrewarded and the evil unpunished, man is duty-bound to act morally merely because he is a man, and each man's conduct implicitly answers the child's question. In terms of Crane's recurring pattern, therefore, the human situation—which the child's question has to imply to any aware adult in Crane's world—is the reality which has been present and available to Peza long before his progression to the awareness of it (which is achieved by the end of the story) even began.

This protagonist, 'a young student who could write sonnets and play the piano quite well', introduces himself with an emotional declamation to a young lieutenant who instantly recognizes him for what he is: unaware, untried, unrestrained, and undirected by anything other than romantic clichés. Crane comments after Peza's outburst:

He paused, breathing heavily. His eyes glistened from that soft overflow which comes on occasion to the glance of a young woman. Eager, passionate, profoundly moved, his first words . . . had been an active definition of his own dimension, *his personal relation to men, geography, life*. Throughout he had preserved the fiery dignity of a tragedian. (p. 243; italics mine.)

Peza is so sentimental that he is womanish, and he does not understand men, geography, and life. He is everything the lieutenant is not: 'The officer was also a young man, but he was bronzed and steady . . . stern, quiet, and confident, respecting fate, fearing only opinion. . . . At the violent cries of his companion he smiled as if to himself' (p. 244). Peza grapples with his illusions concerning men, geography, and life as he progresses toward a confrontation with the reality which he must perceive correctly if he is ever to become a man like the lieutenant.

One of the protagonist's illusions about nature appears only in this story; it introduces his attitudes towards men and life: Peza has the great romantic desire 'to do battle for the land of my father' because, he says, he loves Greece, although he has spent most of his life in Italy. Yet Greece, as the *land* of his father, is just so much insensate dirt. Man's fighting a war, like any other human action, is meaningful in moral terms only as it affects the lives of other men; and Peza fails miserably in his relationship with the men of his fatherland: 'he chooses the grand and senti- mental gesture of becoming a "soldier for Greece"—a role for which he is sublimely unfit—and yet flees in terror from the practical and human task which he could perform, the aiding of the wounded soldier' (Jumper, p. 223). Peza fails because his romantic notions prevent him from seeing whatever is practical: he is never able to consider the men simply as human beings working at an unpleasant task. Thus, at one moment he considers them heroes and infinitely pitiable when wounded—a useless pity which draws a sharp response from the practical lieutenant: 'The officer faced about angrily. "If you are coming with me, there is no time for this." ' The next moment his sensibility leads him to look down upon the common soldier:

these stupid peasants who, throughout the world, hold potentates on their thrones, make statesmen illustrious, provide generals with lasting victories, all with ignorance, indifference, or half-witted hatred, moving the world with the strength of their arms, and getting their heads knocked together, in the name of God, the king, or the stock exchange —immortal, dreaming, hopeless asses who surrender their reason to the care of a shining puppet, and persuade some toy to carry their lives in his purse. (p. 257)

This famous indictment is Peza's, not Crane's, as even a glance at

'War Memories' will prove. The irony within the passage identifies it with the protagonist: Peza should be the last person to condemn others for being 'dreaming, hopeless asses who surrender their reason to the care of a shining puppet'. Also, his whole indictment ironically misses the point and thus, as his ambiguous attitude towards these men should suggest, it reveals more about the protagonist than it does about the men. Peza judges men at war on the basis of grand romantic movements which have little meaning to practical men working at the task of fighting other practical men. Peza distinguishes between men at war largely on a social basis: he sees officers and peasants. Crane judges and distinguishes on the basis of a man's actions which imply his motivations: he portrays blind terror, panic, apathy, cowardly failure, and—in officer and peasant alike—the stoic acceptance of practical responsibility. Thus, when Peza announces to some front-line artillery officers his intention of advancing to a still more perilous position in the rifle-pits he 'felt that he was wandering, with his protestations of high patriotism, through a desert of sensible men'; and *en route* he fails to aid the wounded man in his haste to fight for a portion of geography. When finally he sees a far-off charge advance, his hysterical fear endows corpses and other inanimate things, a bandoleer and a rifle, with the power to drag him down to some romantically horrible Hades beneath the earth; and he runs away followed by the jeers of the practical men.

Crane's insistent and uncharacteristic use of the panoramic scene points to Peza's basic illusion about life in general. When Peza sees 'gunless and jaded men' exhausted from battle he wonders if their state of mind results from an experience comparable to his own in an art gallery:

he had found himself amid heavenly skies and diabolic midnights—the sunshine beating red upon desert sands, nude bodies flung to the shore in the green moonglow, ghastly and starving men clawing at a wall in darkness, a girl in her bath, with screened rays falling upon her pearly shoulders, a dance, a funeral, a review, an execution—all the strength of argus-eyed art; and he had whirled and whirled amid this universe, with cries of woe and joy, sin and beauty, piercing his ears until he had been obliged to simply come away. He remembered that as he had emerged he had lit a cigarette with unction, and advanced promptly to a cafe. (pp. 252–3)

Peza at war is still Peza at the art gallery. This 'theatre for slaughter' is another 'place of pictures', a 'pageant' of panoramic views, and Peza is again gazing without discrimination, restraint, or self-control. He looks at the men and his own role much as he had considered the painted figures: 'The shells killed no one. War was not so bad! He was simply having coffee in the smoking-room of some embassy where reverberate the names of nations' (p. 259). Peza is still whirling in the real universe, various cries still pierce his uncritical sensibility, and he still acts—like George Kelcey or Caspar Cadovan—as if it were possible 'to simply come away' when he becomes surfeited. Peza is not really an intellectual: his education has wrapped him in a sentimental romanticism instead of preparing him for life in the real world, and his sensibility is undirected because it is uncritical. This womanish young innocent has left the protection of the convent, as it were, to blunder out for the first time into an amoral universe where, by chance, men are at the moment trying to kill each other. Hence, the Crane protagonist has again placed himself in a position which entails his eventual experience of the unknown, and for Peza this unknown is best defined simply as reality itself.

Ironically, both times that the realism in the war theatre becomes so overpowering that Peza takes the panic-stricken decision 'to simply come away', his flight is towards the very confrontation that he intended to avoid. Reality, when actually faced, is neither sentimental nonsense nor a corpse drawing one to death beneath the earth: it is merely the implicit question which Peza, in his innocence, thought he had answered before his psychological progression to an awareness of its real significance began. Although the story ends at the climax, Crane implies that Peza will eventually emerge as a man from his enchanted forest. He honestly acknowledges that he is not yet a man, i.e. the 'definition of his misery' which 'could be written on a wee grass-blade' is the brief word 'no' in answer to the child's question. Also, Crane states that 'it did not occur to him, *until later*, that he was now going to battle mainly because at a previous time a certain man had smiled' (p. 255; italics mine). Peza, Crane implies, will recall the bombast of his earlier gospels in the light of his deflating confrontation with reality, and will then despise them; with his intelligence oriented by means of a critical awareness of man's real position in the universe, he will eventually become a man like the young lieutenant who smiled at him.

'The Blue Hotel' (written by February 1898), probably Crane's most difficult story, has been discussed as much as 'The Open Boat' and has evoked far more critical disagreement. The first eight sections, taut and enigmatic, a brilliant, hard-surfaced impressionism, offer such highly charged prose that every aspect of the tale, essential to the main action or not, reverberates into insistent overtones of meaning which seem important in their own right. There is the oddly painted hotel, the temple-like haven of warmth against the rage of the blizzard, the cards, the role of Pat Scully—who is likened to both a priest and a murderer—the Easterner's taciturnity, the long and careful characterization of the gambler, and the puzzling final section which appears to have been added to explain the preceding action. All these elements are important in context, but when a reader centres his attention on one of them it is all too easy to give it more importance than it contributes to this context.[27] The superbly presented blizzard, for example, attracts the naturalistic critic (see Stein, '*Homo Absurdus*', p. 174). Yet man's moral world and external nature's pointless energy are as sharply distinct in this story as elsewhere in Crane's work. Nobody dies in this blizzard; even the Swede has to find a saloon, with men in it, before death comes to him. And Joseph N. Satterwhite, who provides the best treatment of the one conclusion scholars tend to agree upon—that there is a failure of human responsibility and understanding among the men whom the

[27] See particularly James T. Cox 'Stephen Crane as Symbolic Naturalist: An Analysis of "The Blue Hotel" ', *Modern Fiction Studies*, III (Summer 1957), 147–58.

Swede encounters—is sufficiently bothered by the final section to argue that 'the Swede is not the protagonist. . . . The cash-register legend . . . is misleading because it implies the Swede has deliberately sought and deserved his death; actually he has been destroyed by a social environment which has refused or has been unable to understand him.'[28] The small point to be made, at the moment, is simply that all elements of the story need to be considered in terms of the essential action to which, in context, each of them contributes.

The essential action, given the Swede's fear and illusions and the ironic deflation at the end of the eighth section, is based upon Crane's psychological pattern. The Swede is obviously the protagonist, and the unknown which he both fears and—in view of his unexplained trip to Fort Romper—believes he cannot avoid is life in the West as he has come to imagine it through his reading of dime novels: this explanation has to be accepted because it is the only one available; it is provided by the Easterner, who is the most intelligent character; it is confirmed in the upstairs conversation implied by Scully's remark that the Swede 'was from the East, and he thought this was a tough place', by the cowboy's congratulating the Easterner for being right about 'that there Dutchman', and by Crane's important use of wild-West conventions which come straight out of the trash that the Swede is assumed to have read. Because this unknown is itself an illusion, because the wild West of the dime novel does not exist except in the Swede's imagination, it is impossible for this protagonist to experience his unknown in the objective manner of the correspondent's aware passage through the surf. Moreover, this is the only important story in which the protagonist himself is killed; and the mere existence of the final section makes it structurally unique. Such important departures from the norm imply the radical innovation in the pattern itself: 'The Blue Hotel' is Crane's only important story in which the fact of experience entirely fulfils both the protagonist's greatest fear and his wildest illusions. Before his death the Swede actually

[28] 'Stephen Crane's "The Blue Hotel"': The Failure of Understanding', *Modern Fiction Studies*, II (Winter 1956–7), 238.

lives, for a brief while, in the wild-West world of his own imagination.[29] He creates it himself.

He creates it gradually, in three ascending levels of intensity as he climbs through illusion to the reality of death. Scully's whisky ends the first stage and initiates the second, the victory over Johnnie lifts the Swede out of the second stage, and the 'splendour of isolation' of the Swede in the storm is the final level at which he completely realizes his own illusion. During the first stage the Swede is quiescent because his fear dominates his actions; during the second, his fear deadened by Scully's whisky, the illusory world of his imagination swiftly asserts itself as he assumes the bravado of the dime-novel hero; when he whips Johnnie his last trace of fear ('I won't stand much show against this gang. I know you'll all pitch on me.') vanishes, and he immediately leaves the hotel as 'conquering and elate humanity' living entirely within the stormy world of his own violent illusions.

The world of the blue hotel, like that of the saloon, seems best defined simply as reality, the reality with which the Swede is out of touch. Scully ministers in genial proprietorship at his commercial temple. His card-sharping son, the farmer, and the cowboy are familiar types equally at home in the Swede's dime novels, in legitimate fiction of the West, and in reality. The Easterner, although normal, is an outsider (in contrast to the Swede, who is a psychological outsider), and he is distinguished by having a more perceptive intelligence than his fellows and proportionally greater restraint. This world is prosaic enough, but Crane centres the reader's attention on it by the simple expedient of having the hotel painted blue, a colour which causes a heron 'to declare its position against any background'. Crane's comment implies the function of this device: as the story develops, the world of the hotel does declare its position, morally speaking, against the

[29] Walter Sutton, 'Pity and Fear in "The Blue Hotel" ', *American Quarterly*, IV (Spring 1952), 76; Robert F. Gleckner, 'Stephen Crane and the Wonder of Man's Conceit', *Modern Fiction Studies*, V (Autumn 1959), 278; Solomon, *Parody to Realism*, pp. 257–74; Richard A. Davison, 'Crane's "Blue Hotel" Revisited: The Illusion of Fate', *Modern Fiction Studies*, XV (Winter 1969–70), 537–9.

immense background of the terrible blizzard. This hotel in the midst of the snowstorm is analogous to the dinghy in the midst of the sea: both *can become* a haven of refuge where human life is secured from the 'profligate fury' of the natural world. Hence, the hotel 'has the sacred air of a sanctuary about it, its public room being described as a "proper temple" for an enormous stove which hummed with "godlike violence". Over it all Scully presides "like an old priest" who initiates his guests with a ceremonious, baptismal-like washing ritual' (Satterwhite, p. 239). But these images are ironic. Neither boat nor hotel is in itself anything but another piece of the world's external furniture (the blizzard is twice associated with the colour blue to emphasize this fact), and whatever each becomes depends upon human action. The boat becomes a sanctuary because the men work together to make it so, but the hotel does not because the men whom it harbours fail to create the brotherhood a sanctuary requires: 'there can be little of dramatic import in environment. Any room can present a tragic front; any room can be comic' (*Work*, X, 112). As Westbrook claims, all four men understand the Swede quite well enough to realize how they should act towards him: 'all are in agreement. The Swede is a frightened man who deserves kindly treatment' ('Revolt-Search', p. 104). Thus, their failure is primarily one of moral responsibility towards a brother man. Huddled together against the natural fury,

the symbolic nature of their situation makes the failure of the four . . . all the more reprehensible. These characters are less individuals than representatives of various reasons for the failure. . . . For Scully, the Swede is less a human than an economic factor, and the host spends his energies in protecting his profit. . . . Johnnie Scully is emotionally disqualified for . . . he is angry when the Swede first enters the hotel and steadily grows more wrathful. Simple incredulity overwhelms the Cowboy. . . . Habitual restraint and reticence isolate the Easterner and reduce him to the status of reflective observer. (Satterwhite, pp. 239–40)

Crane's painting this hotel blue at once identifies it as an externality that in itself is as amoral as the storm and focuses attention upon the developing human situation within as, confronted with the Swede's actions, the human beings gradually reveal a moral declaration of position.

The Swede immediately challenges the reality of the hotel because his fears isolate him from it. He is introduced as 'shaky and quick-eyed', he does not join the others in washing with Scully's ice water, and he stays out of the general conversation: 'The Swede said nothing. He seemed to be occupied in making furtive estimates of each man in the room. . . . He resembled a badly frightened man' (pp. 94–5). His isolation is stated in the final paragraph of the first section:

he said that some of these Western communities were very dangerous; and after this statement he straightened his legs under the table, tilted his head, and laughed again, loudly. It was plain that the demonstration had no meaning to the others. They looked at him wondering and in silence. (p. 96)

Thus, he never accepts the prosaic reality surrounding him at Scully's table. The violence of his illusion is to the moral world what the storm's violence is to the physical world; and his entry into the hotel among this group of men mocks all allusions to a temple or sanctuary from the enveloping fury. The storm, as it were, is now inside the hotel, lurking beneath the restraint of fear in the Swede's mind but already forcing the others to take action because of it (cf. Gleckner, p. 274).

The second section brings the Swede's general isolation into specific focus. He joins the game of High-Five—which the reader should associate with a typical episode in wild-West fiction—and his strangeness is pin-pointed when he says, 'I suppose there have been a good many men killed in this room.' When the cowboy flings the deck of cards down on the board, a typical dime-novel prelude to catastrophe, the Swede's reaction is violent: 'I suppose I am going to be killed before I can leave this house!' Scully enters, and the Swede's abnormality is openly stated when Johnnie says, 'He's crazy', and Scully tells him, 'Man, you're off your nut.' Hence, when Scully claims he 'will not allow any peaceable man to be troubled' under his roof, his words can hardly apply to the Swede, 'the wildest loon I ever see'. But the point, increasingly evident in succeeding sections, is that none of the others makes an attempt to show the Swede his error and thus help him to become a peaceable man. While Scully, upstairs, tries to reassure a scared guest in order to protect the hotel's reputation, the others, downstairs, 'attempt to identify him, to explain him in terms of his nationality rather than in terms of his bewilderment' (Satterwhite, p. 240). Thus, while the downstairs scene is almost comic in its futility, its irrelevancy is matched by the *non sequiturs* being offered above. To the Swede's fear of imminent death Scully offers first a line of electric streetcars, then pictures of his successful son and dead daughter, and finally—neither offering having proved meaningful to the Swede—whisky. Although the Swede's fear is greatly increased by this ritualistic offer of whisky, he dares not refuse: it is a wild-West convention that horrible consequences follow a refusal to drink upon demand, and this convention is used again in the saloon. Hence, this is no friendly drink: 'the Swede laughed loudly. He grabbed the bottle, put it to his mouth; and as his lips curled absurdly around the opening and his throat worked, he kept his glance, burning with hatred, upon the old man's face' (p. 106).

Scully's whisky submerges the Swede's fear beneath his illusory concept of the West, and he begins to embody the pose of a dime-novel hero: he laughs too loudly at Scully's jokes, bullies and patronizes him, monopolizes the conversation, and walks into the private part of the house to get his own drink. Scully states that his guest is 'all right now' (i.e. not about to run from the hotel), and the others, except Johnnie, forgo responsibility by timidly agreeing. But Johnnie is more correct: 'Other time he was scared, but now he's too fresh.' Throughout sections four and five the Swede imposes his wild-West heroics upon the others, who submit with varying degrees of reluctance until he accuses Johnnie of cheating at cards. Violence then begins with a suggestive passage: 'Of course the board had been overturned, and now the whole company of cards was scattered over the floor, where the boots of the men trampled the fat and painted kings and queens as they gazed with their silly eyes at the war that was waging above them'

(p. 113). Crane implies the relations between cards, men, and the storms both within and without. The order and convention of the game have *not* been overturned only by the Swede, as the reader learns later: the cause of the disruption is Johnnie's cheating, the Swede's refusal to accept it, the Easterner's moral failure of silence, and Johnnie's refusal to acknowledge his own action. Similarly, the order and convention of the blue hotel have been overturned by the Swede's illusory world, the moral failure of the others to act as brothers towards an obviously frightened man, and Scully's failure to accept responsibility for the Swede's recent actions which have been caused, in part, by Scully's whisky (he says, 'I've stood this damned Swede till I'm sick. We'll let them fight'). The men raging above the cards are analogous to the violent storms raging above the men both outside the hotel and within the Swede's mind: their failure of responsibility has left them morally as helpless beneath the onslaught of the Swede's illusory world as the cards beneath their trampling feet; and the implication is plain that if they failed as miserably in coping with the blizzard then some of them would surely die.

The moral failure is emphasized by the Easterner's reaction—his own guilt, as he later admits—to the preliminaries before the great fist-fight: 'The entire prelude had in it a tragedy greater than the tragedy of action, and this aspect was accentuated by the long, mellow cry of the blizzard, as it sped the tumbling and wailing flakes into the black abyss of the south' (p. 117). Yet the failure is sustained. The fight takes place in the midst of a natural fury which ponderously underscores the necessity of moral responsibility among men. With his victory over Johnnie (and, psychologically, over the three others who cheer for Johnnie), the Swede loses all touch with reality: 'There was a splendour of isolation in his situation at this time which the Easterner felt once when, lifting his eyes from the man on the ground, he beheld that mysterious and lonely figure, waiting' (p. 119). The image of the helpless cards is thus reproduced by the helpless men trampled, either physically or morally, by the Swede's energy and their own sins of inaction. From this point until his death the Swede is above all fear and thus above the moral reality of humankind: he merges with the pointless violence of the blizzard and lives completely within the world of his own raging illusion.

Crane's merging of the Swede with the storm fulfils a promise implicit in the story since the beginning. At first the storm is excluded from the hotel just as the Swede's imaginary world is checked by his fear. Scully opens the door to both storms, by leaving to meet the next train and by giving the Swede whisky, and both storms demolish the 'games' in progress within the hotel. The cowboy's criticism of the bar tender, Scully's counterpart in the saloon scene, that if he 'had been any good he would have gone in and cracked that there Dutchman on the head with a bottle in the beginnin' of it and stopped all this here murderin' ', applies also to Scully because, 'ironically, in permitting the fight, he has done the same thing he berated Johnnie for doing: turning on the Swede because he is a badly frightened and quite obnoxious human being' (Westbrook, 'Revolt-Search', pp. 104–5). When the Swede's fear no longer restrains his imaginary world, the reality of the hotel no longer contains the action, and the scene moves out into the storm itself.

After his victory the Swede is identified with the blizzard in one of Crane's most difficult passages:

We picture the world as thick with conquering and elate humanity, but here, with the bugles of the tempest pealing, it was hard to imagine a peopled earth. One viewed the existence of man then as a marvel, and conceded a glamour of wonder to these lice which were caused to cling to a whirling, fire-smitten, ice-locked, disease-stricken, space-lost bulb. The conceit of man was explained by this storm to be the very engine of life. One was a coxcomb not to die in it. (p. 124)

Humanity in Crane's world, if it has any sense, does not consider itself conquering and elate relative to either the natural world or the moral world: the physical forces of nature and chance can always overwhelm man, his weak mental machinery makes life difficult enough even in moral terms, and to picture the human lot otherwise is an illusion which the storm should deflate for any rational person. In the midst of the storm, as in the intensity of the

Swede's imaginary world, it is hard to imagine a peopled earth; and the Swede does not so imagine it because he is now isolated from the peopled earth in his illusory notion that he is the conquering and elate hero of the wild West, as invincible as the storm itself. The Swiftian language of the next sentence defines man from the point of view of a Brobdingnagian creature undismayed by such storms, a conquering and elate giant looking down upon normal men from the towering height of the Swede's fantasy: from such a viewpoint man's mere existence is a marvel which earns a 'glamour of wonder'. Man's human dignity which causes him to persist even in the teeth of a blizzard, when considered from the viewpoint of the unleashed fury of either the storm or the Swede's imagination, seems mere conceit—an implicit and laughable affront to such overpowering forces. Yet man, provided he is not a coxcomb such as the Swede, Scully, Johnnie, the cowboy, or the Easterner, does not normally expose himself through his own failure of responsibility either to a howling tempest, as the Swede does, or to moral domination by the fantasy of an excited imagination, as all five do: the external threat triggers the 'engine' of man's moral force—intelligence, will, purposive action, self-control—and man either overcomes or adapts himself to preserve life as long as he can. Of course the Swede is not to die in this storm: he is safest when most immersed in the storm because he '*is*' a coxcomb, tragically deluded by his imaginative conception of the West and the "proof" he has found for it' (Gleckner, p. 278). But the story does not end at this point:

Had Crane left him in the storm, the Swede would be a romantic hero, winning against all odds, a defender of his own integrity, a giant of a man whose stature is even greater by virtue of his kinship with the blizzard. 'However'—and this is Crane's carefully chosen word—'however, the Swede found a saloon.' (Gleckner, p. 278)

Inside the saloon the Swede identifies himself with the storm in his conversation with the bar tender, and thus implies the innocent but gigantic conceit already exhibited in his actions, the moral equivalent of the pointless force of the blizzard. Illusion then collides head-on with reality when he tries to make the men

conform to his dime-novel world by forcing their acceptance of his
'invitation' to drink with him; and, as usual whenever this clash
occurs in a Crane story, illusion is defeated, pierced as easily as a
melon, by reality. The prosaic nature of reality, compared with
the monstrous illusions of the imagination, is implied by the fact
that the smallest man in the room easily kills the burly and violent
Swede.[30] The sense of chagrin suffered by Crane's protagonist at
the end of his progression is suggested by the excellent tableau
which, strictly in terms of Crane's psychological pattern, provides
the aesthetically proper ending: 'The corpse of the Swede, alone
in the saloon, had its eyes fixed upon a dreadful legend that dwelt
atop of the cash-machine: "This registers the amount of your
purchase." ' This legend is correct as a statement of the final step
in Crane's pattern: the protagonist's fears and his giving in to his
own illusions bring upon him, purchase for him, the disenchanting
experience of reality. In this story, however, the protagonist has a
lot of help, and the fact of experience happens to be death.

Crane's pattern overshoots its mark in 'The Blue Hotel', and
the trouble with the final section is not that it

furnishes a trumped-up theme, but that it violates the economy of the
rigidly selective impressionism of the earlier chapters. . . . Crane, in
his honesty, could not end the story with the dramatic cash-machine,
thereby falsifying the values and avoiding the issue; and yet he could not
find a way to break through the hard surface of his impressionistic
narrative to establish the human values upon which the story rests.
(Jumper, pp. 239–40)

Crane's problem was to shift the reader's attention from the
protagonist to the other characters, a problem complicated by both

[30] Gleckner (p. 280, n. 4) justifies the extensive characterization of the gambler by equating him with all the men in the hotel: 'the gambler is like Scully
in that he disarms his "enemies" with his benevolence and good humor; he is
like Johnnie in his fleecing of farmers, like the Easterner in that he seems to
abhor violence and is "delicate in manner," and like the cowboy . . . in being
a "professional" Westerner, the type called "dude" by the Swede.' For an
analogous relationship between the five men in the hotel and the five in the
saloon, see Richard VanDerBeets, 'Character as Structure: Ironic Parallel and
Transformation in "The Blue Hotel" ', *Studies in Short Fiction*, V (1968),
294–5.

the force of the ending of the eighth section and the fact that the essential 'actions' of the others are really their failures to act. The final section adds only two facts that seem important: Johnnie's dishonesty and the Easterner's failure to expose the cheating he witnessed. The fact of the gambler's punishment alters nothing in the earlier part of the story. But confirmation of Johnnie's cheating helps to establish the multiple cause of the disruption in the hotel, the Easterner's admission of guilt declares his own moral position, and his theorizing opposes the dreadful legend of the cash register. However, as Gleckner argues (p. 280), the reading of this final section is

obscured by the frequent identification of Crane with the Easterner, whose final comment is taken as Crane's 'explanation' of the story. I find no evidence in the story for such an identification. He is a character in his own right, and like all the others . . . he does not completely understand what has happened. Crane does, and his final section is calculated to show the reader not what happened, but why. . . . It is the cowboy, not the Easterner, who speaks the epilogue: 'Well, I didn't do anythin', did I?'

The Easterner does not speak for Crane. Crane is aware that the Swede is living in his own illusory world, and the Easterner reveals no such awareness. Also, his 'fog of mysterious theory' misses the essential point: the only significant thing which could have been done would have been to find a more humane means than a knife-thrust to bring the Swede back to reality from the grip of his illusions, for until he thus returns he is not vulnerable to the actions of the lice on the space-lost bulb.

The final section attempts to balance the ending of the previous section: the dreadful legend pins the responsibility for the Swede's death upon the protagonist himself; the final section pins it upon the others and absolves the Swede. The point should emerge from the equilibrium which unites all of these men in an ironic brotherhood of guilt as the consequence of their failure to manifest real brotherhood when the situation demanded it of them. 'Every sin is the result of a collaboration.' And *six* men—Scully, Johnnie, the Easterner, the cowboy, the gambler, and the Swede himself—

collaborate, with the help of chance, to kill the Swede. The cowboy does indeed speak the epilogue.[31] In Crane's world a man who does nothing, or who does less than his awareness of the human situation demands of him, is not exempted from moral responsibility on the grounds of his inaction whether that man be George Kelcey, the Bowery assassin, Billie Atkins, Caspar Cadogan, or the men in the blue hotel.[32]

'War Memories' (probably written during the summer of 1899) has been neglected because it appears to be merely a rehashing of episodes culled from Crane's dispatches from the Spanish-American War. However, a character named Vernall, not Crane, is the narrator; and although Vernall's memories contain much of Crane's experience—even to having attended Claverack—Berryman (p. 224) noted that Vernall's experience deviates noticeably from the actual events in which Crane participated. Comparison with the news reports reveals that 'War Memories' is carefully selective and contains much that is original, and hence there must have been some sort of artistic purpose behind Crane's writing this piece. The only scholar who has grappled seriously with 'War Memories' argues that it 'is a story about the artist's problem of realism, hinging on a verbal irony: "I have told you nothing at all." But aside from the verbal irony, the structural unity of the individual episode depends upon the urgent intuition: these things happened this way to a single, tortured mind' (Jumper, p. 154). This estimate is essentially correct, and it errs only in calling this piece a story. Because it sets forth a moral reality through a careful use of the techniques of fiction in communicating an actual experience 'War Memories' is one of Crane's finest sketches, a late example of the skills exhibited in 'An Experiment in Misery'.

Like the earlier sketch, 'War Memories' is placed within an opening and closing comment by the viewpoint character whose

[31] See W. B. Dillingham, ' "The Blue Hotel" and the Gentle Reader', *Studies in Short Fiction*, I (Spring 1964), 226.

[32] For further comment, see Hugh N. Maclean, 'The Two Worlds of "The Blue Hotel" ', *Modern Fiction Studies*, V (Autumn 1959), 260–70; West, pp. 225–6; Westbrook, 'Social Ethic', pp. 594–5.

problem is essentially the same one that the youth solved through his experiment:

'But to get the real thing!' cried Vernall, the war-correspondent. 'It seems impossible! It is because war is neither magnificent nor squalid; it is simply life, and an expression of life can always evade us. We can never tell life, one to another, although sometimes we think we can.' (*Work*, IX, 201)

Then, at the end of the episodic body of the sketch, Vernall says, 'And you can depend upon it that I have told you nothing at all, nothing at all, nothing at all.' As in the earlier sketch, but with considerably more irony and subtlety, the framing commentary points the way to a correct reading of 'War Memories'.

Vernall's 'real thing', or simply 'life', is the sort of reality defined by the poems as 'a breath, a wind,/A shadow, a phantom'; it is not the literal fact of magnificence or squalor which is easily communicated in a news dispatch. Vernall's opening statement should recall Crane's exasperation after examining *Battles and Leaders of the Civil War*: 'I wonder that *some* of these fellows don't tell how they *felt* in those scraps! They spout eternally of what they *did*.'[33] What they did is merely the literal fact of action, not the reality of the human experience. Vernall's 'real thing' is also implied when a crucial passage of the sketch repeats the image that illustrated Crane's early advice to Arthur Oliver (who had been discussing his own failures to get the real thing down on paper): Crane tossed a handful of sand to the wind and advised Oliver to 'treat your notions like that', to 'forget what you think about it and tell how you feel about it' (see above, p. 26). In 'War Memories' Vernall ends his comments on Lawton's division going up San Juan Hill: 'One cannot speak of it—the spectacle of the common man serenely doing his work, his appointed work. It is the one thing in the universe which makes one fling expression to the winds and be satisfied to simply feel' (p. 238). The real thing is never seen or heard: it is the moral reality which the aware mind perceives within or beyond the literal event, the life which is masked by the mere fact.

[33] Linson, *My Stephen Crane*, p. 37.

The fact of what happened, however, is never sold short. As in 'An Experiment in Misery', the surface action is vividly presented, immediately interesting and satisfying in itself; the reader never has to probe beyond this surface to respond to the force of the writing. For this reason this sketch seems to me the key-stone of *Wounds in the Rain*, superior to the fiction in this collection: the writing of a sketch instead of a story effectively released Crane from the demands of artistic objectivity which he was not entirely able to meet in these stories. Hence, in 'War Memories' the fact is deliberately given full prominence because it is the vehicle for the reality that Vernall's mind perceives in his experience of the fact. Yet Vernall's ironic repetition at the end means exactly what it says: the real thing, the life that Crane experienced in Cuba, is literally 'no-*thing* at all'. The nameless Regular's expert profession-alism, his stoic acceptance of suffering, his brotherhood, his quiet courage in the face of death, and Crane's overwhelming response to such realities are not *things* which can be communicated in factual reports. Thus, every episode in this sketch begins with the external event, just as the youth's experiment began with his observing the external appearance of a tramp, and it progresses to the moral reality beyond the literal event, just as the youth gradu-ally discerned the tramp's point of view. The reality, implicitly Vernall's understanding and response to the fact, is communicated by bringing each episode to a taut emotional climax expressed either in images of intense silence or in images which exist only within Vernall's haunted mind as it leaps beyond the observed event.

Emotionally intense silence is omnipresent in 'War Memories', and is so deftly interwoven that no one has noticed any strangeness about recollections of a shooting war being so saturated with such a quality. The image is introduced unobtrusively in the first episode when a 'silent, determined, ferocious' bunch of bananas knocks the war correspondents about the cabin of a rolling ship. But when Vernall identifies this incident with his problem of separating reality from the façade of fact—'You see? War! A bunch of bananas rampant because the ship rolled' (p. 202)—the ironic deflation removes the significance from the event itself and places it upon Vernall's understanding of the event: fallible human beings with their usual great expectations have set out to capture the reality of war, and their first campaign, as it were, is this comically stupid duel with the enigmatic antagonist in their cabin. The general structure of succeeding episodes is much the same as this one, and Crane's more serious use of silence begins immediately.

When the *Three Friends* is hit by the *Machias* the adventure begins with a signal from the cruiser: 'Thereafter followed one of those silences which had become so peculiarly instructive to the blockade-runner. Somewhere in the darkness we knew that . . . the men stood at general quarters in silence about the long thin guns, and it was the law of life and death that we should make true answer in about the twelfth part of a second' (p. 203). The signals on the *Three Friends* are so cumbersome that Vernall is acutely aware that their delay in answering may get them blown out of the water. The *Machias* appears, 'silent as death', and after the collision and the hail of inquiry the correspondents hold their breath until the mate reports the damage. A stealthy twenty-five-mile trip behind the Spanish lines takes place in silence because of the nearness of the enemy, but a different sort of silence occurs at the bitter climax when the exhausted and half-starved Cuban guides are cheated by circumstance of the food the correspondents promised them: 'they were not indignant at all. They simply smiled and made a gesture which expressed an habitual pessimism. . . . It was the Americans who refused to be comforted' (p. 224). When Gibbs dies, slowly and horribly, some seven feet away from where Vernall listens lying trapped in the darkness, death comes only after 'intervals of terrible silence in which I held my own breath'. Vernall uses silence to express the suffering on the road back from San Juan Hill:

The trail was already crowded with stretcher-bearers and with wounded men who could walk. One had to stem a tide of mute agony. But I don't know that it was mute agony. I only know that it was mute. It was something in which the silence or, more likely, the reticence was an appalling and inexplicable fact. One's senses seemed to demand that these men should cry out. (p. 233)

This episode closes with 'the awful majesty of a man shot in the face', a soldier with a 'great dragoon moustache' with blood dripping from both tips who 'looked steadily into my eyes' and said nothing. Vernall ends his eulogy: 'Thus they moved at San Juan—the soldiers of the United States Regular Army. One pays them the tribute of the toast of silence' (p. 238).

Silence implies the reality of Admiral Sampson, a 'quiet old man' who 'said no word, kindly or unkindly', in tending to his duty. 'Men behaved badly to him, and he said nothing. Men thought of glory, and he considered the management of ships. All without a sound. A noiseless campaign—on his part. No bunting, no arches, no fireworks; nothing but the perfect management of a big fleet' (p. 226). At least twice silence is pointedly opposed to noise in order to distinguish reality from the surface event. In El Caney the chatter of women—'the vacuous morning screech of a swarm of sea-gulls'—is harshly juxtaposed to Vernall's urgent awareness that 'this town was the death-bed, so to speak, of scores of gallant men whose blood was not yet dry; whose hands, of the hue of pale amber, stuck from the soil of the hasty burial' (pp. 244–5). And when Lieutenant Hobson is exchanged from the Spanish lines,

the men of the regular army . . . arose *en masse* and came to attention. . . . They slowly lifted every weather-beaten hat and drooped it until it touched the knee. Then there was a magnificent silence, broken only by the measured hoof-beats of the little company's horses as they rode through the gap. It was solemn, funereal, this splendid silent welcome of a brave man by men who stood on a hill which they had earned out of blood and death . . .

Then suddenly the whole scene went to rubbish. . . . But the real welcome was that welcome of silence. (p. 251)

When the ship loaded with sick and wounded anchors off Old Port Comfort, a launch comes out and circles it while a small woman frantically searches the deck until Colonel Liscum appears at the rail: 'The little woman saw him, and instantly she covered up her face with her hands as if blinded with a flash of white fire. She made no outcry; it was all in this simply swift gesture' (p. 256). Finally, when the wounded and fever-ridden men are landed, dirty and exhausted, they pass silently through a gaily dressed crowd of holiday-makers who welcome them in stunned silence broken only by 'the sound of women weeping'.

Crane's use of Vernall's consciousness to express an unobservable reality does not occur as often as the image of silence, but its appearance is impressive because it implies Vernall's state of mind—a consciousness that has been battered by just about all the experience it can take. This man's mind is seized so intensely by a particular sight that it seems to leap beyond it to the implicit reality almost as a means of release from the fact. Sometimes this haunted consciousness reveals itself in imagery, as when Vernall's glance shies away from marines landing and fixes upon their destination. The stark prose charges the images of fire, darkness, blue steel, and gore with the burden of an ominous reality beyond the observed fact:

It was at nightfall, and on the eastward point a small village was burning, and it happened that a fiery light was thrown upon some palm-trees so that it made them into enormous crimson feathers. The water was the colour of blue steel; the Cuban woods were sombre; high shivered the gory feathers. The last boat-loads of the marine battalion were pulling for the beach. (pp. 206–7)

Sometimes Vernall's awareness struggles unsuccessfully, as when he attempts to fix the reality of a man seen a mile away, behind the enemy lines, who seems to be striding the very fire of a thunderous battle. And when he comes upon a red-headed Spanish corpse his mind gropes helplessly after a sensed reality it cannot grasp: 'Sleep well, red-headed peasant. You came to another hemisphere to fight because—because you were told to, I suppose. Well, there you are, buried in your trench on San Juan Hill. . . . Sleep well, red-headed mystery' (p. 239).[34] But the most striking use of this technique occurs when Vernall's mind races beyond the already vivid fact of the church-hospital:

[34] Cf. Ernest Hemingway, *Death in the Afternoon* (New York, 1932), p. 20.

The interior of the church was too cave-like in its gloom for the eyes of the operating surgeons, so they had had the altar-table carried to the doorway, where there was a bright light. Framed then in the black archway was the altar-table with the figure of a man upon it. He was naked save for a breech-clout, and so close, so clear was the ecclesiastic suggestion that one's mind leaped to a fantasy that this thin, pale figure had just been torn down from a cross. The flash of the impression was like light, and for this instant it illumined all the dark recesses of one's remotest idea of sacrilege, ghastly and wanton . . . something meaningless and at the same time overwhelming, crushing, monstrous. (pp. 245–6)

In each episode the implicit reality of the experience is the cause of the intense silence at the climax, the shock of recognition which sends Vernall's mind reeling beyond the fact. Whichever way it is presented, this 'life' remains the nothing at all which Vernall insists he *has* conveyed to the reader. 'War Memories' contains some of Crane's best prose, it is easily his most artistic presentation of his own attitudes towards men at war, and reality—in this sketch published six months before his death just as in the 'Experiment' written early in his career—is once more shown to be the moral shadow the fact casts within the mind of the aware perceiver.

'An Episode of War' (published December 1899) provides an excellent and late example of Crane's pattern used with only minor variations. A lieutenant is shot in the arm, and the wound immediately separates him, psychologically, from the unwounded:

A wound gives strange dignity to him who bears it. Well men shy from this new and terrible majesty. It is as if the wounded man's hand is upon the curtain which hangs before the revelations of all existence . . . and the power of it sheds radiance upon a bloody form, and makes the other men understand sometimes that they are little. (*Work*, IX, 130–1)

This man's hand is indeed upon the curtain before a revelation, but this revelation does not concern all existence, and men are always little even if they are not always aware of it. However, the protagonist in this story is the wounded man himself.

With his wound the lieutenant is immediately possessed with a fear of losing his arm, a fear which is unformulated, unrealized by the lieutenant himself until, at the climax, it becomes defined in his words to the surgeon: 'I guess I won't have it amputated.' Because the doctor has not even hinted at amputation, or said or done anything to justify this reaction, the lieutenant's statement in this context implies the cause of his psychological isolation during his walk through the rear lines to the field hospital. The imminent loss of an arm is an unknown experience to this man, yet with the fact of his wound it is impossible for him to avoid going to the hospital for treatment; thus, the lieutenant's vague fear evokes illusions about the gravity of his wound:

One timidly presented his shoulder and asked the lieutenant if he cared to lean upon it, but the latter waved him away mournfully. He wore the look of one who knows he is the victim of a terrible disease and understands his helplessness. . . . He held his right wrist tenderly in his left hand as if the wounded arm was made of very brittle glass. (p. 131)

These illusory notions function more or less as a psychological crutch; i.e. if his situation is as grave as all this, then he must be a brave man to walk straight to the hospital, an 'old schoolhouse, as sinister to him as the portals of death'. After his ineffectual struggle with the doctor he undergoes his feared experience, and the story ends: 'When he reached home, his sisters, his mother, his wife, sobbed for a long time at the sight of the flat sleeve. "Oh, well," he said, standing shamefaced amid these tears, "I don't suppose it matters so much as all that" ' (p. 134). The fact of experience has removed the curtain from the only revelation this man gained from his wound. He stands shamefaced before these feminine tears because the reality of his experience has fallen far short of what his imagination had conceived it would be, and his fears and illusions before the fact have now deflated to a memory of which he is somewhat ashamed.

In this story, however, Crane seems to exchange intensity for subtlety in his ironic handling of the protagonist's perceptions. During that part of the protagonist's progression in which his emotional state usually leads him to distort the reality he perceives,

Crane here stresses the unusual clarity of the lieutenant's awareness of external events. This emphasis results in some excellent
impressionistic sketching—for example, Crane's superb description of a battery racing into firing position (pp. 131–2)—but it also
prepares for the climax of the lieutenant's experience. At the
hospital he is not at all deceived by the surgeon's assurance that
the arm will not be amputated; otherwise the hospital would not
seem 'as sinister to him as the portals of death'. But neither is his
perception of his own situation correct: his fears are fulfilled only
so far as the literal fact which results from his experience is concerned. The extent of his shame at home among the sobbing women
is the measure of how far the perception of this man—who sees so
sharply the picturesque composition of the meeting between the
general and his aide, the speeding battery, the coming of death to
the grey-faced man—failed to grasp the reality of the experience
which was soon to come to him.

It is singularly appropriate that the last major work from a man
who always strove for brevity and compression should be 'The
Upturned Face' (written by November 1899), about fifteen
hundred words long and one of Crane's best stories. The prose
bristles with tension because the protagonists, Timothy Lean and
the adjutant, are caught right at the edge of hysteria; and their
hysteria is fully justified by Crane's combining the ghastly nature
of the experience they cannot avoid and the awful illusion that
seizes them because of their situation. In accordance with the
military code by which they live, these officers have to bury the
body of a good friend who has just been killed, and the entire
action takes place while the men are under rifle fire from enemy
sharp-shooters; but this situation in itself, bad as it is, does not
explain the men's hysteria. The adjutant's opening question,
'What will we do now?', clearly implies that burying the body of a
comrade is a hitherto unknown experience to these men, a fact
which is confirmed by their hesitation in searching the body, their
uncertainty about the burial service and when it is spoken. Their
unavoidable task, however, is made almost unbearable by their
illusions about the corpse: Lean and the adjutant refuse to accept

the fact of death even though this fact is harshly forced upon them by the necessity of an immediate burial before they can withdraw and save their own lives. Hence their hysteria: the fact is—literally, in this story—staring them in the face, and they do not accept it.

The story is loaded with actions which imply this particular hysteria. The corpse is always personal—*his* clothes, see what *he's* got, *his* sword. Lean says, 'we've got to bury old Bill.' When Lean says that 'it would be better if we laid him in ourselves', he means that it will be more meaningful to Bill if he is laid in his grave by his two friends rather than by the two privates who have dug the grave. Both Lean and the adjutant are 'particular that their fingers should not feel the corpse', so they get it into the grave by touching only its clothing. Afterwards, 'the two officers, straightening, looked again at each other—they were always looking at each other.' Then the adjutant says, 'let us say something—while he can hear us.' And after the grotesque service which finally comes down to the single word 'Mercy'—a plea as much for themselves as for their dead friend—neither Lean nor the adjutant wants to see the earth shovelled upon the upturned face of the corpse in the grave.

Then the soldier emptied his shovel on—on the feet.

Timothy Lean felt [significantly] as if tons had been swiftly lifted from off his forehead. He had felt that perhaps the private might empty the shovel on—on the face. It had been emptied on the feet. There was a great point gained there—ha, ha!—the first shovelful had been emptied on the feet. How satisfactory!

The adjutant began to babble. 'Well, of course—a man we've messed with all these years—impossible—you can't, you know, leave your intimate friends rotting on the field.' (*Work*, IX, 169–70)

Then, when the privates have been sent to the rear and Lean has completed the job to the extent that the next shovelful must land on the face, their hysteria becomes so intensified that Lean curses his superior.

The men fear to cover the face with its open eyes because this act will, to them, finally make the fact of death irrevocable. Similarly, they refuse to touch the corpse because their touch would confirm the fact they refuse to accept. Thus, the tension mounts steadily as their illusion becomes increasingly threatened until story, tension, hysteria—all—are brutally ended by the final word as the earth lands upon the upturned face: 'plop'. The prosaic fact—this flat 'plop'—does away with their fear because it signifies their safe completion of the action they feared; and it reveals their hysteria for the absurdity that it is. This corpse was after all but a corpse: it was not Bill, it owned no sword or clothes, it could hear no prayer, and whatever happened to it could happen to any other piece of inanimate clay with exactly the same significance.

VII

READER'S NOTES

CRANE'S world is reality as he perceived it, externally amoral matter subject to chance upheavals of purposeless violence and therefore ultimately unknowable and for ever beyond man's complete control; the mere fact that human life has to be lived in such a world places full responsibility for all moral values upon man alone, and thus the separation between the physical world and man's moral world is absolute. This perception, so far as I can determine, underlies everything Crane wrote— fiction, poems, newspaper pieces—because, apparently, it had come to him 'in that vague unformulating way in which I sometimes come to know things' (*Letters*, p. 101), and he was working on the basis of it, before he examined it intellectually by sorting out its various elements and implications to form the secure, thoroughly understood philosophical position which he found tenable—an intellectual process which was well advanced before he finished work on *The Red Badge* and was completed with *The Black Riders*.

Crane's protagonists, from Uncle Jake to Timothy Lean, have freedom of the will to choose their own commitments from whatever alternatives their awareness of the particular situations they confront makes available to them: 'Free will does not mean the power to control events; it means the power to control belief and effort' (Westbrook, 'Revolt-Search', p. 103). Because Crane's adult characters possess this freedom they are without exception— honest or dishonest, aware or innocent—held morally responsible for whatever choices their actions imply that they have made; and the best people in this world, those who are both honest and aware of the human situation that man has to accept, also hold themselves personally responsible for their own shortcomings even if such weaknesses are unperceived or misunderstood by other men. And because the precarious human situation in the moral desert is at best difficult, no man escapes moral responsibility by simply doing nothing: failure to act in this situation is itself an action freely chosen, and it is morally condemned. Only children are exempt from moral responsibility, and they are excused only long enough to acquire a minimal awareness of the reality with which all adults have to cope. Because the separation between man's moral world and external nature is absolute, Crane's characters are morally never subject to externality; human desires and intentions have to be carried out in the external world, and the ultimate success or failure of any human action is therefore contingent upon externals, but the moral value inherent in the choice of the action is not determined by externality. Morally, Crane's physically puny man is able to stand against the mountains and prevail. Crane's recurring pattern would not be meaningful without the morally responsible protagonist who is free to choose his own actions: he is confronted with an unknown because he has chosen to place himself in such a position that, often with the help of chance, this unknown becomes unavoidable; he suffers because of his own weaknesses; and his shamefaced deflation by the fact of experience could not occur if he did not hold himself morally responsible for his own past actions. Hence, the naturalistic frame of reference is far too narrow to contain even Crane's early Bowery writings.

Crane was aware of naturalistic doctrines and techniques and mocked them in 'Why Did the Young Clerk Swear?' But his early development seems best described in terms of his own increasing awareness of the implications present in his own perception of reality. In the Sullivan County tales, written when he was merely 'clever', the little man's deflating experiences do not bring awareness; and in *Maggie*, where only hypocrites triumph and even existence seems to require personal dishonesty, Crane apparently wrestles with the cynicism which he later called 'uneducated' a 'little, little way' along the road to wisdom. But the little man and Maggie are different only in degree, not in kind, from the later protagonists—for example, Henry Fleming and the correspondent —who learn and succeed only because they are more completely human, not because they live in an external world which differs in any significant way from the world inhabited by the little man and Maggie. Crane wrote only one brief story, 'The Snake' (published 1896), which it is at least possible to read as naturalism without either distorting or ignoring anything he has to say in it; and this story is not typical because the essential action is an external fight between a man and a snake, the cause is hereditary hatred and fear, and the prose offers few indications of having been written by an ironist. Elsewhere, truth or reality for Crane is mental and moral, even in the early work, and thus his ironic awareness is free to explore his own perceptions of man's weak mental machinery as it struggles to carry human desire and intention into external effect. As at least one excellent scholar has perceived, 'the disappearance of irony as a prevailing tone is worth attention as a difference between Realism (Howells, Fuller) and Naturalism (Norris, Dreiser). It is a change in which the felt presence of the author's taste and reservations about human nature is succeeded, with an accompanying loss of incisiveness, by a truly faceless impersonality which is uncritical.'[1]

If Crane's recurring psychological pattern implicitly rejects naturalism, it also militates against the attempt to explain his work by means of image clusters or interrelated symbols. If the pattern provides the essential structure of the story then Crane's powerful imagery is not primarily conceptual. The isolated image may well have stimulated Crane's imagination—the dreadful legend of the cash register must have lurked in Crane's mind before it became part of the structured whole which constitutes 'The Blue Hotel'— but if symbols exist only in context the recurring pattern conceptually forms the structural context that determines the function of any image or symbol contained within it. The phrasing of Crane's comment to Willa Cather, that he only had one trump, implies a motif which is transferable to various settings or situations

[1] James B. Stronks, '*A Modern Instance*', *American Literary Realism 1870– 1910*, No. 4 (Fall 1968), n.p.

and able to survive loss or gain of particular incident; thus, the sort of imagery which appears within a given story arises naturally out of the particular situation Crane has chosen as a means of embodying his conceptual pattern. Crane varies his pattern conceptually and manipulates it to express his meaning from story to story; and his meaning in a particular story, once conceived in terms of structure, merely becomes intensified and enriched through his conspicuous craftsmanship with image and symbol. In short, an understanding of Crane should best be approached by way of the structural pattern itself.

Such an approach at least suggests possible explanations for some of the matters which trouble Crane's readers. For example, the recurring pattern accounts for the notable absence from Crane's work of moral commitments beyond those of the individual protagonist. *The Red Badge* gives no hint of the broad moral issues behind the Civil War, such humanistic purposes as freeing the slaves or preserving the Union as an instrument of order— purposes which Crane himself obviously would have affirmed, and which must have helped some of the soldiers in Fleming's situation to stand fast and shoulder their more immediate responsibilities. *Maggie* offers no suggestions for social reform, there is no external programme which might regenerate George Kelcey, no help for the assassin's drunkenness, no humanitarian means of relief for the suffering of Dr. Trescott—such omissions are constant in Crane's work: he, apparently, affirms an individual moral responsibility which is absolute, and simultaneously ignores the broader issues by means of which the individual translates his own efforts into specific social and political accomplishment. Crane's protagonists, however, progress to awareness of an already existing reality, and their struggle depends partly upon their lack of knowledge, partly upon their fear, and partly upon their distortions of reality because of their own weaknesses. Crane could hardly present the broad moral issues as illusions, as the unknown cause of fear, or reveal a character's lack of knowledge by means of them. More importantly, until Crane's protagonists gain an awareness of reality and suffer the chastening of ego that their experiences entail, they—like the pines to whom the shell speaks—are not morally fit to bear the responsibility of such issues. Crane's pattern, in other words, analyses the individual's progression to a moral posture which is prerequisite to a significant affirmation of moral issues beyond his own personal honesty, humility, and acceptance of the human situation. Thus, there should be nothing strange about Crane's omission of these greater responsibilities from his protagonist's progression towards the capability of assuming them.

The recurring pattern also helps to explain the scarcity of romantic love and memorable young female characters in Crane's work. Romantic love would seem difficult for anyone to portray by means of a structural pattern which acquires its aesthetic force from the impact of an ironic deflation. Joyce may have performed such a feat in 'Araby', but the best Crane could do was 'The Pace of Youth' and 'A Grey Sleeve'. Crane's protagonist usually makes rather an ass of himself before experience deflates his swelling illusions to an unpleasant recollection, and editors in the 1890s were not anxious to see such a thing happen to beautiful young ladies in the fiction they published. Howells conducted beautiful young Irene Lapham through an experience similar to the ones suffered by Crane's protagonists; but the misfortunes of Irene are cushioned by the rich context of an extremely well-made novel and, as Crane's trump made him primarily a writer of short stories, the well-made novel was not for him.

Much of the peculiar intensity of Crane's best work can be credited to his recurring pattern. During the greater part of the protagonist's journey to awareness he labours in an unstable nightmare-world of fear, vanity, desire, incompetence—an illusory world created from the distortion wrought by his excited imagination. Because this distortion usually increases until the deflating fact of experience, the intensity of his best portrayals of the protagonist's nightmare—perhaps *The Red Badge*, 'Death and the Child', 'The Blue Hotel', 'The Upturned Face'—rises towards the level of hallucination as his protagonist edges closer and closer to panic. But provision for such intensity is built into the pattern itself for an author who utilizes the third-person limited narrative technique. Thus, the presence of such intensity in Crane's work need not imply the unconscious expression of hidden compulsions; it more reasonably suggests the labour of craftsmanship by an artist who was well aware of what he was pursuing—the greater the intensity of the protagonist's distortion, the greater the impact of the 'plop' when experience suddenly slams him back to reality.

Finally, a knowledge of the recurring pattern and Crane's dependence upon it should provide a viable approach to the enigma of Crane the man. Crane seems to me neither genius nor Oedipal monstrosity, but a brilliant, brutally hard-working craftsman whose powers of perception were much greater than his depth of intellect. He did not spring into life fully armed except in terms of his ironic vision—and even this had to hone its edge on experience. His writings, particularly during the first half of his career, reveal that he had to work hard to turn an angular, disjointed prose style into flexibility and smoothness; and the measure of his success can be taken by anyone who compares 'The Open Boat' with a Sullivan County sketch, or the sustained understatement and restraint of the final section of 'The Bride Comes to Yellow Sky' with the shrill irony of *Maggie*. Yet Crane's pattern implies that his approach to fiction was determined by his own acute perception, and thus at least a partial explanation of why he has proved such an uneasy subject for the literary historian is available. The structural core of Crane's work is timeless and universal, and not dependent upon whatever his literary background may have been. The realization that man's imagination is powerfully stimulated by fear is at least as old as Seneca's *dubia plus torquent mala*. The same realization, together with an awareness that the creations of the imagination further increase fear, is exploited in *Macbeth* and *Othello*. Fielding describes this psychological state:

Indeed, fear is never more uneasy than when it doth not certainly know its object; for on such occasions the mind is ever employed in raising a thousand bugbears and phantoms, much more dreadful than any realities, and, like children, when they tell tales of hobgoblins, seems industrious in terrifying itself.

Hazlitt examines the same condition:

the imagination is that faculty which represents objects, not as they are in themselves, but as they are moulded by other thoughts and feelings, into an infinite variety of shapes and combinations of power. . . . It conveys the impression which the object under the influence of passion makes on the mind. Let an object, for instance, be presented to the senses in a state of agitation or fear—and the imagination will distort or magnify the object, and convert it into the likeness of whatever is most proper to encourage the fear.[2]

Crane had no need to read these authors to discover the principal elements of his pattern for himself: all he had to do was train his own perception upon his own reactions to fear and, assuming he was a normal human being, analyse them. If Crane's career anywhere reveals the flash of genius it is in his aligning these universal human reactions to fear into a sharply ironic pattern that turns upon the sufferer's awareness, and in his immediate perception of the artistic possibilities inherent in his one trump. Literary historians have made excellent contributions to a knowledge of Crane's education, social surroundings, factual matters of biographical and bibliographical interest, his attitudes toward specific institutions of his day (such as Gullason's study of the 'yellow journalism' Crane loathed), and the various influences which touched him; but the conceptual pattern itself is not likely to be caught in the standard nets of literary history.

At first glance, Crane's 'narrowness of interest'—mourned by readers from his own time to the present—seems confirmed by his dependence upon his recurring pattern. So long as he uses a structure based upon a psychological progression to awareness he is obliged to confine his subject-matter to those areas of man's inner life which his pattern can express: fear, vanity, ignorance, honesty or dishonesty, chagrin, the activity of the imagination, the necessity for self-restraint and brotherhood, the increase in

---

[2] Seneca, *Agamemnon*, III, i, 29; Fielding, *Amelia*, Book VI, ch. 4; Hazlitt, *Lectures on the English Poets*, Lecture I, 'On Poetry in General'.

awareness that results from an abrupt deflation of expectation. But such a subject-matter lies right at the foundations of man's moral life, and fashionable lamentation over the narrowness of an author intensely concerned with it therefore suggests a certain innocence. Crane's interests, of course, are not nearly as narrow as they are presumed to be, and readers who believe otherwise probably have not read or have not understood the poems, his major work apart from his one trump. The full thrust of Crane's mind cannot be measured in his fiction alone. The recurring pattern, through the consistency of Crane's attitudes towards man's moral life which it reveals, clearly implies a frame of reference greater than itself. The pattern catches the protagonist as he undergoes the crucial process of growing up psychologically to responsible manhood, and to be a man in Crane's world entails a great deal more than mere awareness that reality is after all but reality. As Crane himself suggested, the full scope of his thought is available in his poems: a mature philosophy—thoroughly examined and subjected to proof in the furnace of his irony—which has the satisfying solidity of completeness, the whole moral truth which Crane's perception allowed him to accept, and which was not to be shaken by either natural forces, the inevitability of final death, or the actions of other men. Crane's poems reveal a man who looked carefully at the realities of human life and judged wisely. The recurring pattern in his fiction concerns the most dramatic incident in the normal individual's progress towards the body of truth set forth in the poems, and thus it should point the reader towards that whole which defines the full significance of the fictional protagonists' archetypal experience.

Most interesting of all, perhaps, are a couple of loose analogies which may be drawn between the recurring pattern and Crane's stoic humanism, analogies which admittedly are more suggestive than conclusive. Crane's moral code, like the pattern itself, seems to be less an intellectual construction than a consequence of his perception. In itself, apart from the manner in which the poems and stories present it, it is neither particularly complex nor subtle, and—with the possible exception of Marcus Aurelius' *Meditations*

—there seem to be no strong reasons for believing it derived from important sources other than Crane's own perception of the human situation. But if his stoic humanism is primarily a creation of his own perception, then the biographer who attempts to stalk Crane's mind by way of the various influences to which he was subjected is roughly in the position of the literary historian who approaches Crane's work by means of historical and literary sources. Crane did not grow up in a vacuum: he was affected by the Methodism of his parents, the American Protestant evangelical tradition, his association with painters in New York, what Kwiat calls his 'newspaper experience', the hardship of his early years, the humanity of Howells—but so far as Crane's own philosophy is concerned, such influences often seem to form part of the 'enormous repudiations' noted by H. G. Wells. Whatever contradictions exist can be attributed to Crane's ironic perception: although each of these influences helped to sharpen his vision, the vision itself would necessarily have been turned back upon the influence, and Crane—always the discriminating, organizing, repudiating ironist—in each instance must have accepted only that which his own perception told him was valuable. The result, as implied by the poems, is a common-sense moral position which Crane could continually justify on the basis of his continuing perception of the human situation, and a repudiation of whatever his perception could not affirm as acceptable. Hence, the essential Crane should continue to elude the investigator of the influences upon his life until the ironic vision is recognized as a constant factor in whatever biographical equation is used. Crane, that is, is not at all the result of influences A, B, and C: he is the result of *only* what his perception allowed him to accept from *each* of these influences at the time he was subjected to it.

Such a claim is suggested by Crane's lifelong use of his one trump in his fiction. The pattern is ultimately only a codification or organization, for artistic purposes, of the ironic vision itself. The distinctive function of an ironic perception is the same as that from which Crane's structural pattern acquires its aesthetic force: the piercing or deflation of appearance to bring about an awareness of reality. The ironist moves through the world as something of a psychological alien only because his perception makes constantly available to him precisely the bleak awareness of reality that Crane's protagonists can acquire only by passing through the unpleasant experiences of the pattern. Thus, whatever his work rejects as illusory normally figures as part of the enormous repudiations in Crane's own life. The code of values set forth in the poems and fiction, in other words, constitutes the philosophical position which Crane's perception affirmed as the one most likely to save him from suffering exactly the sort of deflation his protagonists experience. Crane the man, in brief, seems to me remarkably consistent with his work.

Crane's penetrating awareness and untiring labour were concentrated upon the moral realities of human life in this world. So long as that life continues, so long as moral values survive as realities, Crane's work will remain, as he wished, a benefit to his kind.

BIBLIOGRAPHY

This bibliography contains only those books by Crane which are cited in the text; those fugitive pieces by Crane which are either obscure, uncollected, of unconfirmed authorship, or mentioned by date in the text; and critical works cited. Later editions and collections of Crane's writings cited in the text appear below under the name of the editor.

WORKS BY CRANE

Active Service. New York: Frederick A. Stokes, 1899.

The Black Riders and Other Lines. Boston: Copeland and Day, 1895.

George's Mother. New York and London: Edward Arnold, 1896.

Great Battles of the World. Philadelphia: Lippincott, 1901.

The Little Regiment and Other Episodes of the American Civil War. New York: Appleton, 1896.

Maggie, A Girl of the Streets, by 'Johnston Smith'. New York: privately printed, 1893.

Maggie, A Girl of the Streets. New York: Appleton, 1896.

The O'Ruddy, completed by Robert Barr. New York: Frederick A. Stokes, 1903.

The Red Badge of Courage, An Episode of the American Civil War. New York: Appleton, 1895.

The Third Violet. New York: Appleton, 1897.

War Is Kind. New York: Frederick A. Stokes, 1899.

Wounds in the Rain. New York: Frederick A. Stokes, 1900.

'Asbury Park as Seen by Stephen Crane', New York *Journal*, 16 August 1896, p. 33.

'Bear and Panther', New York *Tribune*, 17 July 1892, p. 18.

'Billy Atkins Went to Omaha', New York *Press*, 20 May 1894, part 4, p. 3.

'Crowding into Asbury Park', New York *Tribune*, 3 July 1892, p. 28.

'Daughters and Sons of the King', New York *Tribune*, 7 August 1891, p. 7.

'An Experiment in Misery', New York *Press*, 22 April 1894, part 3, p. 2.

'Great Bugs in Onondaga', New York *Tribune*, 1 June 1891, p. 1.

'Howells Discussed at Avon-By-The-Sea', New York *Tribune*, 18 August 1891, p. 5.

'Howells Fears Realists Must Wait', New York *Times*, 28 October 1894, p. 20.

'Hunting Wild Hogs', New York *Tribune*, 28 February 1892, p. 17.

'Joys of Seaside Life', New York *Tribune*, 17 July 1892, p. 18.

'The Last of the Mohicans', New York *Tribune*, 21 February 1892, p. 12.

'The Last Panther', New York *Tribune*, 3 April 1892, p. 17.

'Meetings Begun at Ocean Grove', New York *Tribune*, 2 July 1892, p. 4.

'Meetings for Worship at Asbury Park', New York *Tribune*, 6 July 1891, p. 2.

'Nebraskans' Bitter Fight for Life', Philadelphia *Press*, 24 February 1895, part 3, p. 25.

'Not Much of a Hero', New York *Tribune*, 1 May 1892, p. 15.

'On the Banks of Shark River', New York *Tribune*, 11 July 1891, p. 5.

'On the Boardwalk', New York *Tribune*, 14 August 1892, p. 17.

'On the New-Jersey Coast', New York *Tribune*, 21 August 1892, p. 22.

'Regulars Get No Glory', New York *World*, 20 July 1898, p. 6.

'A Reminiscence of Indian War', New York *Tribune*, 26 June 1892, p. 17.

'Services by the Seaside', New York *Tribune*, 20 July 1891, p. 3.

'The Snake', *Pocket Magazine*, II (August 1896), 125–32.

'Stephen Crane's Own Story', New York *Press*, 7 January 1897, p. 1.

'Sullivan County Bears', New York *Tribune*, 1 May 1892, p. 16.

'Travels in New York: The Broken-Down Van', New York *Tribune*, 10 July 1892, p. 8.

'Two Men and a Bear', New York *Tribune*, 24 July 1892, p. 17.

'Waiting for the Spring', *Prairie Schooner*, XXXVIII (Spring 1964), 15–26 (from Nebraska *State Journal*, 24 February 1895).

'The Way in Sullivan County', New York *Tribune*, 8 May 1892, p. 15.

CRITICAL WORKS CITED

ÅHNEBRINK, LARS. *The Beginnings of Naturalism in American Fiction.* Upsala: Upsala University Press, 1950.

ADAMS, R. P. 'Naturalistic Fiction: "The Open Boat" ', *Tulane Studies in English*, IV (1954), 137–46.

BARNES, ROBERT. 'Crane's "The Bride Comes to Yellow Sky" ', *Explicator*, XVI (April 1958), item 39.

BASSAN, MAURICE. 'An Early Draft of *George's Mother*', *American Literature*, XXXVI (January 1965), 518–22.

BEER, THOMAS. *Stephen Crane: A Study in American Letters*, introduction by Joseph Conrad. London: Heinemann, 1924.

BERRYMAN, JOHN. *Stephen Crane*. New York: Sloane, 1950.

BLUM, MORGAN. 'Berryman as Biographer, Stephen Crane as Poet', *Poetry*, LXXVIII (August 1951), 298–307.

BRENNAN, JOSEPH X. 'Ironic and Symbolic Structure in Crane's *Maggie*', *Nineteenth-Century Fiction*, XVI (March 1962), 303–15.

— 'Stephen Crane and the Limits of Irony', *Criticism*, XI (Spring 1969), 183–200.

BROWN, CURTIS. *Contacts*. London: Cassell, 1935.

BUITENHUIS, PETER. 'The Essentials of Life: "The Open Boat" as Existentialist Fiction', *Modern Fiction Studies*, V (Autumn 1959), 243–50.

BUSHMAN, JOHN C. 'The Fiction of Stephen Crane and Its Critics', unpublished Ph.D. thesis (Illinois, 1943).

CADY, EDWIN H. *The Realist At War: The Mature Years, 1885–1920, of William Dean Howells*. Syracuse: Syracuse University Press, 1958.

— *Stephen Crane*. New York: Twayne, 1962.

— 'Stephen Crane and the Strenuous Life', *English Literary History*, XXVIII (December 1961), 376–82.

CARLSON, ERIC W. 'Stephen Crane's *The Red Badge of Courage*', *Explicator*, XV (March 1958), item 34.

CATHER, WILLA. 'When I Knew Stephen Crane', *Prairie Schooner*, XXIII (Fall 1949), 231–7.

CAZEMAJOU, JEAN. 'Stephen Crane et ses esquisses de vie new-yorkaise', *Caliban*, no. 1 (janvier 1964), 7–24.

— 'Stephen Crane: Pennington Seminary: Étape d'une éducation méthodiste', *Études Anglaises*, XX (avril–juin 1967), 140–8.

COLVERT, JAMES B. 'Stephen Crane's Magic Mountain', *Stephen Crane: A Collection of Critical Essays*, ed. Maurice Bassan. Englewood Cliffs: Prentice Hall, 1967. pp. 95–105.

— 'Stephen Crane: The Development of His Art', unpublished Ph.D. thesis (Louisiana, 1953).

— 'Structure and Theme in Stephen Crane's Fiction', *Modern Fiction Studies*, V (Autumn 1959), 199–208.

— 'Style and Meaning in Stephen Crane: *The Open Boat*', *Texas Studies in English*, XXXVII (1958), 35–45.

COX, JAMES T. 'Stephen Crane as Symbolic Naturalist: An Analysis of "The Blue Hotel" ', *Modern Fiction Studies*, III (Summer 1957), 147–58.

CRANE, HELEN R. 'My Uncle, Stephen Crane', *American Mercury*, XXXI (January 1934), 24–9.

CUNLIFFE, MARCUS. 'Stephen Crane and the American Background of *Maggie*', *American Quarterly*, VII (Spring 1955), 31–44.

DAVIS, RICHARD HARDING. 'Our War Correspondents in Cuba and Puerto Rico', *Harper's*, XCVIII (May 1899), 938–48.

DAVISON, RICHARD A. 'Crane's "Blue Hotel" Revisited: The Illusion of Fate', *Modern Fiction Studies*, XV (Winter 1969–70), 537–9.

DILLINGHAM, W. B. ' "The Blue Hotel" and the Gentle Reader', *Studies in Short Fiction*, I (Spring 1964), 224–6.

ELCONIN, VICTOR A. 'Stephen Crane at Asbury Park', *American Literature*, XX (November 1948), 275–89.

FERGUSON, S. C. 'Crane's "The Bride Comes to Yellow Sky" ', *Explicator*, XXI (March 1963), item 59.

FITELSON, DAVID. 'Stephen Crane's *Maggie* and Darwinism', *American Quarterly*, XVI (Summer 1964), 182–94.

FOLLETT, WILSON S. Introduction, *The Work of Stephen Crane*. New York: Knopf, 1925–7. III, ix–xxii.

— ed. *The Work of Stephen Crane*. New York: Knopf, 1925–7. 12 vols.

FREDERIC, HAROLD. 'Stephen Crane's New Book', New York *Times*, 1 May 1898, p. 19.

FRIEDMAN, NORMAN. 'Criticism and the Novel', *Antioch Review*, XVIII (Fall 1958), 356–61.

FRYCKSTEDT, OLOV W. 'Crane's *Black Riders*: A Discussion of Dates', *Studia Neophilologica*, XXXIV (1962), 282–93.

— 'Henry Fleming's Tupenny Fury: Cosmic Pessimism in Stephen Crane's *The Red Badge of Courage*', *Studia Neophilologica*, XXXIII (1961), 265–81.

— 'Stephen Crane in the Tenderloin', *Studia Neophilologica*, XXXIV (1962), 135–63.

— ed. *Stephen Crane: Uncollected Writings*. Upsala: Upsala University Press, 1963.

GARGANO, JAMES W. 'Crane's "A Mystery of Heroism": A Possible Source', *Modern Language Notes*, LXXIV (January 1959), 22–3.

GARLAND, HAMLIN. 'An Ambitious French Novel and a Modest American Story', *Arena*, VIII (June 1893), xi–xii.

GEISMAR, MAXWELL. *Rebels and Ancestors: The American Novel 1890–1915*. Boston: Houghton Mifflin, 1953.

GILDER, JEANETTE. 'Romance by Swinburne and Realism by Crane', New York *World*, 31 May 1896, p. 20.

GLECKNER, ROBERT F. 'Stephen Crane and the Wonder of Man's Conceit', *Modern Fiction Studies*, V (Autumn 1959), 271–81.

GREENFIELD, STANLEY B. 'The Unmistakable Stephen Crane', *PMLA*, LXXIII (December 1958), 562–72.

GULLASON, THOMAS A. 'The Cranes at Pennington Seminary', *American Literature*, XXXIX (January 1968), 530–41.

— 'The Jamesian Motif in Stephen Crane's Last Novels', *Personalist*, LXII (January 1961), 77–84.

— 'New Light on the Crane–Howells Relationship', *New England Quarterly*, XXX (September 1957), 389–92.

— 'The Significance of "Wounds in the Rain" ', *Modern Fiction Studies*, V (Autumn 1959), 235–42.

— 'Some Aspects of the Mind and Art of Stephen Crane', unpublished Ph.D. thesis (Wisconsin, 1953).

— 'A Stephen Crane Find: Nine Newspaper Sketches', *Southern Humanities Review*, II (Winter 1968), 1–37.

— 'Stephen Crane's Private War Against Yellow Journalism', *Huntington Library Quarterly*, XXII (May 1959), 201–9.

— 'The Symbolic Unity of "The Monster" ', *Modern Language Notes*, LXXV (December 1960), 663–8.

— ed. *The Complete Novels of Stephen Crane*. Garden City: Doubleday, 1967.

HART, ANDREW W. 'Stephen Crane's Social Outlook as Revealed in His Writings', unpublished Ph.D. thesis (Michigan State, 1955).

HEMINGWAY, ERNEST. *Death in the Afternoon*. New York: Scribner's, 1933.

HOFFMAN, DANIEL G. *The Poetry of Stephen Crane*. New York: Columbia University Press, 1957.

— 'Stephen Crane's First Story', *Bulletin of the New York Public Library*, LXIV (May 1960), 273–8.

— 'Stephen Crane's Last Novel', *Bulletin of the New York Public Library*, LXIV (June 1960), 337–43.

'Holland' [ELISHA JAY EDWARDS]. 'Society Leaders' Suffrage Crusade', Philadelphia *Press*, 22 April 1894, p. 5.

HOLTON, MILNE. 'The Sparrow's Fall and the Sparrow's Eye: Crane's *Maggie*', *Studia Neophilologica*, XLI (1969), 115–29.

HOWARTH, WILLIAM. '*The Red Badge of Courage* Manuscript: New Evidence for a Critical Edition', *Studies in Bibliography*, XVIII (1965), 229–47.

HOWELLS, WILLIAM DEAN. 'Editor's Easy Chair', *Harper's*, CXXX (April 1915), 796–9.

258 *Bibliography*

— 'Frank Norris', *North American Review*, CLXXV (December 1902), 769–78.
— 'New York Low Life in Fiction', New York *World*, 26 July 1896, p. 18.
ITABASHI, YOSHIE. 'The Modern Pilgrimage of *The Black Riders*', *Tsuda Review*, no. 12 (November 1967), 1–41.
JOHNSON, W. F. 'The Launching of Stephen Crane', *Literary Digest and International Book Review*, IV (April 1926), 288–90.
JONES, CLAUDE. 'Stephen Crane at Syracuse', *American Literature*, VII (March 1935), 82–4.
JUMPER, WILL C. 'Tragic Irony as Form: Structural Problems in the Prose of Stephen Crane', unpublished Ph.D. thesis (Stanford, 1958).
KAHN, SY. 'Stephen Crane and the Giant Voice in the Night: An Explication of "The Monster" ', *Essays in Modern American Literature*, eds. R. E. Langford, Guy Owen, and W. E. Taylor. Deland, Florida: Stetson University Press, 1963. pp. 35–45.
KANTOR, MACKINLAY. 'The Historical Novel', *Three Views of the Novel*, by Irving Howe, John O'Hara, and MacKinlay Kantor. Washington, D.C.: Library of Congress, 1957.
KATZ, JOSEPH. ' "The Blue Battalions" and the Uses of Experience', *Studia Neophilologica*, XXXVIII (1966), 107–16.
— 'Cora Crane and the Poetry of Stephen Crane', *Papers of the Bibliographical Society of America*, LVIII (1964), 469–76.
— 'The *Maggie* Nobody Knows', *Modern Fiction Studies*, XII (Summer 1966), 200–12.
— ed. *The Poems of Stephen Crane*. New York: Cooper Square Publishers, 1966.
— ed. *The Red Badge of Courage*, by Stephen Crane. Gainesville, Florida: University of Florida Press, 1967.
KIERKEGAARD, SØREN. *Concluding Unscientific Postscript*, trans. David F. Swenson and Walter Lowrie. Princeton: Princeton University Press, 1941.
KINDILIEN, CARLIN T. 'Stephen Crane and the "Savage Philosophy" of Olive Schreiner', *Boston University Studies in English*, III (Summer 1957), 97–107.
KWIAT, JOSEPH J. 'The Newspaper Experience: Crane, Norris, and Dreiser', *Nineteenth-Century Fiction*, VIII (September 1953), 99–117.
— 'Stephen Crane and Painting', *American Quarterly*, IV (Winter 1952), 331–8.

LABOR, EARLE. 'Crane and Hemingway: Anatomy of Trauma', *Renascence*, XI (Summer 1959), 189–96.

LANG, JEAN V. E. WHITEHEAD. 'The Art of Stephen Crane', unpublished Ph.D. thesis (Cornell, 1944).

LENEHAN, WILLIAM T. 'The Failure of Naturalistic Techniques in Stephen Crane's *Maggie*', *Stephen Crane's Maggie: Text and Context*, ed. Maurice Bassan. Belmont, California: Wadsworth, 1966. pp. 166–73.

LIEBLING, A. J. 'The Dollars Damned Him', *New Yorker*, XXXVII (5 August 1961), 48–72.

LINSON, CORWIN KNAPP. *My Stephen Crane*, ed. Edwin H. Cady. Syracuse: Syracuse University Press, 1958.

LIVELY, ROBERT A. *Fiction Fights the Civil War*. Chapel Hill: University of North Carolina Press, 1957.

LYNSKEY, WINIFRED. 'Crane's *Red Badge of Courage*', *Explicator*, VIII (December 1949), item 18.

MACLEAN, HUGH N. 'The Two Worlds of "The Blue Hotel" ', *Modern Fiction Studies*, V (Autumn 1959), 260–70.

MANE, ROBERT. 'Une Rencontre Littéraire: Hamlin Garland et Stephen Crane', *Études Anglaises*, XVII (janvier–mars 1964), 30–46.

MARCUS, MORDECAI. 'The Three-Fold View of Nature in "The Open Boat" ', *Philological Quarterly*, XLI (April 1962), 511–15.

MARSHALL, EDWARD. 'New York Tenements', *North American Review*, CLVII (December 1893), 753–6.

McDERMOTT, JOHN J. 'Symbolism and Psychological Realism in *The Red Badge of Courage*', *Nineteenth-Century Fiction*, XXIII (December 1968), 324–31.

MILLER, RUTH. 'Regions of Snow: The Poetic Style of Stephen Crane', *Bulletin of the New York Public Library*, LXXII (1968), 328–49.

NELSON, HARLAND S. 'Stephen Crane's Achievement as a Poet', *Texas Studies in Literature and Language*, IV (Winter 1963), 564–82.

NOXON, FRANK W. 'The Real Stephen Crane', *Step Ladder*, XIV (January 1928), 4–9.

O'DONNELL, BERNARD. 'An Analysis of Prose Style to Determine Authorship: *The O'Ruddy*, a Novel by Stephen Crane and Robert Barr', unpublished Ed.D. thesis (Harvard, 1963).

OLIVER, ARTHUR. 'Jersey Memories—Stephen Crane', *New Jersey Historical Society Proceedings*, n.s. XVI (October 1931), 454–63.

OSBORN, SCOTT C. 'Stephen Crane's Imagery: "Pasted Like a Wafer" ', *American Literature*, XXIII (November 1951), 362.

OVERMYER, JANET. 'The Structure of Crane's *Maggie*', *University of Kansas City Review*, XXIX (Autumn 1962), 71–2.

PAINE, RALPH D. *Roads of Adventure*. Boston: Houghton Mifflin, 1922.

PECK, HARRY THURSTON. '*George's Mother*', *Bookman*, III (July 1896), 446–7.

PHELPS, WILLIAM LYON. Introduction, *The Work of Stephen Crane*. New York: Knopf, 1925–7. V, ix–xiii.

PIZER, DONALD. 'The Garland–Crane Relationship', *Huntington Library Quarterly*, XXIV (November 1960), 75–82.

— 'Romantic Individualism in Garland, Norris and Crane', *American Quarterly*, X (Winter 1958), 463–75.

— 'Stephen Crane's "Maggie" and American Naturalism', *Criticism*, VII (Spring 1965), 168–75.

PRATT, LYNDON UPSON. 'An Addition to the Canon of Stephen Crane', *Research Studies, State College of Washington*, VII (March 1939), 55–8.

— 'The Formal Education of Stephen Crane', *American Literature*, X (January 1939), 460–71.

RAHV, PHILIP. 'Fiction and the Criticism of Fiction', *Kenyon Review*, XVIII (Spring 1956), 276–99.

RALPH, JULIAN. 'The Bowery', *Century*, XLIII (December 1891), 227–37.

RANDEL, WILLIAM. 'From Slate to Emerald Green: More Light on Crane's Jacksonville Visit', *Nineteenth-Century Fiction*, XIX (March 1965), 357–68.

REMORDS, GEORGES. 'Un Précurseur des romanciers américains contemporains: Stephen Crane (1871–1900)', *Bulletin de la Faculté des Lettres de Strasbourg*, XXVIII (1950), 190–202, 249–62, 351–67; XXIX (1950–1), 158–66, 182–95.

RIIS, JACOB. *How the Other Half Lives*. New York: Scribner's, 1890.

ROSENFELD, ISAAC. 'Stephen Crane as Symbolist', *Kenyon Review*, XV (Spring 1953), 310–14.

SAFRANEK, WILLIAM P. 'Crane's *The Red Badge of Courage*', *Explicator*, XXVI (November 1967), item 21.

SATTERWHITE, JOSEPH N. 'Stephen Crane's "The Blue Hotel": The Failure of Understanding', *Modern Fiction Studies*, II (Winter 1956–7), 238–41.

SCHOBERLIN, MELVIN, ed. *The Sullivan County Sketches of Stephen Crane*. Syracuse: Syracuse University Press, 1949.

SHANE, MARION L. 'The Theme of Spiritual Poverty in Selected Works of Four American Novelists: Twain, Crane, Fitzgerald, and Dreiser', unpublished Ph.D. thesis (Syracuse, 1953).

SHROEDER, JOHN W. 'Stephen Crane Embattled', *University of Kansas City Review*, XVII (Winter 1950), 119–29.

SIDBURY, EDNA CRANE. 'My Uncle, Stephen Crane, as I Knew Him', *Literary Digest and International Book Review*, IV (March 1926), 248–50.

SOLOMON, ERIC. *Stephen Crane: From Parody to Realism*. Cambridge, Mass.: Harvard University Press, 1966.

— 'Stephen Crane's War Stories', *Texas Studies in Literature and Language*, III (Spring 1961), 67–80.

— 'The Structure of "The Red Badge of Courage" ', *Modern Fiction Studies*, V (Autumn 1959), 220–34.

SOLOMON, M. "Stephen Crane: A Critical Study", *Masses and Mainstream*, IX (January 1956), 25–42 (March 1956), 31–47.

STALLMAN, R. W. 'Crane's "Maggie": A Reassessment', *Modern Fiction Studies*, V (Autumn 1959), 251–9.

— *Stephen Crane: A Biography*. New York: George Braziller, 1968.

— 'Stephen Crane: Some New Sketches', *Bulletin of the New York Public Library*, LXXI (1967), 554–62.

— 'Stephen Crane: Some New Stories', *Bulletin of the New York Public Library*, LX (September 1956), 455–62 (October 1956), 477–86; LXI (January 1957), 36–46.

— ed. *Stephen Crane: An Omnibus*. New York: Knopf, 1952.

— ed. *Stephen Crane: Sullivan County Tales and Sketches*. Ames, Iowa: Iowa State University Press, 1968.

— and E. R. HAGEMANN, eds. *The New York City Sketches of Stephen Crane and Related Pieces*. New York: New York University Press, 1966.

— and LILLIAN GILKES, eds. *Stephen Crane: Letters*. New York: New York University Press, 1960.

STEIN, W. B. 'Stephen Crane's *Homo Absurdus*', *Bucknell Review*, VIII (May 1959), 168–88.

'Stephen Crane', *Bookman*, I (May 1895), 229–30.

STONE, EDWARD. 'The Many Suns of *The Red Badge of Courage*', *American Literature*, XXIX (November 1957), 322–6.

STRONKS, James B. '*A Modern Instance*', *American Literary Realism 1870–1910*, No. 4 (Fall 1968), n.p.

— 'Stephen Crane's English Years: The Legend Corrected', *Papers of the Bibliographical Society of America*, LVII (1963), 340–9.

SUTTON, WALTER. 'Pity and Fear in "The Blue Hotel" ', *American Quarterly*, IV (Spring 1952), 73–8.

TAYLOR, GORDON O. *The Passages of Thought: Psychological Representation in the American Novel 1870–1900*. New York: Oxford University Press, 1969.

VANDERBEETS, RICHARD. 'Character as Structure: Ironic Parallel and Transformation in "The Blue Hotel" ', *Studies in Short Fiction*, V (1968), 294–5.

VAN DOREN, CARL. Introduction, *The Work of Stephen Crane*. New York: Knopf, 1925–7. IV, ix–xv.

— ed. *Twenty Stories by Stephen Crane*. New York: Knopf, 1940.

VON ABELE, RUDOLPH, and WALTER HAVIGHURST. 'Symbolism and the Student', *College English*, XVI (April 1955), 424–34, 461.

WALCUTT, CHARLES CHILD. 'Harold Frederic and American Naturalism', *American Literature*, XI (March 1939), 11–22.

WELLS, H. G. 'Stephen Crane from an English Standpoint', *North American Review*, CLXXI (August 1900), 233–42.

WERTHEIM, STANLEY. 'Stephen Crane and the Wrath of Jehova', *Literary Review*, VII (Spring 1964), 499–508.

WEST, R. B. 'Stephen Crane: Author in Transition', *American Literature*, XXXIV (May 1962), 215–28.

WESTBROOK, MAX R. 'Stephen Crane and the Personal Universal', *Modern Fiction Studies*, VIII (Winter 1962–3), 351–60.

—'Stephen Crane and the Revolt-Search Motif', unpublished Ph.D. thesis (Texas, 1960).

—'Stephen Crane's Poetry: Perspective and Arrogance', *Bucknell Review*, XI (December 1963), 24–34.

— 'Stephen Crane's Social Ethic', *American Quarterly*, XIV (Winter 1962), 587–96.

— 'Stephen Crane: The Pattern of Affirmation', *Nineteenth-Century Fiction*, XIV (December 1959), 219–29.

WHITE, WILLIAM. 'A Stephen Crane Letter', *The Times Literary Supplement*, no. 3108, 22 September 1961, p. 636.

WICKHAM, HARVEY. 'Stephen Crane at College', *American Mercury*, VII (March 1926), 291–7.

WILLIAMS, HERBERT P. 'Mr. Crane as Literary Artist', *Illustrated American*, XX (18 July 1896), 126.

WILMER, RICHARD H. 'Collecting Civil War Novels', *Colophon*, n.s. III (Autumn 1938), 513–18.

WINTERICH, JOHN T. 'Romantic Stories of Books: *The Red Badge of*

Courage', *Publishers' Weekly*, CXVIII (20 September 1930), 1303–7.

WINTHER, SOPHUS KEITH. *The Realistic War Novel*, University of Washington Chapbooks, No. 35, ed. G. Hughes. Seattle: University of Washington Bookstore, 1930.

WRIGHT, A. H. 'Irony and Fiction', *Journal of Aesthetics and Art Criticism*, XII (September 1953), 111–18.

WYATT, EDITH. 'Stephen Crane', *New Republic*, IV (11 September 1915), 148–50.

INDEX OF FIRST LINES

GENERAL INDEX